CW00403564

*English Life in the
Nineteenth Century*

English Life
in the
Nineteenth Century

Roger Hart

"A mighty mass of brick, and smoke, and shipping
    Dirty and dusky, but as wide as eye
Could reach, with here and there a sail just skipping
    In sight, then lost amidst the forestry
Of masts; a wilderness of steeples peeping
    On tiptoe through their sea-coal canopy;
A huge dun cupola, like a foolscap crown
    On a fool's head – and there is London Town!"
    (Lord Byron, *Don Juan*, 1822)

THE ENGLISH LIFE SERIES

Britain Between the World Wars 1918–1939
Marion Yass
The Edwardians
Christopher Martin
English Life in the First World War
Christopher Martin
English Life in the Nineteenth Century
Roger Hart

Frontispiece: A busy London thoroughfare at the time of Charles Dickens.

First published in 1971 by
Wayland (Publishers) Ltd
61 Western Road, Hove
East Sussex BN1 3JD
© Copyright 1971 Roger Hart
2nd impression 1988

ISBN 1 85210 584 4

Printed and bound at
The Bath Press, Avon

Contents

PREFACE

Although the nineteenth century is a well-documented one, there is much about English life from 1800 to 1900 which remains baffling and complex. How, in an age of enormous material progress, could so many people actually have grown poorer? How, in an age of improved communications, could parts of the country seem so set apart? Why did Victorian England never give way to violent revolution as so many predicted, and as sometimes happened in Europe? Why did such a gulf lie between moral ideals and social realities? The answers to such questions are not easy to find. The intention of the present volume is to create a living panorama of English society in the age of Dickens and Mayhew, making extensive use of contemporary illustrations and documents, in the hope of illuminating some of the complex attitudes of English men and women of every class of society.

R. W. H.

1 Rural Rides

The Industrial Revolution of the nineteenth century put agriculture second place in national life. This change was most strongly marked by the repeal of the Corn Laws in 1846. Introduced in 1815, the Corn Laws had been designed to protect the interests of the great land-owners by preventing the importation of corn from overseas unless the price had risen to a high level in the home market. But after the repeal of the Corn Laws, agriculture – like industry – was put on the basis of free trade. The landed interests were no longer to be regarded as paramount in English life. Nevertheless, agriculture continued to provide the livelihood of millions of Englishmen, for at that time England still largely had to feed herself. But farmers at home now had to face growing competition from corn growers overseas.

Farm workers cutting swedes for winter food

Life on the Land

In the first three or four decades of the century, standards of living in the countryside were actually falling. During these years, England was still primarily a farming nation rather than a manufacturing one. When harvests were bad, or farming was depressed for other reasons, farm workers were the first to suffer. Even in "good" years, most farm workers and small tenants had little more than a subsistence living. This was a major cause of the great migration which took place toward the towns, where work was easy to find, and where there was less financial uncertainty.

Ever since the outbreak of the French Wars (1793–1815) farming had been unstable. The years after 1793 had witnessed a population explosion which forced up the price of bread; the new issues of war-time paper currency helped inflation; and during much of the Napoleonic period, England was under a partial maritime blockade. In the eighteenth century, many farm workers had been boarded and fed by their employers, but as the demand for cash crops grew employers were reluctant to part with goods in kind. Instead, they placed their employees on weekly wages, where they were at the mercy of rising prices.

When the French Wars finally ended with Napoleon's fall at Waterloo in 1815, an agricultural slump followed. Not even the economic protection given by the Corn Laws could hold up the price of corn. By 1822 the price of corn had plummeted to less than half that of 1813. One farmer complained to the rural writer William Cobbett: "What we need is another war!"

Rural life was made still worse by the operation of the Poor Laws. Since a famous legal case – the Speenhamland Case decided by Berkshire magistrates in 1795 – poor families were to receive a cash "allowance" based upon the number of children in the family, and upon the prevailing price of bread. With the great price rise during the war period, the so-called Speenhamland system had the effect of artificially subsidizing large families, with serious long-term social effects. When bread prices fell after 1815, the situation grew still worse. Hundreds of small farms closed down and let their land go out of cultivation; thousands of people went out of work.

A government survey of agricultural wages (1824) found enormous variations from one part of the country to another. The Survey Committee heard evidence from many people, including one farm worker Thomas Smart. Aged forty-six, Smart had seven surviving children (out of thirteen), and by a combination of hard work and good luck had stayed in work for nearly all his life. In 1812, just before the depression, his wage had been twelve shillings a week; in 1824 it was down to eight shillings a week. His diet was almost entirely made up of bread and cheese; he seldom ate meat or bacon. He had no pig, but grew potatoes in a small garden; he drank tea and, very occasionally, milk. His house cost £5 a year.

The classic account of the agricultural troubles of these years is William Cobbett's *Rural Rides* (1830). A passionate lover of the English countryside, and a hater of "the great Wen" as he called London, Cobbett was deeply saddened to find the countryside filled with derelict farmhouses and uncultivated fields. In many villages, the old parish churches were far too large for the remaining populations who gathered there each Sunday morning.

Cobbett declared that the lowest classes of farm workers were "the worst used labouring people upon the face of the earth. Dogs and hogs and horses are treated with more civility, and as to food and lodging, how gladly would the labourers change with them!" Cobbett estimated that the minimum living wage for a farm-worker's family was £62 a year, three times that received by Thomas Smart. Wages were so low that the overseer of the Warminster parish poor was employing twelve men to dig a field at ninepence a day, as it was cheaper than horse-drawn ploughing. Observing them, Cobbett wrote, "I really am ashamed to ride a fat horse, to have a full belly, and to have a clean shirt upon my back when I look at these wretched countrymen of mine; while I actually see them reeling with weakness; when I see their poor faces present me nothing but skin and bone."

Many contemporary writers produced books of advice for those living in the country, such as Esther Copley's *Cottage Comforts* and *Cottage Cookery* of the 1820s and 1830s. Esther Copley wrote that "the want and misery of many families arise more from want of discretion in managing their resources than from the real scantiness of their income." But many people would have disagreed.

In 1834 a new Poor Law placed poor relief on a new footing. The old "allowance" was scrapped in favour of workhouse relief. In addition, as the parish was no longer responsible for finding work for the unemployed, most families living in rural areas were forced to become more independent. In some ways the unmarried man was worst off, as a family man had a wife and children to put to work.

The 1840s saw a period of great agricultural depression and unemployment, which since 1904 has been popularly known as the "Hungry Forties". (In 1904 a graphic body of evidence about these years was published in a volume entitled *The Hungry Forties*.) One farm worker, Charles Astridge of Midhurst, said that during this period "we mostly lived on bread, but 'twasn't bread like 'ee get now; 'twas that heavy and doughy 'ee could pull long strings of it out your mouth. They called it 'growy bread'. But 'twas fine compared with the porridge we made out of bruised beans; that made you inside feel as if 'twas on fire, and sort of choked 'ee. In those days we'd see children from Duck Lane come out in the streets of Midhurst an' pick up a bit of bread, and even potato peelings."

Left A farm worker. *Right* An English village street scene

In 1843 an official Report presented a vivid picture of the hard conditions of rural life. A man might earn no more than eight shillings a week, which could be made up to as much as eighteen shillings if his wife and children also worked. Many of them suffered from chronic dietary troubles. A physician from Calne, Wiltshire, noted that four out of every five of his female patients suffered from a diet "insufficient in quantity and not good enough in quality". He added that when everything was taken into account, "I am always more and more astonished how the labourers continue to live at all." A Bexwell priest, who also gave evidence in 1843, reported that most of his parishioners lived on bread, potatoes and tea: "I have no hesitation in saying that no independent labourer can obtain the diet which is given in the Union Workhouse."

A cottage and garden of a farm worker

The Report of 1843 gave many examples of a weekly family budget. This was one:

Name	Age	Earnings	Weekly Expenditure	
Robert Crick	42	9s. 0d.	Bread	9s. 0d.
			Potatoes	1s. 0d.
Wife	40	9d.	Rent	1s. 2d.
			Tea	2d.
Boy	12	2s. 0d.	Sugar	3½d.
			Soap	3d.
Boy	11	1s. 0d	Blue	½d.
			Thread, *etc.*	2d.
Boy	8	1s. 0d.	Candles	3d.
			Salt	½d.
Girl	6	nil	Coal and wood	9d.
			Butter	4½d.
Boy	4	nil	Cheese	3d.
Total earnings		13s. 9d.	Total expenditure	13s. 9d.

Most families, especially in the southern counties of England, had a diet which was both frugal and monotonous. But some did have small perquisites such as a rent-free cottage and garden, or a small plot of land on which to pasture a pig or cow, or grow potatoes.

Throughout the nineteenth century, one finds a curious contrast between the depressing official reports, and the romantic views of rural England held by many people apparently unaware of the social realities. One writer, Francis George Heath, who hiked through the West Country in 1873, wrote lyrically: "A peep over the hedge revealed just a glimpse of the whitewashed walls and the low thatched roof of a cottage. . . . Down one side of the lane gurgled a limpid stream of water. . . . Facing the cottages there was a row of little gardens over-shadowed by fruit trees. Here and there rustic beehives were scattered over these gardens, which contained flowers and shrubs in addition to their little crops of vegetables." Yet inside one of these cottages, Heath was appalled to find a family whose father earned only ten shillings a week, and his small son a few pennies a day. The cottage leaked and was in a slum condition; the family lived in rags, and some of the children lacked shoes. This was the truth which was so often overlooked in the legends of an idyllic rustic England. One Canon Edward Girdlestone remarked that farm workers "did not live in the proper sense of the word, they merely didn't die." Between 1851 and 1901, it has been estimated that the agricultural population of England and Wales fell from some 1,340,000 to 970,000, so poorly did conditions seem to compare with those in the smoky new industrial towns.

A Dorset farm worker earning six shillings a week in 1850 described a day's diet: after tending to his horses he ate a breakfast consisting of flour and butter with water poured over; working in the fields at mid-day he ate a piece of bread, and occasionally cheese. His supper consisted of bread or potatoes, and water, sometimes with a little bacon. At harvest time his master gave him an allowance of beer. Joseph Arch

Above and *below:* the inside of a farm-worker's cottage

recalled: "In many a household even a morsel of bacon was considered a luxury." Even those families who received some payment in kind (bread, beer, bacon) were usually off-loaded with the worst of the available produce, since farm prices were so high in the second half of the century. Not surprisingly, poaching and theft of stock was widespread. The Game Laws were most severe, and until as late as 1857 poaching of hares or rabbits could be punished with transportation (deportation to the colonies) for life. Many a worker returned from the fields after dusk carrying stolen turnips, only to be heavily fined, and often ruined.

A farm worker turf-cutting

In a report of 1863, Dr. Edward Smith found that bread was so important as a staple diet, that the average consumption per head was over twelve pounds weight per week; the average consumption of potatoes was six pounds weight, and of meat and bacon only one pound. (The term meat rarely implied butcher's meat, but items such as cows' and sheep's heads.) Dr. Smith collected many case reports of actual diets. These are some of them:

DEVON (Case no. 135). *Breakfast and supper* tea kettle broth (bread, hot water, salt and ½ pint of milk), bread and treacle. *Dinner* pudding (flour, salt and water), vegetables and fresh meat. No bread.
DORSET (Case no. 191). *Breakfast* water broth, bread, butter, tea with milk. *Dinner* husband has bread and cheese, family take tea besides. *Supper* fried bacon and cabbage, or bread and cheese.
LINCOLNSHIRE (Case no. 248). *Breakfast* milk gruel, or bread and water, or tea and bread. *Dinner* meat for husband only, others vegetables only. *Tea and supper* bread or potatoes.
NOTTINGHAMSHIRE (Case no. 255). *Breakfast* children eat thickened milk, others tea or coffee, and bread and butter with cheese sometimes. *Dinner* little milk and potatoes. *Supper* bacon or tea.
DERBYSHIRE (Case no. 281). *Breakfast* coffee, bread and butter. *Dinner* hot meat, vegetables and pudding daily. *Tea* tea, bread and butter. *Supper* hot, when not hot dinner.

Altogether, the Report of 1863 presented a depressing picture. The English village had always been an isolated unit, having little contact with the wider world apart from important local market centres in the provinces. Communications were poor; the stage-coach services which had sprung up in the later eighteenth century, and which prided themselves on their fast journey times, did more to link together the major provincial centres such as Bristol, York, Norwich, Oxford, Exeter and Bath, than to reach remote villages. It was an irony that in the nineteenth century, with all its road services, railways and canals, the villages grew even more isolated. For the new railway services were beginning to put out of business even those coach services which did help the villages.

Nevertheless, one should not exaggerate the regret felt by villages themselves. The English villages were, generally speaking, close-knit and inward-looking communities. They handed down their attitudes and traditions from one generation to the next, and looked on every outsider as a stranger. Making use of the corn gleaned after the harvest, some farm workers were able to live well enough, and indeed in many

A woodcutter

cases could live more securely and healthily than the workers in the new industrial towns. Drink was often home-made, for example, ale, cider, and flower or fruit wines. Tea was an expensive imported product, and seldom drunk. Vegetable soups could be made cheaply enough, and helped out with dumplings they provided a filling if plain meal. The poorer families would often have "kettle broth" at breakfast and supper; this was a thin brew made of boiling water poured over pieces of bread and fat.

Like food, fuel was a home product, and easy enough to come by. Most people burned wood, except in areas close to one of the new coal mining districts, perhaps in Nottinghamshire, Derbyshire or South Wales, where coal was cheap. Where the village family found most difficulty was in buying manufactured goods, such as shoes and clothing; these had to be paid for out of very limited cash resources. Clothes were usually passed down from father to son, and if they were primitive and lacking in any elegance, at least these leather jerkins, smocks and breeches were toughly made and likely to withstand a good deal of wear and tear. The womenfolk wore woollen dresses and shawls in the winter months and cotton dresses and bonnets in the spring and summer.

Working on the Land

Until the protective Corn Laws were repealed in 1846, most English corn growers prospered. Even after 1846 corn growing remained quite a profitable business. The ruin which many people had foretold had not come about. Nevertheless, the later nineteenth century was not a very happy time for the corn growers. Overseas competition from the vast granaries of Canada, the United States, Australia and South Russia was becoming fierce, and was unchecked in this age of free trade. In addition, the 1870s saw one bad harvest after another, culminating in the great crop failure of 1879.

Nevertheless many Victorian farms recorded a steady growth in improvements. The old primitive wooden plough was being replaced in many areas by iron ploughs of more complex designs, tailored to the soil conditions of different regions. Drilling machines were being used on a wider scale to sow seeds; cultivating machines were being used to prepare the soil for sowing. Specially useful was the reaping machine, which appeared in the middle of the century, and promised a new efficiency in gathering in the harvests. The first reaping machines were simple vehicles with a cutting apparatus, and a platform on which the cut corn was collected. When the platform was full, the driver threw down the corn behind him, leaving other workers to gather and bind it into sheaves. A self-delivery reaper soon followed, which automatically threw down the corn to one side. Like many early examples of Victorian engineering, these reapers were crudely built and frequently broke down. They also attracted the anger of farm workers who feared that they would be thrown out of work. This fear of technical progress was shared by many people in different occupations.

A further objection to the new reaping machines was that they

A peasant sitting on a stile

A demonstration of ploughing
by steam

reduced the gleanings traditionally gathered by the village poor when
the harvest had been taken. After a field had been raked over by the
harvesters, a gleaning bell was often sounded as a signal for the gleaning to begin. Many families gleaned corn to make enough bread to see
them right through the winter. For a few pence, the local miller would
grind the corn for them.

At harvest time, the farmer would employ women and girls from
nearby villages to follow the reaping machines around the field, to help
gather in the harvest, and bind up the crops into sheaves. Many of
these seasonal workers were Irish; they came to England just for the
harvest, slept in communal lodgings provided by the farms, and then
returned home again.

A horse hoe

A corn and seed drill

A Garrett's reaping machine

13

A harvest celebration

When the corn had been harvested it had to be threshed and winnowed. Threshing was a laborious affair, carried out with a hand flail, usually made of stout ash, and jointed. The corn was laid on the barn floor and threshed by one or two men until all the grain was separated from the straw. The grain itself then had to be freed of the chaff by "winnowing". Often this was done by shaking the grain through a sieve. Threshing and winnowing machines were apparently first used in Scotland, but came to be used south of the border from the early 1800s. Threshing machines were first powered by horses or water mills, and later by steam and oil engines. Threshing gangs would often travel about country areas with these machines at harvest time, and do in a day what had once taken the local workers weeks to do.

Apart from reaping, threshing and winnowing machines, the Victorian farmer also began to use other contrivances – mowing machines, sweep-rakes, elevators, balers, trussers and swathe-turners. Agricultural chemistry began to advance. A variety of soil fertilizers were traditionally used – animal manures, lime, chalk, marl, potash (made from wood ash), sugar-baker's scum, soap-boiler's ashes, hog's hair, malt dust, and horn shavings. Founded in 1843, the Rothampstead Experimental Station in Hertfordshire fostered a whole new science of soils. Under its encouragement, farmers began to look further afield for fertilizers: potash from Germany, guano from Peru, nitrogen from gasworks' refuse, and the slag from steel works. Many farmers were suspicious of these new products, but in time their value was generally understood by the farming community. The Government insisted that every diseased animal had to be killed by its owner and buried or burned: and from 1866, the final year of the rinderpest epidemic – a form of cattle plague – compensation was paid out at the rate of £10 per cow. These measures helped, too, to reduce outbreaks of foot-and-mouth disease.

Dairy farming took place on a large scale. A typically prosperous dairy farm might have three or four dozen cows, which were milked

Below Hop pickers resting for a meal. *Below right* Hop pickers at work

Making apple cider

twice a day. The fresh milk was poured into large earthenware dishes, to allow the cream to separate from the milk, which was then used for pig swill, or sold off cheaply to the poor village women. The cream was hand-churned, or occasionally churned by horsepower, and the butter washed and patted into pound or half-pound portions for sale in the market. Dairy farmers were on the whole slow to experiment with mechanization; most churning was done by hand; and not until 1879 were machines used to skim the cream from the milk, on the centrifugal system. Milking machines do not seem to have appeared until 1895. Many farmers were unwilling to install expensive new equipment, especially when farm wages were so low. Cheese-making was an important activity in some regions of Britain, for example in Cheshire and in the Cheddar Valley. The milk was first curdled, and the curds separated from the whey; the curds were pressed into tubs and placed in a special cheese room where they eventually ripened. The whey was used to make whey-butter.

For centuries wool had been one of Britain's greatest exports, and in the nineteenth century home grown wool continued to be an important commodity. No doubt the life of the shepherd had changed little from the life led by his forebears in the seventeenth and eighteenth centuries. Working perhaps on the slopes of the Pennines, he worked alone except for his sheep dog. A shepherd's life was at its hardest and busiest in the winter months, up to the end of March, which included the lambing season. The summer was a full one, too, for the sheep had to be washed, shorn of their coats, and dipped. Sheep farming, like other types of farming, was not much mechanized in the nineteenth century, and most sheep shearing was performed by hand. When this work was over, many villages held sheep shearing festivals, at least until the middle part of the century. A shepherd was usually paid partly in kind, as he had been for centuries past, perhaps with a lamb, or with lambs' tails cut off at tailing time; these tails were considered a great delicacy.

Below left Hop pickers waiting to be paid. *Below* Hop pickers being paid

An *Illustrated London News* cartoon of a London dairy show

Left Birmingham dairy show

Village horse and cart

The villages contained people in many other occupations apart from dairy, crop or cattle farming. There were blacksmiths, cobblers, thatchers, wheelwrights, coopers (barrel makers), hurdle makers, masons, carriers, saddlers, tailors, butchers, and usually an innkeeper and perhaps a small general storekeeper. It was the wheelwright who made the carts and wagons for local use; the thatcher who covered the roofs of village houses with straw thatch of wheat, rye or reeds, whose thick but open-structured form kept the interiors warm in winter and pleasantly cool in summer. Thatched roofs always involved a fire risk, and iron hooks were often kept near at hand in order quickly to demolish the roof if a fire should break out. Their ends were closely woven together at the ridge of the roof, and were fastened to the rafters by tarred twine; these thatched roofs were surprisingly noise-resistant and weatherproof, as well as attractive to the eye.

The blacksmith was an important figure in village life. As well as forging all the bars, hooks, nails, hinges and other ironwork needed, his main task was to shoe the horses, a task which called for a good deal of experience and skill. In practice the blacksmith often acted as veterinary surgeon, and offered a diagnosis and cure for lame horses. Many men earned their living as woodworkers of one kind or another, making chair legs, poles and pegs on their lathes, or shaping wooden bowls, spoons, walking sticks, fence posts, or clogs to which the blacksmith added iron tips.

Basket-making was another important craft in some counties of England, for example Berkshire and Somerset. This craft commanded some respect; since it could not yet be replaced by machinery, the craftsmen felt secure in their jobs. Basket-making was performed by many cottagers who grew their own osiers, cutting and stripping the rods themselves, seasoning them, peeling and preparing them from the point of view of appearance. A number of special tools were needed for the work, for example the brake (a forked implement used to strip the rods), bodkins, knives and mauls. Sometimes, baskets were made of rushes instead of osiers. The womenfolk in some areas plaited straw for use in the new hat factories, especially in Luton, Bedfordshire. Certain other trades or crafts were dominated by the women, such as glove-making in Oxfordshire and Worcestershire, quilting and lace-making in Nottinghamshire.

Basket-sellers

Left The farrier. *Right* The basket-maker

A neo-gothic country mansion, Westwood, near Droitwich

The Rich

The contrast between the life led by the poorer classes on the land, and that led by the rich was immense. In the nineteenth century, in the days before crippling death duties, a few families owned huge tracts of the countryside, some of them amounting to hundreds of thousands of acres, and containing hundreds of villages, and stretching across several counties. The large estates were managed by a large staff, responsible to a steward. Such estates supported their proprietors in great luxury, and provided them with the very best that the English countryside had to offer, both in terms of its produce, and its sports. It was the ambition of many successful industrialists or merchants to acquire landed status, and to mix with the country gentry on equal terms. The ownership of land brought both social and political power.

The great country houses of England devoted their weekends to large house parties. The most socially important of these were those given by the Prince of Wales (later King Edward VII) at his residence at Sandringham, where some 10,000 pheasants were bred for shooting each year. At the start of each season, the guests were led out by sixty uniformed beaters each bearing a flag, to begin the first shoot. It is recorded that in the season of 1896–97 the Sandringham guests shot 13,958 pheasants, 3,965 partridges, 836 hares, 6,185 rabbits, 77 woodcock, 52 teal, 271 wild duck, 18 pigeons and 27 "various birds". Dozens of species of birds were specially bred for shooting. This was entertainment on the most spectacular and extravagant scale.

The Game Laws designed to stop poaching were severely, even savagely, enforced. The local parish justices and landowners were often one and the same. Landowners would set trip-wire guns ("spring guns") in woods and thickets to discourage the unwary. Sydney Smith found "a sort of horror in thinking of a whole land filled with lurking engines of death – machinations against human life under every green tree – traps and guns in every dusky dell and bosky bourn . . . the lords of the manors eyeing their peasantry as so many butts and marks, and panting to hear the click of the trap and to see the flash of the gun." The Game Laws created a small and privileged class licensed to shoot game, requiring such people to own an estate worth at least £100 a year. Only the eldest sons of the gentry were allowed to hunt and sell game (unless it was a gift of the landlord). R. B. Thornhill wrote in the *Shooting Directory* (1804) that the Game Laws were designed not only "for the prevention of idleness and dissipation in husbandmen, labourers, artificers and others of lower rank," but to prevent "popular insurrection by disarming the bulk of the people". If contemporaries found these laws irksome, there can be little doubt of the debt owed to them by modern gun-free English society.

Poachers being caught by a landowner

Opposite Hunting scenes at the royal hunting lodge at Sandringham

Above Hawking. *Above right*
Grouse-shooting

During the early years of the century several attempts were made to ban spring guns, but until 1827 the reformers were always defeated by the landowning classes represented in Parliament. In 1827, however, the campaign was successfully reopened. The promoter of the Spring Guns Bill, Charles Tennyson, pictured the game-preserving squire, "sitting in his hall, surrounded like an ogre by death-dealing machines". After extended debates in both Houses of Parliament, the Bill finally became law, and one of the more dangerous and unpleasant aspects of rural life was removed. Those landowners who defied the law in the later years could be, and sometimes were, prosecuted under the Offences Against Persons Act of 1861.

2 *A Nation on the Move*

Coach Travel

During his lifetime, Charles Dickens would have seen a great rise in coaching traffic on the streets of London, some of it leaving for far destinations. The first London mail-coach had set out for Exeter in 1785; and in 1806 the Holyhead mail-coaches were covering the 126-mile journey from London in a little over a day. Thirty years later the time had been cut to a fast sixteen hours. Such coaches were the marvel of the age. The early years of the stage-coaches have an almost legendary quality about them. The best coaching companies prided themselves on well-kept stables and luxurious equipment, and their highly trained coachmen and grooms competed eagerly in reducing journey times. One London–Brighton coachman, a Cambridge graduate, served his passengers with sherry and sandwiches from a silver luncheon box. But these romantic days were to be brought to an end with the advent of the railways.

By 1800 London's roads had shown much improvement. Complaints about rut-holes and broken axles were becoming more scarce, as many thoroughfares were fitted with wooden block surfaces. By the time of the Great Exhibition (1851) most of London's roads were paved, cobbled, or tarmacadamed. Horse-drawn omnibuses and hansom cabs were becoming a familiar sight in the traffic, too. Some omnibus proprietors would go to almost any lengths to provide comfort and service, for example providing refreshment or books and newspapers aboard their vehicles. But as the daily traffic grew, these early standards of service began to decline and satires on rude drivers and conductors ("cads") were common in the pages of *Punch*.

By 1886, licences were being granted to some 7,000 hansom cabs and 4,000 four-wheelers (or "growlers"); and within seven years of first appearing, there were some 400 omnibuses. But despite the growth of public and private transport, the streets were still congested with pedestrians. Most Londoners still walked to work, often from terraces and villas in Islington, Walworth and other suburbs.

The Railway Revolution

The pride of Victorian England was her railways, which seemed to represent the sum of all human ingenuity, daring and endeavour. One of the leading railway pioneers in Britain was the Cornish engineer,

A four-in-hand (1857)

A tandem (1883)

A pony phaeton (1850)

The crowded thoroughfare of London Bridge in 1872

Top Richard Trevithick's
locomotive. *Above Puffing Billy*

Richard Trevithick (1771–1833). Trevithick was the first man to build a steam engine which could move along by its own power. In 1804, this primitive locomotive hauled a train of five wagons, carrying a cargo of iron and some passengers, for the distance of nine miles from the Pen-y-Darren Foundry at Merthyr Tydfil in South Wales. But Trevithick ran into endless difficulties. The flanged cast-iron rail tracks were not strong enough to hold the train, and frequently buckled under the weight of the locomotive and wagons. Trevithick might have done better to flange the wheels of the engine instead of the track itself, as the colliery railways did. This, indeed, was the solution finally adopted by the railway engineers.

Soon after Trevithick had demonstrated his locomotive, colliery owners were trying out their own machines. They already operated stationary steam engines, for example to work the lift shafts in the mines to bring up the coal to the surface. They began to adapt these as railway locomotives. An early example was *Puffing Billy*, built in 1813. This was a locomotive of ungainly appearance, having a great deal of its locomotive gear mounted externally. *Puffing Billy* was stoked from the front, and had to be preceded by a wagon containing a water tank, coal box and fireman.

The first true passenger railway was, however, the famous Stockton and Darlington Railway, which linked these two south Durham towns. Darlington was a coal-mining town, and Stockton its outlet on the River Tees. The line was opened in 1825. At first the railway directors were not much interested in carrying passengers as well as coal, but finally agreed to attach passenger wagons to the coal wagons in the train. Before then, private operators had been licensed to run horse-drawn trains along the line on payment of a fee.

The second true railway to open (in 1830) was the Liverpool and Manchester line which from the start combined freight and passenger operations. After much-publicized steam locomotive trials at Rainhill near Liverpool the year before, the directors of the company agreed to install steam locomotion, and not horsepower as some had first advised. The winner of the Rainhill trials was the famous *Rocket* built by George Stephenson (1781–1848) and his son Robert. The *Rocket* was in fact the only competing locomotive to pass the tests laid down by the railway company directors; it averaged a speed of fourteen miles per hour, and up to forty miles per hour when travelling light. The *Rocket* reduced excessive steam pressure – a serious problem to engineers of the time – by a pressure gauge, and two safety valves on the top of the six-foot boiler. The *Rocket* required careful handling for other reasons; all the moving parts in the machine had to be lubricated by hand; and it had no brakes. Railway "policemen" patrolled the railway line, operating the points, and signalling by flags: red for stop, green for caution, white for go. Lamps of the same kind were used at night. After a time mechanical semaphore signals were erected, which could be operated from a signal box some distance away.

The actress Fanny Kemble (1809–93) was the first woman to travel by rail. She made her journey in 1830 on the Liverpool–Manchester line in company with George Stephenson. She wrote to a friend: "A common sheet of paper is enough for love, but a foolscap extra can alone contain a railroad and my ecstasy. . . . We were introduced to the little engine which was to drag us along the rails. She (for they make these curious little fire-horses all mares) consisted of a boiler, a stove, a small platform, a bench, and behind the bench a barrel, containing enough water to prevent her being thirsty for fifteen miles. . . . The reins, bit and bridle of this wonderful beast is a small steel handle, which applies or withdraws the steam from the legs or pistons, so that a child might manage it. The coals, which are its oats, were under the bench. . . . This snorting little animal, which I felt inclined to pat, was then harnessed to our carriage, and, Mr. Stephenson having taken me on the bench of the engine with him we started at about ten miles an hour." Fanny added: "You can't imagine how strange it seemed to be journeying on thus, without any visible cause of progress other than the magical machine, with the flying white breath and rhythmical un-varying pace, between those rocky walls. . . . I felt as if no fairy tale was ever half so wonderful as what I saw."

Robert Stephenson, the locomotive engineer

The success of the Liverpool and Manchester Railway prompted many financiers and engineers to join together in similar enterprises, with the hope of quick and large profits. Often, they came unstuck. One of the main problems was the purchase of land, since many land-owners were unwilling to sell, or, as they thought, to jeopardize the health of their cows at calving time, or run the risks of engine sparks setting their crops alight. As a result of these fears railway companies were often induced to pay absurdly high prices for land. Noisy opposi-tion to railways was put up by canal proprietors and turnpike trustees. Not surprisingly, many of the first promoters fell by the wayside. Another great expense which had to be met was to launch the private Act of Parliament needed to sanction every new line. Lawyers had to be hired, Members of Parliament lobbied, and public support drummed up. All this cost time, and a great deal of money.

Above Robert Stephenson's *Rocket. Below* Isambard Kingdom Brunel

The company which, more than any other, made a success of its fortunes at the height of the railway mania, was the Great Western Railway. It owed its success mainly to the tireless genius of its talented young engineer, Isambard Kingdom Brunel (1806–59). Brunel was a man of extraordinary ambitions, and planned the railway on the grandest possible scale. The very wide gauge (7 feet and $\frac{1}{4}$ inch) seemed to challenge the 4 feet $8\frac{1}{2}$ inches standard set by Stephenson; and Brunel's iron railway bridges were monumental memorials to his engineering spirit.

As the railways spread through the country, comparisons were often made between railways and stage-coaches. George Stephenson's biographer, Samuel Smiles, wrote that many deplored the inevitable downfall of the old stage-coach system. There was an end to "that delightful variety of incident" which usually attended a journey by road. The rapid scamper across a fine country on the outside of the four-horse "express" or "highflyer", the journey amid open green fields, through smiling villages and fine old towns where the stage stopped to change horses and the passengers to take their supper: all this had been very delightful in its way, and many people regretted that this old-fashioned and pleasant style of travelling was about to pass away.

"But it had its dark side, too," Smiles added. "Anyone who remembers the journey by stage from London to Manchester or York, will associate it with recollections and sensations of not unmixed delight. To be perched for twenty hours, exposed to all weathers, on the outside of a coach, trying in vain to find a soft seat – sitting now with the face to the wind, rain, or sun, and now with the back – without any shelter such as the commonest penny-a-mile parliamentary train now daily provides – was a miserable undertaking, looked forward to with horror by many whose business required them to travel between the provinces and the metropolis." (A parliamentary train was a train service required by law to run at least once a day at a maximum charge of a penny per mile, third class, for the benefit of the poorer classes.)

In the very early days of railways, little attention was paid to passenger comfort; indeed, little seemed necessary. The main point was to move from one place to another, and it mattered little whether the cargo was coal or people. Third class passengers had to travel standing up in open trucks. Straw was sometimes thrown on the floor in frosty weather; and a few holes were drilled in the truck floors to let the rain-water out. Second class passengers at least had the benefit of wooden benches, but one had to travel first class to have the benefit of coaches covered at the sides as well as overhead.

Left Dining car on the Great Northern Railway. *Right* The Metropolitan underground railway in London at the opening in 1863

Partly owing to increased competition for passengers and for national status, and partly owing to government intervention, the railways were forced to pay more attention to standards of service, comfort and safety. From 1845, for example, they were all forced to run at least one train a day in each direction along their lines with third class accommodation at not more than a penny a mile. In protest many railway proprietors ran these "parliamentary trains" at the most inconvenient times of day in order to discourage people from using them. Other companies made the best of the situation, and went all out to capture extra business. Not until 1872, however, did any railway company allow third class passengers aboard its prestigious express trains. Two years later, the London and North Western Railway ran the first sleeper car service, between London and Glasgow. In 1879, the Great Northern Railway installed a dining-car service – the first – on its London to Leeds line. Both sleepers and dining cars were at first reserved for first class passengers only. Corridor trains with toilet facilities were first run in the 1890s, and promoted express non-stop runs from one distant city to another.

The most prominent landmarks in many Victorian towns and cities were the new railway stations. When the great Doric colonnade of Euston Station was erected in 1837, the year of Queen Victoria's accession, it was hailed as the eighth wonder of the world; and St. Pancras was similarly praised later on. Dr. Carus, a German doctor who visited London in 1844, noted that Paddington Station had greatly changed the lives of those who lived nearby, not only by increasing local traffic, but by the eviction of tenants whose homes lay in the path of the proposed railway. As the first tracks were put down, housing began to develop by their side; these were to be the smoky slums of the next generation. Charles Manby Smith wrote in his *Curiosities of London Life* (1853) of "the deep gorge of a railway cutting, which has ploughed its way through the centre of the market gardens, and burrowing beneath the carriage road, and knocking a thousand houses out of its

path, pursues its circuitous course to the City." It was reckoned for example that the North London Railway Company once demolished nine hundred houses for the sake of building a mere two miles of track; and *The Working Man* estimated that by 1856 twenty thousand people had been displaced by the building of the Euston terminal. The railway companies were supposed to rehouse the homeless, but this often took months or years, and the new accommodation was usually at higher rents. But the railways helped to solve some social problems, too. With the rise of fairly cheap services, many families were able to migrate

Left The Metropolitan underground being constructed in London. *Right* Farringdon Road Station in London (1866)

Top King's Cross railway terminus of the Great Northern Railway in London. *Above* Inside King's Cross Station (1863)

from London into villages in Surrey, Sussex, Middlesex and Kent, and travel to work each day. These villages laid the foundations of the so-called "commuter belt" of London suburbia.

The labourers – many of them Irish – who built the railways, were named "navvies". The biographer Samuel Smiles found the navvies a "remarkable class". During the pioneer days of the railways and after, the navvy wandered about from one place of work to another, apparently belonging to no country and having no fixed home. His typical dress was a white felt hat with the brim turned up, a velveteen or "jean square-tailed coat", a scarlet plush waistcoat with little black spots, and a bright red neckerchief about his Herculean neck. He wore corduroy breeches tied and buttoned at the knee, displaying beneath a solid calf and foot encased in strong high-laced boots.

"Working together, eating, drinking and sleeping together, and daily exposed to the same influences, these railway labourers soon presented a distinct and well-defined character, strongly marking them from the population of the districts in which they laboured. Reckless alike of their lives as of their earnings, the navvies worked hard and lived hard. For their lodging, a hut of turf would content them; and in their hours of leisure the meanest public house would serve for their parlour. Unburdened, as they usually were, by domestic ties, unsoftened by family affection, and without much moral or religious training, the navvies came to be distinguished by a sort of savage manners, which contrasted strongly with those of the surrounding population."

Smiles added: "Yet ignorant and violent though they may be, they were usually good-hearted fellows in the main – frank and open-handed with their comrades, and ready to share their last penny with those in distress. Their pay nights were often a saturnalia of riot and disorder, dreaded by the inhabitants of the villages along the line of works."

By the end of the century, the steam railways of Britain had achieved a high degree of sophistication, comfort, safety and speed. They were no longer regarded with the same fear and fascination as when they had first appeared. About 22,000 miles of track were in use, and more than 1,000 million journeys undertaken each year. The *Sphere* noted in 1900 that, "The Great Western Railway had made very material improvements in the railway service between London and Cork. . . . They have built certain corridor trains with first, second and third class carriages, all of various stages of luxury. The first class carriages have a luxurious arrangement of white and gold, the second of mahogany and velvet, and the third a most effective arrangement of oak and red wool." A corridor ran down the whole length of the train, through the middle of the coaches; and the passengers could not only dine, but summon an attendant to serve light refreshments by pushing a bell at the side of their seats.

An English provincial railway station (Marlow in Buckinghamshire)

All the railway companies took great pride in their service, and identified themselves with liveries. The London, Brighton and South Coast Railway, with terminals at London Bridge and Victoria, had engines of brilliant *gamboge* and brass fittings, which later gave way to a more sober chocolate colour. The Midland Railway, which operated from St. Pancras in London, had coaches and engines of crimson lake, while the South Eastern and Chatham preferred a simple green and brass livery. The locomotives of the Great Western Railway and Great Central Railway were both painted in green, and the Great Western coaches in chocolate and cream.

Underground railways, too, were making their appearance and rendering a valuable service to London commuters. In 1900 there were three underground electric railway companies in London. The City and South London electric railway, which opened in 1890, ran for three and a half miles. The City and Waterloo, which was also electric, was opened in 1898 and ran for a mile and a half. In 1900, the Prince of Wales opened the third railway, the Central London (popularly known as the "twopenny tube"). This ran from the Bank of England to Shepherd's Bush, and was built at a cost of nearly four million pounds. A fourth line was also under construction at this time, the Baker Street and Waterloo Railway of three miles. These lines were the foundation of London's modern network of underground railways.

Rowland Hill

Left The "Penny Black", the world's first adhesive postage stamp. *Right* Inside the London post office (1875)

The Penny Post

Before 1840, postal charges on letters and packets depended partly upon the distance they were sent, not inside the country and abroad, and upon their weight. But after Rowland Hill (1795–1879) had introduced the standard Penny Post postal business greatly increased, to the benefit of the community as a whole. Hill's idea was that, instead of having a complicated scale of charges, and all the difficulties and delays that such a system involved, the public should be able to send a half-ounce letter anywhere within the United Kingdom for a fixed charge of a penny. Many people were sceptical of the plan, but Hill was proved right. The expansion of business which resulted not only reduced postal charges, but made the postal service much more widely available. (Previously, the average scale charge per letter had been

POSTING PARCELS

DIVISIONAL SORTING

DESPATCHING ROOM

LOADING VANS

THE

around seven pence.) Rowland Hill himself later became secretary in the Post Office, immediately responsible to the Postmaster-General.

As before 1840, Hill's scheme allowed the postage to be either prepaid, or paid on delivery. Prepayment was shown by sticking a small stamp to the envelope. The stamps were red, black or blue, and carried a small portrait of Queen Victoria. The first pillar boxes were put up in London in 1855; postcards and the halfpenny stamp were introduced fifteen years later. Money orders had been in use since as early as 1838, although postal orders not until 1881. Another important innovation was the Post Office Savings Bank, founded in 1861. The Post Office made full use of railways and steam ships, as well as stage-coaches, to deliver post, and itself became nationally responsible for telegraphy in 1869, and telephones in 1912. The first airmail was carried from London to Windsor in 1911.

The Horseless Carriage

Railways had lost much of their novelty by the end of the nineteenth century. In contemporaries' eyes, the most spectacular new development was the horseless carriage. European inventors like Nicholas Cugnot, Jean Lenoir, Emile Levassor, the Marquis de Dion and others in France, and Germans like Karl Benz and Gottlieb Daimler, were perfecting these remarkable new machines. In Britain, too, John Dunlop had made an important contribution in the form of a pneumatic tyre.

The development of motor-car engineering in England was held back by the existing transport laws, which prohibited any mechanically propelled vehicle from travelling faster than four miles an hour on the public highways. To make matters worse, every such vehicle had to be manned by at least three persons, one of whom had to walk at least twenty yards ahead to warn other road users of its approach. This low speed limit was not raised (to fourteen miles per hour) until as late as 1896, by the Locomotives on Highways Act. To celebrate this new found freedom, the Motor Car Club staged a ceremonial run from London down to Brighton on the south coast, a route which is still run once a year in commemoration of the new dawn of motoring. The first London to Brighton run took place on 14th November, 1896.

The first petrol engine made by Benz in 1886

The first Daimler motor car

Opposite A sketch from the *Illustrated London News* of the first day of the parcel post (1883)

Top An early motor van used by a London department store (1897). *Above* A Gardner Serpollet built for Edward VII

Below Horseless carriage in London (1896). *Bottom* Horses versus the motor car

If her laws had prevented Britain from making much progress in the new field of transport, as compared with Europe or the United States, many people were fully aware of the potential of the horseless carriage, whose success had after all been shown in other countries. During a cab drivers' strike in London in 1896, *Punch* warned:

> *Hansoms and growlers together,*
> *Fares don't care for your love or your war!*
> *In this coming November*
> *Just please to remember*
> *You've a rival – the new motor car!*

There was much popular scepticism about the reliability of the new machines. Much of it was amply justified. Breakdowns were frequent, and an owner had to be a fairly skilled mechanic if he hoped to stay on the road. Petrol (gasoline) stations ("petrol stockists") were few and far between, as were automobile services of any kind. In 1900 *Punch* pictured a proud car owner driving his wife to Epsom in a motor car, but taking his horses along with him as well in case the motor car broke down.

Most of the 10,000-odd cars on English roads in 1900 were still of foreign manufacture, mostly French, German or American. One of the most popular cars in this early period of British motoring was the German Daimler, which from 1893 operated in Britain as the Daimler Motor Syndicate, and three years later as the Daimler Motor Company Limited. The first Daimler appeared in Britain the following year. The new company, operating under licence, began to prosper under royal patronage, which began with the Prince of Wales' purchase of a Daimler in 1900 on the advice of Lord Montagu of Beaulieu.

The new contraption was given a great deal of popular publicity in 1900 when the newspaper proprietor Alfred Harmsworth sponsored, through the *Daily Mail*, a 1,000-mile rally from London to Edinburgh and back. Eighty-five cars entered the run, of which all but twenty finished the course, mostly with one or more breakdowns on the way. At this time, the most popular model was the Wolseley Voiturette, an English car which sold for around £225. The Wolseley won a prize in the 1900 run, as the best model of its class. There was much opposition to automobiles, as indeed there had been to railways a few decades before. Moving at speeds of up to fifteen miles an hour, the motor car was thought to pose a great danger to life and limb, especially in urban areas, and a car travelling at such a speed was often described as a "runaway". Many a motor-car owner fell foul of the law for driving too fast, or without proper attention to other road users, or for frightening horses and cattle. But by the early 1900s the motor car had firmly established itself as the essential adjunct to smart living. The *Brighton Season* reported in 1907 that on Sunday each week "weirdly masked, furred and goggled, scores if not hundreds of the Smart Set came whirling down from the metropolis to lunch perhaps at one or other of the big hotels on the front, lounge the afternoon away on the piers, sip early afternoon tea, and whizz back again to town in time for dinner."

Buses, Trams, Cabs and Bicycles

The city streets were crowded with horse-drawn omnibuses, some of which were reserved as express services. One type of omnibus was the "knife-board", so called on account of the vertical seat-dividers on the top of the vehicle. The "knife-boards" were outmoded by 1900, although they still ran on certain routes. One of the pioneers of the horse-drawn omnibus in London was Thomas Tilling, who opened his business in 1829 with a capital of a few pounds. After an early bankruptcy and other difficulties, Tilling opened a suburban service from Rye Lane into Oxford Circus, a distance of five or six miles, which took slightly under an hour and cost eighteen pence. The service was highly personal, and business men expected the bus actually to call at their house, and would send their servants out to summon it. One of Tilling's reforms was to end this practice, and make the passengers come to the bus. His grand-daughter recalled: "Those early buses were somewhat clumsy contraptions. Their wheels were iron-shod – the two front ones being much smaller than those behind; and they must have been very noisy. They could carry twenty-six people, twelve inside and fourteen outside. The seats on the roof were reached by an almost perpendicular iron ladder, which was considered neither safe nor modest for ladies to mount, which is not to be wondered at, as they wore crinolines."

Below A horse-drawn omnibus in London in 1881 with open top. *Bottom* An electric omnibus of 1897

In wet weather, the bus conductor would invite the gentlemen to give up their dry seats inside the bus, and climb upstairs into the open to make way for the ladies. A music hall song referred to this practice:

> *'Blige a lady, 'blige a lady, 'blige a lady, sir?*
> *Said I, "Old chap, she can have my lap,*
> *But I wouldn't get drenched for 'er."*
> *A little fat man with a little fat voice,*
> *From the opposite corner cried:*
> *"If she isn't content with a full-sized lap,*
> *Let her jolly well ride outside!"*

A painter's view of Victorian progress

A horse-drawn tram in Southport, Lancashire

Even as late as 1900, all Thomas Tilling's buses were still horse-drawn. His 7,000 horses cost him a weekly fortune to feed (each bus required some ten horses, working turn and turn about, in pairs or threes). Tilling did not take delivery of his first motor omnibus until 1904.

By the end of the century, a number of different kinds of tram were adding to the road congestion in the cities. There were horse-drawn trams, steam trams, and some electric trams. Trams had first been brought to England by the American G. F. Train, who installed tram lines in 1861 at Bayswater, Victoria, and from Westminster out to Kennington. Train also founded tram routes in the provinces, for example in Birkenhead, Darlington, and in the Potteries in Staffordshire. Steam trams first appeared in Govan, Scotland, in 1877, and cable trams in Edinburgh in 1899.

London was slow to adopt electric trams, compared with some European capitals like Berlin, and major cities in the United States of America. The London County Council had nothing but horse-drawn trams until as late as 1905. Omnibuses, hansom cabs and other forms of horse-drawn transport gave employment to about 30,000 people in London by the end of the century according to the Public Carriage Office – as hackney drivers, stage drivers and conductors. Countless others obtained a lean living as street cleaners.

For those, however, who preferred private to public transport, there was the hansom cab. In Central London the fares at the end of the century were a shilling for the first two miles, and sixpence a mile or part of a mile thereafter. For journeys beyond a radius of four miles from Charing Cross, the fare rose to a shilling a mile. A scale of extra charges covered such items as luggage, and waiting time, which at one time depended upon whether the cab had two or four wheels. Large private parties to the races or the seaside travelled by horse-drawn

Below An electric tram at Northfleet, Kent (1889). *Below right* Steam trams like this one in London did not catch on

An early Oppermann
electric motor carriage

A Daimler oil motor
carriage

An electrical cab

charabanc or horse-brake – a wagonette capable of carrying thirty
people. Wealthy people still maintained their own private carriages
and four-in-hands, and Londoners took much pleasure in exercising
them in Rotten Row in Hyde Park on Sunday mornings.

The bicycle rendered a great service to ordinary life, in giving
factory workers and clerks the means of travelling rapidly and cheaply
about the countryside, giving them the opportunity to find fresh air
and explore the English countryside. A good machine, such as the
Triumph, cost about ten pounds, although cheaper models were
available. Tandems were popular, too. As the internal combustion
engine was developed, cycles became mechanized, and one of the most
striking attractions at the Cycle Show in London in 1899 was the
motorcycle.

The new fangled tandem bicycle was celebrated by the music hall
artiste Katie Lawrence in 1892, suitably clad in bloomers and woollen
stockings:

> *Daisy, Daisy, give me your answer true.*
> *I'm half crazy, all for the love of you!*
> *It won't be a stylish marriage,*
> *I can't afford a carriage,*
> *But you'll look sweet*
> *Upon the seat*
> *Of a bicycle made for two!*

From City to Suburb

The growth of new travel services began to change the working lives of
many people. In 1860 for example, some 300,000 people travelled into
the City of London each day from the suburbs, and by the end of the
century this number rose to about 400,000. They included clerks and
other working people from their crowded terrace homes in Dalston,

Below left A curious kind of
tandem bicycle of the 1880s.
Centre The first motorcycle
(1887). *Right* A form of penny-
farthing bicycle of 1885

Brixton, New Cross, Forest Hill, Walthamstow and Tottenham; small tradesmen from Kennington, Stockwell and Camberwell; and the more affluent classes from Balham, Sydenham, Highgate, Hampstead, Barnes and Richmond. The housewives and their families who stayed behind in these new suburbs had thousands of new shops and local services of all kinds. For suburban recreation and education, many new Institutes, Free Libraries, Clubs and Guilds sprang up – societies and clubs for bicycling, rambling, football, cricket, or rowing on the Thames, orchestral and choral societies. Sir Walter Besant wrote with approval that "many of the Nonconformist Chapels provide a continuous round of these amusements. They keep the young men occupied in the evening, and they generally advocate, if they do not enforce, total abstinence from strong drink; they are developing a kind of young man very superior to his predecessor – better read, better behaved, of better physique." The womenfolk no doubt benefited, being "less frivolous, much healthier; they know a great deal more; they take broader views of life; they are even taller and stronger."

Steam Ships

The growing knowledge of steam power, which made possible the growth of the railways in the first part of the nineteenth century, also made possible the rise of the steam ship. The steam ship rapidly came to dominate English mercantile traffic and to win for England more than half the world's shipping tonnage by the middle of the nineteenth century. Two men who pioneered steam ships were William Symington (1763–1831) and Henry Bell (1767–1830) of Glasgow. In 1802, Symington successfully launched a prototype steam ship, the *Charlotte Dundas*, based upon a patent he had taken out as early as 1789. The *Charlotte Dundas* towed two barges of seventy tons a distance of twenty miles along the Forth and Clyde Canal, in the face of extremely adverse weather. Shortly afterwards Symington demonstrated the vessel to the great canal proprietor, the Duke of Bridgewater. But the Duke did not have long to live, and Symington himself despaired of making further progress, plunged as he was in debt. Henry Bell had watched Symington's trials with interest, and in 1812 he built a rather larger steam ship, whose 4·5 horsepower engine operated two paddles amidship. This was the *Comet* which ran a ferry service along the River Clyde in Scotland, and then between Glasgow, Oban and Fort William. The *Comet* was wrecked in 1820 (by sea, not by explosion as some people had predicted).

In 1838, a year after the young Queen Victoria had come to the throne, the first trans-Atlantic crossing was made by steam ship. The ship was the *Sirius*, which left with a cargo of coal and forty passengers on 4th April from Cork in Ireland. The *Sirius* arrived in New York eighteen days later, to a wildly enthusiastic reception. She had beaten her larger rival, Isambard Brunel's *Great Western*, by only a few hours (although the *Great Western* had not set out from Bristol until 7th April, and actually made a faster crossing than the *Sirius*).

The trans-Atlantic steam-ship crossings of the later 1830s attracted wide publicity on both sides of the Atlantic. This was largely because of the growing traffic of emigrants from England to the New World in the years of depression. In 1840 a Nova Scotia merchant won an official contract to run a regular service on the route from Liverpool (England) to Halifax (Nova Scotia) and thence to Boston: this was Samuel Cunard. One of Cunard's early passengers was Charles Dickens, who sailed to America aboard the steam ship *Britannia* in 1842, and recorded his experiences in his *American Notes*. The crossing, which took about ten days, did not much appeal to him. "Before descending into the bowels of the ship," he wrote, "we had passed from the deck into a long narrow apartment, not unlike a gigantic hearse with windows in the side; having at the upper end a melancholy stove, at which three or four chilly stewards were warming their hands, while on either side, extending down its whole dreary length, was a long, long table, over each of which a rack, fixed to the low roof, and stuck full of drinking glasses, and cruet stands, hinted dismally at rolling seas and heavy weather." At midnight, during the voyage, Dickens wrote, the *Britannia* shipped a heavy sea which crashed down through the skylights and flooded down into the ladies' cabin, much to the consternation of his wife and other passengers, who were in great fear of being struck by lightning.

In the same year (1840) that the *Britannia* entered service, an important new maritime company was formed, the Peninsular and

Building the *Great Eastern* steam ship in 1857

The *Cutty Sark*

Oriental, which served routes to the East, and from 1852 to Australia. People wishing to travel to India would sail first to Alexandria in Egypt, and cross overland to Port Suez on the Red Sea to take a second vessel. After the Suez Canal had been opened in 1869, the voyage could be undertaken by a single ship.

The *Britannia*, like all the early steam ships, carried sail as well, since it was not envisaged in the early days that steam would entirely replace sail. Indeed, some of the greatest sailing ships of history were built in the nineteenth century, for example the *Cutty Sark* (1869), which could sail from Sydney, Australia, to England in as little as seventy-five days, reaching speeds of $17\frac{1}{2}$ knots. The opening of the Suez Canal drove the clippers away from the China tea trade, and the *Cutty Sark* and other ships like her began to concentrate upon the Australian wool trade. The *Cutty Sark* was no mere maritime showpiece; she could carry a cargo of two million pounds of wool, as could the *Thermopylae*, another famous vessel. The *Cutty Sark* is now on display in dry dock at Greenwich, London. The steam ships helped to bring the most distant places within reach of London, and to create communications and new markets for manufactured goods which beforehand had hardly been dreamed of.

The Great Exhibition

One of the most spectacular events in the widening Victorian world was the Great Exhibition of 1851. The Exhibition was a great show-piece for contemporary science and invention, and it attracted hundreds of thousands of visitors from all parts of the world. The Exhibition building – the Crystal Palace – was fittingly opened by Queen Victoria on 1st May, 1851. Next day *The Times* reported: "There was yesterday witnessed a sight the like of which has never happened before, and which, in the nature of things, can never be repeated. . . . In a building that could easily have accommodated twice as many, twenty-five thousand persons, so it is computed, were arranged in order round the throne of our Sovereign. Around them, amidst them, and over their heads was displayed all that is useful or beautiful in nature or in art. Above them rose a glittering arch far more lofty and spacious than the vaults of even our noblest cathedrals. On either side the vista seemed almost boundless."

The writer added, "Some saw in it the second and more glorious inauguration of the Sovereign, some a solemn dedication of art and its stores; some were most reminded of that day when all ages and climes shall be gathered round the throne of their Maker. . . . All contributed to an effect so grand, and yet so natural, that it hardly seemed to be put together by design, or to be the work of human artificers."

The Great Exhibition of the Works of Industry of All Nations – to give it its full title – originated in the series of industrial exhibitions organized from 1847 by the two leading figures in the Society of Arts, Prince Albert and Henry Cole. Their first exhibition in 1847 drew 20,000 visitors and another the following year 70,000, while that in 1849 topped 100,000. Cole and the Prince Consort then had the idea

Inside the Great Exhibition Hall the crowds await the arrival of Queen Victoria for the opening ceremony on 1st May, 1851

of staging the first international exhibition, in Hyde Park. The plan was a bold and imaginative mixture of idealism and materialism; for not only did the Great Exhibition serve as a fine monument to human progress, it also produced a healthy profit. Enthusiastic support was gained for the whole project when the designer Joseph Paxton put forward his plan for a great glass palace in the pages of the *Illustrated London News*. The Executive Committee soon invited tenders, and work was begun on laying the site's foundations. An opponent of the plan – Colonel Sibthorp – declared that "the dearest wish of my heart is that that confounded building called the Crystal Palace might be dashed to pieces." Despite all the gloomy predictions of architects, engineers and others, rapid progress was made by the 2,000 workmen, and the great structure began to rise into the sky. The public grew excited at this leviathan in their midst, and the more so when the cartloads of strange exhibits began to pour in. Prince Albert wrote, "Just at present I am more dead than alive from overwork."

The last of many public rows which beset the Great Exhibition was sparked off by an official decision (in the interest of royal security) to open the Exhibition in private; only Queen Victoria and an invited audience were to attend. But this was too much for public opinion. *The Times*, as usual, offered a piece of firm advice: "What an unworthy part would these nervous advisers cause the Queen of England to play! Surely Queen Victoria is not Tiberius or Louis XI, that she should be smuggled out of a great glass building under cover of the truncheons of the police and the broadswords of the Life Guards. Where most Englishmen are gathered together, there the Queen of England is most secure." So, the public were admitted, although in view of the demand only season-ticket holders were allowed in. Apparently, these numbered more than 25,000. Queen Victoria wrote in her journal (1st May): "This day is one of the greatest and most glorious days of our lives, with which to my pride and joy the name of my dearly beloved Albert is forever associated! It is a day which makes my heart swell with thankfulness."

But plans for the Exhibition got off to a shaky start. The first hurdle was overcome when Queen Victoria gave her permission for Hyde Park to be used as the site, and personally contributed £1,000 toward the

The Great Exhibition housed in its Crystal Palace

Prince Albert

Erecting the Great Exhibition hall in 1850

Queen Victoria and Prince Albert opening the Great Exhibition on
1st May, 1851

Dakin's patent coffee-roasting
apparatus, one of the thousands
of pieces of mechanical ingenuity
on display at the Great
Exhibition

Exhibition building fund. But when the full details of the building
plans became public, a great uproar broke out. Surely it was not
seriously proposed to destroy sixteen acres of London's most central
and popular open space? To do so would be an act of sheer public
vandalism. On 25th June, 1850, *The Times* declared: "The whole of
Hyde Park and, we will venture to predict, the whole of Kensington
Gardens, will be turned into the bivouac of all the vagabonds of
London so long as the Exhibition shall continue. . . . The annoyance
inflicted upon the neighbourhood will be indescribable." And two
days later, *The Times* loudly drew attention to the fact that the
building was to be no mere "booth" or "timber shed", but "a solid,
substantial edifice of brick, and iron and stone, calculated to endure
the wear and tear of the next hundred years." In fact it was to be as
large as Buckingham Palace itself. "Once more we entreat the Prince
and his adviser to pause ere it be too late."

The attack in Parliament was led by an eccentric reactionary,
Colonel Charles Sibthorp, the 67-year-old Member for Lincoln. He
protested in the House of Commons: "The object of its promoters is to
introduce amongst us foreign stuff of every description, live and dead

The Crystal Palace at Sydenham (1854)

stock, without regard to quality or quantity. It is meant to bring down prices in this country, and to pave the way for the establishment of the cheap and nasty trash and trumpery system. . . . I would advise persons residing near the Park to keep a sharp lookout after their silver forks and spoons and servant maids." But vocal though the opposition was, it was not strong enough and the plans went ahead to accommodate the 14,000 exhibitors.

And so the Exhibition began, organized incidentally under a moral code which earned the Queen's approval: it was to be closed on Sundays, alcoholic liquor was not to be sold (only soft drinks and filtered water), and smoking was forbidden.

The Exhibition represented the zenith of technical, scientific and artistic achievement from every part of the world; the products on show ranged from a modest clock to the enormous Koh-i-Noor diamond. Between its opening in May 1851, and its official closing in October, more than six million people visited the Exhibition. The Crystal Palace was taken down in 1852 and reassembled in a modified form outside London at Sydenham, where it was finally destroyed by fire in 1936.

Sheffield steel figured prominently in the Great Exhibition of 1851. Here is a craftman's case of saws, axes, adzes, augers, chisels, knives *etc.*

41

3 *The Labouring Classes*

The Labouring Classes

In the early 1800s, most English people were leading much the same kind of lives that their parents and grandparents had. In the towns, the menfolk worked as shopkeepers and tradesmen, or as craftsmen such as tailors and bootmakers, carpenters and masons. Others worked as watermen or wagoners and carriers, or in great houses as domestic servants, grooms, ostlers, cooks and footmen. Before the young Queen Victoria came to the throne in 1837 far more men and women worked in traditional occupations than in the new cotton mills, or coal and iron mines. But the numbers employed in heavy industry were visibly growing. The first steam operated loom in Manchester had been installed in 1806, but by 1837 there were some 85,000 power looms in England as a whole. The first steam-driven printing press was built in 1814 and was for a time regarded as a strange novelty.

At the same time as these technical innovations were being made, improvements were being seen in communications. Two great Scottish engineers, Thomas Telford (1757–1834) and John McAdam (1756–1836), pioneered the remarking and resurfacing of the country's main highways; new canals were enabling heavy goods, notably coal, ores and industrial machinery, to be moved cheaply and easily from the coal fields to the sea ports. A developing banking system generated finance and credit for expensive new projects of all kinds.

Hand-in-hand with industrialization went a dramatic increase in population, providing more labour and more markets for new projects. In 1811 the official census had put the population at twelve millions, but by 1851, the year of the Great Exhibition, the figure had risen to more than twenty-one millions. London itself grew from 960,000 in 1801 to some 2,400,000 by 1831, and like other cities began to draw outlying hamlets and villages within its orbit.

This table shows how five major towns and cities were growing:

	1801	1831
London	960,000	2,400,000
Liverpool	82,000	202,000
Leeds	53,000	123,000
Manchester	59,000	238,000
Glasgow	77,000	193,000

Opposite: above and below Nineteenth-century labourers

Bricklayers building terraced houses

Perhaps the main reason for this population explosion was the decrease of child mortality. Despite continuing social problems, many people were better fed, clothed and housed, and were realizing the value of proper sanitation and hygiene.

The novelty of urban growth in the 1830s and 1840s was a source of never-ending wonder to the Victorians. It was a wonder compounded of fear and fascination. In *Dombey and Son* (1847), Charles Dickens had referred to the "disorderly crop of beginnings of mean houses, rising out of the rubbish, as if they had been unskilfully sown there." In the shadow of the industrial revolution which was growing apace, thousands of families who had lived for centuries on the land were either drawn into the towns by the lure of better paid jobs, or found their own localities swallowed up in the meandering urban districts that arose on the great new coal and iron fields or textile centres. The industrial Midlands, of Lancashire, Derbyshire, Warwickshire and Nottinghamshire became aptly known as "the Black Country".

Left A coal pit worked by a woman. *Right* Early nineteenth-century dustman

Urban Poverty

By the middle of the century, thousands of new and cheaply built houses had been put up to house mine and factory workers. As Charles Eastlake observed in his *Hints on Household Taste* (1868), "no one need be surprised to find the meadow land which he walked in spring laid out in populous streets by Christmas." By the great new coal mines, dreary brick and slate-roofed terraces sprang up, often built back-to-back, and having little or no water supplies or sanitary facilities. Thousands of such terraces were built either by mine and mill owners or by property speculators, and in most cases no thought was given to making the properties attractive. Building and town planning regulations were more or less non-existent. The windows and doors were small, and hardly seemed to welcome the light and air. The French historian François Guizot, who visited London in 1840, wrote that the "public buildings, houses and shops, all appeared to me little, monotonous, and meanly ornamented."

The terraced houses in the Midlands and northern industrial towns like Manchester, Salford, Bolton or Doncaster were only seen by the employers as a way to enabling their workers to live close to their place of work. Many of these houses were seriously overcrowded, and were in perpetual danger from the hazards of typhus, cholera and smallpox. These were England's first real urban slums, many of which still mark the face of the country today.

In 1844 the Society for Improving the Condition of the Labouring Classes, whose President was Prince Albert, was one body to take action. The Society built a set of two-storey "model dwelling houses" at Bagnigge Wells, to house twenty-three families and thirty spinsters. Soon after, Pickfords Freight Company built lodging houses in Camden Town, London, for some of their employees. Until control of housing became recognized as the responsibility of the government, remedies lay more or less entirely in the hands of charities, or of private enterprise.

Left Ironwork chimneys in Glasgow at St. Rollosc (1859). *Right* Working-class slum in Birmingham in the 1870s

Below left In the days before town planning people often lived in the middle of industrial areas. *Below* Colliers' slate-roofed cottages near the coal pits. *Bottom* Model dwelling houses erected by philanthropists in London (1852)

A steel factory in Sheffield

The London of Dickens and Mayhew

London remained far and away the greatest city in England. Overseas visitors were struck by the endless social contrasts of the twin cities of London and Westminster: riches and poverty, traditions and innovations, vice and religion. The London bustle was a constant marvel to the young Charles Dickens. In *Household Words* (1853) he recalled: "When I was a very small boy indeed, both in years and stature, I got lost one day in the City of London." He wandered about, "staring at the British merchants, and inspired by a mighty faith in the marvellousness of everything. Up courts and down courts, in and out of yards and little squares, peeping into counting house passages and running away, poorly feeding the echoes in the court of the South Sea House with my timid steps, roaming into Austin Friars, and wondering how the Friars used to like it, ever staring at the British merchants, and never tired of the shops, I rambled on all through the day."

But the marvels of the great public buildings, the banks and commercial offices, the fine houses along the Strand, had to be set against the squalor of the poor quarters. In his *Sketches by Boz* (1836) Dickens wrote that the filthy and miserable aspect of some parts of London was hardly to be believed, even by those who knew of them. Wretched houses with broken windows patched with rags and paper; every room tenanted by a different family and often two or three families; barbers and fish sellers operating in the front parlours, and cobblers in the back; filth everywhere; "a gutter before the houses and a drain behind, clothes drying and slops emptying from the windows . . . men and women, in every variety of scanty and dirty apparel, lounging, scolding, drinking, smoking, squabbling, fighting and swearing."

In 1844, the Society for Improving the Condition of the Labouring Classes began enquiring into housing conditions throughout London. In the parish of St. George's, Hanover Square, the Society found 1,465 families living in 2,174 rooms. One room measuring twenty-two feet by sixteen housed some fifty people, "besides dogs and cats". But as in so many other spheres of social reform, much remained to be done until the turn of the century, when the first London County Council was formed, and housing reformers like Octavia Hill had helped to publicize the problem.

But even then the housing problem remained acute. A Methodist minister, Joseph Ritson, spoke out strongly against overcrowding in London. In the 1890s, he pointed out that more than 500 of the 700 families living in the borough of Marylebone were forced to live in single rooms. He went on: "In London alone, there are nearly 50,000 families each occupying only a single room, and in most of them the conditions of health and morality are utterly absent." Ritson found one room where the "walls and ceilings are black with the secretions of filth which have gathered upon them through the long years of neglect. It is exuding through the cracks in the boards overhead, it is running down the walls, it is everywhere. What goes by the name of a window is half of it stuffed with rags or covered by board to keep out wind and

An electric time-ball and clock, in the Strand, London (1852)

Lord Shaftesbury, the social reformer

Opposite: above The Prince Regent's pavilion at Brighton on the south coast of England. Under his patronage Brighton soon became a fashionable resort. *Below* Fashionable people taking the seaside air on one of Brighton's piers

Left Charles Dickens. *Right* A dark London slum about 1840

rain; the rest is begrimed and obscure so that scarcely any light can enter or anything be seen outside."

Many people were not even lucky enough to share a single room. London had thousands of homeless people. Patrick Colquhoun, a London magistrate who died in 1820, had estimated that London contained 20,000 people without shelter, apart from what they could find in common lodging houses, or in alleys, warehouses, or under arches. In 1843, the great reformer Lord Shaftesbury (1801–85) told the House of Commons how he had found a boy living inside a lawn roller in Regent's Park. Those who made their living on the River Thames as watermen and fishermen often had no other home than their small river craft. At night London's parks were filled with hundreds of vagrants, who slept under the shelter of the trees.

In the summer, many of them slept on the Thames Embankment, and even on the bridges over the river. "Indeed," Ritson said, "it is a sight to cross London Bridge after midnight, and to look at the recesses filled with poor homeless ones in all attitudes, trying to snatch a few hours' relief from life's misery. Where several families are in one house, the street door is left open, and in the morning seven or eight persons will be found in the passage or on the stairs."

Of all those who have portrayed London life, from Charles Dickens to Charles Booth at the end of the century, one of the greatest was Henry Mayhew, whose book *London Labour and the London Poor* (1851), is a classic of its kind. Many of the characters in its pages are unmistakably cockney. Mayhew himself described his book as "the first attempt to publish the history of a people, from the lips of the people themselves." It was designed "to give the rich a more intimate knowledge of the suffering, and the frequent heroism under those sufferings, of the poor."

A dirty London street about 1850

Left Sleeping rough in London

Top Family of beggars in London's East End (1872)

Above The hurdy-gurdy man, London (1872)

Mayhew interviewed hundreds of the London poor while compiling his book. One of the groups he described were the "running patterers". These were down-and-outs or urchins who paraded up and down the streets selling scurrilous penny papers, whose purple accounts of the latest murder or society scandal were eagerly purchased by the lower middle classes. These stories were often pure fiction, and known as "cocks" (cock-and-bull stories). Mayhew reckoned that the public paid out more than £3,000 each year to the hundred-odd London patterers. One well-known "cock" was *The Scarborough Tragedy*, a pamphlet which remained in print for over a generation. One patterer who stocked it explained: "*The Scarborough Tragedy* is very attractive. It draws tears to the women's eyes to think that a poor clergyman's daughter, who is remarkably beautiful, should murder her own child; it's very touching to a feeling heart. There's a copy of verses with it, too." Murders were the most popular subject of patters, together with real or imagined gallows-confessions. Such was the Victorian Londoner's appetite for sensationalism.

More select than the running patterers were the ballad-sellers. These men often had a smattering of education and a fondness for late-eighteenth-century poets like Oliver Goldsmith. Sometimes they would recite verses aloud on street corners, or write and distribute their own ballads to passers-by. One, called *A Husband's Dream*, dealt with a subject very close to the heart of Victorian London, alcoholism:

> *Oh, Dermot, you look healthy now,*
> *Your dress is neat and clean;*
> *I never see you drunk about,*
> *Then tell me where you've been.*
>
> *Your wife and family, are they well?*
> *You once did use them strange:*
> *Oh, are you kinder to them grown,*
> *How came this happy change?*

The reason, apparently, was that Dermot had had a nightmare in which his alcoholism had been punished by the death of his wife. Dermot replied:

> *I pressed her to my throbbing heart*
> *Whilst joyous tears did stream;*
> *And ever since, I've heaven blessed*
> *For sending me that dream.*

The stronger the moral, the higher the sale. The author of *A Husband's Dream* claimed to have sold 10,000 copies, although the local printer had given him only five shillings for it.

The River Thames was an integral part of London life. The Port of London, filled with ships and merchantmen of all nations, was one of the greatest in the world. The river was not only a great artery of trade; it was also an important thoroughfare for the capital, and carried thousands of small craft. The Thames gave a livelihood to many very poor people, including the "mudlarks". The mudlarks, who were usually children, combed the dirty shores of the river at low tide to collect scraps of coal or wood, or any other debris worth a few pence, scattered by the flotilla of vessels which used the river each day.

Mayhew spoke to two Irish boys aged thirteen and eleven years, who were working as mudlarks. The elder of the two told of their work. He was dressed in a brown fustian coat and vest, greasy canvas trousers, a striped shirt, and peaked cap. "When the bargemen heave coals to be carried from their barge to the shore, pieces drop into the water among the mud, which we afterwards pick up. Sometimes we wade in the mud to the ankle, at other times to the knee. Sometimes pieces of coal do not sink, but remain on the surface of the mud; at other times we seek for them with our hands and feet. . . . The most I ever gathered in a day was a shilling's worth. . . . I sell the coals to the poor people in the neighbourhood."

The mudlarks kept a sharp lookout for pieces of iron such as rivets, nails and washers, which could be sold for scrap at a farthing per pound. Copper was a relatively rich prize, since it fetched three half-pence a pound. The mudlarks were continually harried by the Thames police, and by the watermen – not surprisingly, since the boys used to steal aboard the anchored barges to push lumps of coal into the mud, where they could claim it as debris. The Irish boy ended: "I have been in the habit of stealing pieces of rope, lumps of coal and other articles for the last two years, but my parents do not know of this. I have never been tried before the police court for any felony. It is my intention to go to sea, as my brothers have done, so soon as I can find a captain to take me on board his ship. I would like this much better than to be a coal-heaver on the river."

A mudlark

Left Taking the population census in a crowded London tenement. *Right* Mudlarks by the River Thames at low tide

Manchester: Symbol of Progress

One of the great new Victorian cities was Manchester. Already in the eighteenth century, Manchester had begun to prosper through the cotton trade. Between 1801 and 1831 she more than doubled in size. Her affairs were dominated by the great local textile magnates, the land-owners, and the factory owners. With no machinery of local govern-ment to regulate her expansion, Manchester grew and multiplied. As

The dense smoke of industrial Manchester

early as 1808, a visitor to the town had commented: "The steam engine is pestiferous, the dye houses noisesome and offensive, and the water of the river as black as ink or the Stygian lake."

But most people were impressed, rather than offended. An article in *Chamber's Edinburgh Journal* fifty years later declared: "Manchester streets may be irregular, and its trading inscriptions pretentious, its smoke may be dense, and its mud ultra-muddy, but not any or all of these things can prevent the image of a great city rising before us as the very symbol of civilization, foremost in the march of improvement, and grand incarnation of progress."

For Victorians, the word "progress" had a semi-mystical meaning. Not until the sprawling foundations of England's great cities had been laid, well into the second half of the century, did contemporaries begin to feel that urban development ought to be taken in hand. They ceased to marvel at "a principle of life centred on a wholly new principle", and began to give some thought to the dreary quality of life which these towns imposed upon so many of their citizens, in their housing, work and public health.

In the early years of the century, Manchester had enjoyed a great economic boom; work was easy to find and relatively well paid. But in the late 1820s the easy times came to an end. From 1829 onward Manchester was the scene of bitter and violent social discontent, earning for itself an unenviable reputation as a city ripe for violent revolution. It is often said that if Victorian England had ever had a revolution, it would have been sparked off in Manchester.

Manchester had no popular Parliamentary representation, and the vocal discontent of her citizens could not find constitutional expression. The great Whig Parliamentary reform movement of 1831–32, culminating in a small middle-class extension of the franchise, was irrelevant to

Nineteenth-century Manchester

Manchester's needs, and indeed those of other new industrial towns. The people of Manchester were concerned with bad housing, starvation wages and oppressive employment – not with votes. In the general election of 1832, the two members returned by the minority middle-class voters of Manchester were both seen as diehard enemies of the working class.

A tract called the *Reformer's Prayer* parodying the litany was widely circulated in Manchester during 1831: "From all those damnable bishops, lords and peers, from all those bloody murdering Peterloo butchers, from all those idle drones that live on the earnings of the people, good Lord deliver us." The language of the class struggle in Manchester at that time was bitter and unrestrained. The *Manchester Guardian* was accused by its radical rival the *Manchester Advertiser* as "the common heap in which every purse-proud booby shoots his basket of dirt and falsehood . . . foul prostitute and dirty parasite of the worst portion of the mill owners."

Part of the fear of Manchester, in middle- and upper-class circles, arose from the lack of protection and security. There was no real police force, no real local government. In an emergency the authorities would have no other resort than armed troops. The mere threat of this fostered a mood of civil war.

Violence and riots: this was one aspect of life in Manchester. But if the town was feared by the authorities, it was glorified by many other people who saw in her cotton mills and textile factories an economic blueprint of the future. The historian Thomas Carlyle (1795–1881) found Manchester "every whit as wonderful, as fearful, as unimaginable, as the oldest Salem or prophetic city." But this thriving city was rapidly creating a new feudal society, where the manor was the factory, the peasant the mill worker, the aristocracy the mill owners.

Left The charitable distribution of clothing in Manchester (1871). *Right* The unemployed cotton operatives in Manchester (1862)

A Manchester family living in one bare room (1862)

A textile dyeing machine (1844)

Industrial Workers

What were conditions like in the new industrial localities in the days before industrial welfare? In his book *The Manufacturing Population of England* (1833), Peter Gaskell produced a damning indictment of first-generation factory life. Many workers lived in greater poverty and hardship, and ran greater risks of disease and mortality, than they had known in the rural districts from which many of them came. Any man, Gaskell wrote, who has visited a factory at the end of the day must have noticed the ugly and sallow appearance of the people passing through the gates. "Their stature low, the average height of four hundred men, measured at different times and at different place being five feet six inches. Their limbs slender, and splaying badly and ungracefully. A very general bowing of the legs." Many women and girls, he noted, were lame, or suffered from spinal defects; most had flat feet.

These unfortunate people were little better off than slaves. They had to rise at four or five o'clock in the morning, eat a hasty and frugal breakfast, and did not have their first break (of forty minutes) until eight o'clock. At noon, an hour's break was allowed for the midday meal. Then: "Again they are immured from one o'clock till eight or nine, with the exception of twenty minutes, this being allowed for tea, or baggin-time as it is called. This imperfect meal is almost universally taken in the mill: it consists of tea and wheaten bread, with very few exceptions." Gaskell added: "During the whole of this long period they are actively and unremittingly engaged in a crowded room and an elevated temperature, so that, when finally dismissed for the day, they are exhausted equally in body and mind."

The writer added that much of the work in factories was dangerous, and uncontrolled by legislation of any kind. Dangerous steam-powered machinery was often unfenced and unsupervised. "The most common accident is the squeezing off of a single joint of a finger, somewhat less common is the loss of the whole finger. . . . Lockjaw very often follows." Those who worked in cotton mills, coal mines, ironworks, brick factories and other industries noted for their bad air, often contracted chest diseases. "The air is filled with fibrous dust, which produces chest infection especially among workers in the carding and combing rooms [of the mills]. The most common effects of this breathing of dust are blood-spitting, hard noisy breath, pains in the chest, coughs, sleeplessness . . . ending in the worst cases of consumption."

Below Dangerous unfenced machinery in a Victorian locomotive works. *Below right* Smoky railways made urban slums worse

Child Cruelty

Many of the new factories and mines depended upon child workers, who in northern England and Scotland were often ruthlessly exploited. A government report of 1833 disclosed some appalling cases of child cruelty. The factory overseers responsible for the juvenile workers were notorious of their brutality, and for their use of whips. Children often worked as many hours as the adults, and fell asleep over their machines from sheer exhaustion. One man who gave evidence to a government commission, himself a factory official, reported: "I have seen them fall asleep, and they have been performing their work with their hands while they were asleep, after the billy [spinning machine] had stopped, when their work was over. I have stopped and looked at them for two minutes, going through the motions of 'piecening' fast asleep, when there was really no work to do, and they were really doing nothing."

Children also worked in coal mines, and suffered high mortality through accident and disease. Boys worked as trappers of the coal wagons, or watched the doors in the underground tunnels, girls helped to sort and grade the excavated coal. The *Children's Employment Commission Report* (1842) found that "children are taken into these mines to work as early as four years of age, sometimes at five, and between five and six, not unfrequently between six and seven, and often from seven to eight, while from eight to nine is the ordinary age at which employment in these mines commences. . . . In several districts female children began to work in these mines at the same early ages as the males."

The *Coal Commission Report* of the same year found cases where coal workers had been denied food and rest for as long as thirty-nine hours. These were admittedly extreme cases, but they showed what could happen if conditions of work remained unchecked and uncontrolled. In the early nineteenth century, coal miners still had no protection from their employers against the risks of fire, flooding, explosion or other disasters. Small boys rotated sparking wheels to give a dim light at the coal face itself, where candles would have been too dangerous in view of the coal gas. Safety lamps of the kind devised by Humphry Davy were as yet unknown. Women, too, were employed to drag the coal wagons by chains fastened to their waists. One visitor to a mine remarked that he had not realized that the workers were female until he had noticed their ear-rings.

Below a Northumberland collier with pick-axes. *Bottom* A child coal worker with a naked gas lamp in his hat

Left Hauling coal wagons underground. *Right* Female coal workers, from the *Coal Commission Report* of 1842

A coal mine disaster in the Rhondda Valley of Wales (1887)

Boy machine operative (1844)

Boy chimney sweep

One of the worst examples of child exploitation was the use of children as chimney sweeps. The hazards undergone by children aged only five or six were great: lung poisoning, injury from falling masonry, the stunting of natural physical growth. This was to say nothing of the general discomfort of spending hours in a chimney flue filled with soot and fumes. Probably the worst affliction was "chimney sweeps' cancer", a scrotal disease. Climbing boys were chosen for their small size. One master chimney sweep, William Burges, announced on his trade card that he "flatters himself in having boys of the best size for such branches of business suitable for a Tunnel or Chimney, and that it is now in his power to render his assistance in a more extensive manner than he usually has done. He also carries his boys from room to room occasionally, to prevent them staining or marking any room floor with their feet."

Changing styles of architecture added to the hardship: Victorian chimneys tended to be narrower than those of previous times. In a multi-storey mansion, a child could easily become lost in the black labyrinth of flues forty or fifty feet up. Apprentice sweeps learned their trade by standing on the shoulders of larger sweeps, and later on were forced by pins or live coals to climb up inside by themselves. The young sweep in *Oliver Twist* remarked "there's nothing like a good blaze to make 'em come down with a run." To minimize cuts and bruises, the sweeps hardened their skin by rubbing it in brine. Chimney fires were often put out by child sweeps. A House of Lords Committee was told in the early 1800s that the proper payment for this was supposed to be five shillings, but that half this was more often paid. Sydney Smith remarked acidly: "What is a toasted child, compared to the agonies of the mistress of the house with a deranged dinner?"

The need for reform was obfuscated by the romantic nonsense of those like Charles Lamb, who spoke of "tender novices, blooming through their first nigritude, the maternal washings not effaced from their cheek" (*Praise of Chimney Sweeps*). Sir Walter Scott, on the other hand, was more practical. When he built his new house at Abbotsford he took "particular care, by the construction of the vents, that no cruelty shall be practised within its precincts." Scott's solution was to make his chimneys impossible to climb in the first place.

But even before 1800, the great reformer and philanthropist Jonas Hanway had begun to rally public opinion against these practices, for example in his *Sentimental History of Chimney Sweeps* (1785). Primitive cannibals, he said, "roast their children for food but they certainly kill them first; they are not tortured with fire and soot, hunger and thirst, cold and nakedness." Within three years an Act of Parliament was passed, fixing a minimum age for chimney sweeps of eight years. But like so many other reforming measures of the time, the Act was ignored for want of enforcement. Later, William Tooke, and others formed the Society for Superseding the Necessity of Climbing Boys, which promoted George Smart's "Scandiscope", a jointed chimney brush given free to master sweeps who objected to the cost of such equipment.

The propertied classes represented in Parliament opposed any attack on their rights as employers, whether of climbing boys or anyone else. Some towns like Sheffield made reforms on a local level, but not until 1834 was any further progress made nationally, when an Act banned the apprenticing of chimney sweeps under ten years of age; six years later this was raised to twenty-one. But even this did not always help what the reformer Lord Ashley (later Lord Shaftesbury) termed "the most oppressed, degraded and tortured creatures on the face of the earth." In 1853 he complained that the Act was being evaded by the simple ruse of employing climbing boys who were not apprentices. Ten years later, after a series of gruesome government reports and the publication of Charles Kingsley's *Water Babies*, a further attempt was made at legislation, now supported by middle-class opinion. At last, in 1875, long after child chimney-sweeping had been banned in France, North America and elsewhere, Lord Shaftesbury brought in a Bill requiring all master chimney sweeps to be licensed. If they defied the law now, their living could be taken away.

Laissez-faire *and Reform*

Industry was thought to depend for its prosperity upon *laissez-faire* and lack of controls. Artificial controls might upset the natural balances of the economy. The new industrialists argued that government "meddling" might have immeasurable consequences, and do irreparable harm. Nor should employers be forced to lift wage levels above those of the free market. The great fear of every entrepreneur in this age of expansion was of pricing himself out of the market; and in the age of *laissez-faire* he could not expect the government or anyone else to protect him.

The fact that legislative controls of various kinds were steadily introduced was less a product of advanced economic thinking, than of national conscience deeply shocked by the disclosures of bodies like the 1842 Coal Commission, and the social writings of men like Charles Dickens. Nevertheless, some proof was needed that spending on improvements did not necessarily mean lower profits. One man to do this was the owner of the New Lanark Mill, Robert Owen (1771–1858), who was generally regarded as the most advanced cotton spinner in the country. When Owen bought the New Lanark Mill, it employed some 2,000 people, a quarter of whom were children. The Mill had a terrible reputation for brutality and disorder. Owen introduced a number of reforms for the benefit of his employees – better local housing, better hygiene, and physical and mental welfare. But Owen's co-directors disliked his policies, and the reformer left to establish his own mill, which attracted visitors from all over the world.

One of the early landmarks of government legislation for industry was the Factory Act of 1833, which appointed inspectors to see that its welfare provisions were properly carried out. Children aged below nine years were not to be employed at all, those under thirteen were not to work more than eight hours a day, and those of eighteen or less were not to work more than twelve hours a day. Proper time for meals had to be set aside during the day. Children aged between nine and

Top A cartoonist's view of the tensions of working-class life

Above The same cartoonist's view of middle-class gentility

Female workers in a cotton
mill (1851)

thirteen were also to have two hours' education each day. The employer
had to keep registers and see that independent certificates were issued;
if not he faced prosecution. One inspector alone obtained 1,550 con-
victions between April and December, 1839. But most of the fines were
too small to be an effective deterrent. In the ensuing decades a series of
similar Acts were passed, extending the legislation to cover a wider
range of premises, and reducing children's working hours still more.
Further Acts laid down that dangerous machines must be properly
fenced, sanitation provided, and rules of hygiene observed. A whole
code of safety regulations concerning dangerous machines and substances was steadily evolved, largely under the sponsorship of Lord
Shaftesbury.

Chartists and Unionists

These were some of the pressures for reform from above; but there
were also pressures from below. In the first half of the century, the
worsening conditions of industrial urban life helped to produce a vocal
body of working-class discontent. This was most loudly voiced by the
Chartist movement which lasted for some ten years from 1838. The
Chartist leader Ernest Jones (1819–69) wrote a poem called *The Song
of the Lower Classes*, cynically proclaiming that the lower classes were not
fit to enjoy the products of their own toil:

> *We plough and sow – we're so very, very low*
> *That we delve in the dirty clay*
> *Till we bless the plain – with the golden grain*
> *And the vale with fragrant hay.*
> *Our place we know – we're so very low,*
> *'Tis down at the landlord's feet,*
> *We're not too low the bread to grow,*
> *But too low the bread to eat.*
>
> *We're low, we're low, we're very, very low,*
> *Yet from our fingers glide*
> *The silken flow and the robes that glow*
> *Round the limbs of the sons of pride.*
> *And what we get, and what we give,*
> *We know and we know our share:*
> *We're not too low the cloth to weave,*
> *But too low the cloth to wear.*

The Reform Act of 1832 had given the vote to certain sections of the
middle classes, but it gave none to the working classes in the towns and
countryside; and the newly-enfranchised middle classes, who were
often landlords, farmers or factory owners, were as unwilling as the
upper classes to see the uncouth, unwashed, inhabitants of the towns
given a share in the government of the nation. In 1838 the Chartists
drew up a "People's Charter", setting out six expressly political
demands.

(1) All adult males to have the vote (which was not achieved until 1918).
(2) Voting by secret ballot paper, instead of openly, to discourage intimidation and bribery by landlords and employers. (This was not achieved until
the Ballot Act of 1872.)

(3) Abolition of the rule that only landowners could enter the House of Commons. (This rule was not abolished until 1858.)
(4) Annual Parliaments. (This is one Chartist demand which was never realized. A Prime Minister with a majority in the House of Commons is not bound to call a General Election until five years have elapsed since the previous General Election.)
(5) Members of Parliament to receive a salary, so that poor working class Members were not at a financial disadvantage. (Members now receive salaries.)
(6) Equal electoral districts. (Partly owing to apathy, partly to continuing shifts in population, electoral districts remain unequal.)

But many working-class leaders saw little hope in political reforms. There seemed small point in fighting to share a system of government evolved to protect the propertied middle and upper classes. For many centuries, various sections of working people in the towns had "combined" to take direct action to enforce claims for higher wage rates and better working conditions. In 1799, however, Parliament had passed a Combination Act which banned workers from combining together in any way. In 1824, however, this Act was repealed. This was due in large measure to the efforts of Francis Place (1771–1854), a master tailor who had known a good deal of poverty and hardship in his youth. Place felt that the old Act was unduly harsh in preventing workers from trying to improve their conditions. He met a good deal of opposition in 1824 from mill and mine owners, and from craft masters whose own livelihood depended upon the low wages of apprentices and others.

Francis Place

With the Combination Act repealed, working people could now combine, and a number of unions were formed in the following years. But they could still not strike, and did not acquire a legal right to do so until 1874. Robert Owen was one of those to attempt large-scale union organization, with his grand National Consolidated Trades Union, which claimed more than half a million members. But it was grandiose and inefficient, and wielded little effective power.

Nor did the repeal of 1824 have the effect of legalizing very much union organization. In 1834 came the case of the so-called Tolpuddle Martyrs, a group of Dorsetshire farm workers led by George Loveless, who were all prosecuted for administering "unlawful oaths". The "martyrs" were sentenced to transportation for seven years (although they were granted remission two years later). Robert Owen disbanded his own Union, and turned instead to the co-operative movement, which was to make its own important mark on the history of collective bargaining.

Robert Owen

In 1874, a limited right to strike was conferred by an Act of Parliament. By this time unions, co-operatives, and other self-help organizations had grown in strength and influence, helped largely by a generation of prosperity. These bodies included the Miners' Association (1841), the National Association of United Trades for the Protection of Labour (1845), the Amalgamated Society of Engineers (1851), the London Working Men's Association (1866) and the Co-operative Wholesale Society (1864). A national meeting of union delegates representing

118,000 people took place at Manchester in 1868, and became formally known as the Trades Union Congress when it reassembled the following year.

The 1870s saw a great number of strikes. The law relating to picketing, obstruction, intimidation and molestation was still an acute problem for union leaders, but there was no doubt that the right to strike was coming to be regarded as fundamental. After the eight weeks' London dockers' strike in 1889, unskilled workers believed the same. By the end of the century, millions of working people belonged to the main unions, and economists were noting with alarm the effect of rising wages on price levels. The power and influence of the trades unions seemed to advance steadily until 1901, when a High Court decision in the famous Taff Vale case held that a union was financially liable for damage caused during a strike of its workers. As every union had only limited funds, the implications of this judgement were serious. But in 1906 the unions were to establish their freedom from such liability in the Trades Disputes Act.

Rowntree took a detailed note of one family's budget for half a year:

Income

Wages (26 weeks at fifteen shillings)	19	10	0*d.*
Wife's income from outside housework	3	11	9*d.*
	£23	1	9*d.*

Expenditure

Food and beverages	13	13	9½*d.*
Rent	4	4	6*d.*
Coal, etc.	1	19	1*d.*
Oil and candles		1	0½*d.*
Soap, etc.		6	1½*d.*
Sundries		1	2½*d.*
Life insurance		10	10*d.*
Clothing		11	4*d.*
Boots	1	6	0½*d.*
Tobacco and matches		5	2*d.*
Stamps, stationery and papers		4	2*d.*
	£23	3	3½*d.*

The Chartists march on the House of Commons to petition for their Charter of Rights

The resulting deficit was made up by weekly borrowings of a few pence. The founder of the Salvation Army, General William Booth, angrily referred to the "multitudes who struggle and sink in the open-mouthed abyss", and who lived and died "in the midst of unparalleled wealth, and civilization, and philanthropy of this professedly most Christian land". It has been estimated that between a third and a half of the men who volunteered to fight in the Boer War were rejected by the army on the grounds of ill-health.

Benjamin Rowntree estimated that a family of five could not possibly maintain its health on an income of less than about £56 a year. He added that an income as low as this would not allow the family to spend anything on rail or bus fares, to buy a newspaper, contribute to the church collection, take holidays, or incur any exceptional expenditure. Despite England's immense national wealth and power, and despite the growth of a strong union movement, there were still the most severe social evils to eradicate.

4 *Social Reforms*

The Government of England

Apart from the small percentage of the population who made up the upper classes, the people of England as a whole had little part in the government of the country, or in electing Parliament. Even where local people did have a vote in the county elections by virtue of their property, they were often openly influenced and intimidated by their wealthy landlords, or employers. Some boroughs, which were no more than obscure names on a map and still elected Members to Parliament, were said to be "rotten". Many Members of Parliament in the early nineteenth century owed their seats in the House of Commons to such rotten boroughs. Benjamin Disraeli, the inspirer of "Tory democracy", found nothing strange in the fact that England should be governed by an aristocracy. In his *Life of Lord George Bentinck* (1852), he explained that the English aristocracy was not an exclusive class: "It is not true that England is governed by an aristocracy in the common acceptation of that term. England is governed by an aristocratic principle. The aristocracy of England absorbs all aristocracies, and receives every man in every order and every class who defers to the principle of our society: which is to aspire and to excel."

The year 1832, however, saw the first real milestone along the road of political reform. In that year, Lord Grey's Whig government brought in a Reform Bill which destroyed many of these rotten boroughs, and gave the vote to a wider section of the affluent middle classes. In 1867, the franchise was widened still further, when the vote was given to every male ratepayer, and certain other classes of townspeople. The Third Reform Act (1884) extended these developments beyond the confines of the large towns. Not until 1918, however, did the vote really become fully democratic. In that year, all men aged twenty-one or more were enfranchised, regardless of whether they were ratepayers or not, as were women aged thirty years or more.

Most nineteenth-century ministers of the crown regarded themselves as an "administration" rather than a "government"; the safeguarding of interests was considered more important than the planning of national policies. The political economist John Stuart Mill wrote: "The great majority of things are worse done by the intervention of Government." Many thinkers of the Victorian age felt that it was unnecessary,

Opposite An airless Victorian slum

even wrong, for the authorities to interfere in social problems. The historian Lord Macaulay (1768–1859) wrote: "Our rulers will best promise the improvement of this nation by strictly confining themselves to their own legitimate duties." They must leave "capital to find its own most lucrative course, commodities their fair price, industry and intelligence their natural reward, idleness and folly their natural punishment, by maintaining peace, by defending property . . . and by observing strict economy in every department of the State. Let the government do this: the people will assuredly do the rest." The *Economist* newspaper strongly echoed this theme in an article of May 1848, the same year incidentally in which many other European states were plunged in revolution: "Suffering and evil are Nature's admonitions; they cannot be got rid of; and the impatient attempts of benevolence to banish them from the world by legislation . . . have always been more productive of evil than good."

But in the later part of the century, certain liberals began strongly to reject these arguments. They argued that society had a great moral responsibility toward those less able to help and defend themselves, whether through want of education or want of opportunity, neither of which they should be blamed for. Joseph Chamberlain, who rose to prominence as a reforming Mayor of Birmingham, declared in 1885: "I believe that the reduction of the franchise will bring into prominence social questions which have been too long neglected, that it may force upon the consideration of thinking men of all parties the conditions of the poor – aye, and the contrast which unfortunately exists between the great luxury and wealth which some enjoy, and the misery and destitution which prevail amongst large portions of the population." Chamberlain added that he did not believe that Liberal policy would ever remove the security which property rightly enjoyed, or prevent industry and thrift finding their due reward. "But I do think that something may be done to enlarge the obligation and the responsibility of the whole community towards its poorer and less fortunate members." On another occasion, Chamberlain declared: "Squalid homes, unhealthy dwellings, overcrowding: these are the causes . . . of the crime and immorality of great cities. They are the direct result of a system which postpones the good of the community to the interest of individuals, which loses sight altogether of the obligations of property in a servile adulation of its rights."

Introducing the great parliamentary Reform Bill of 1832 in the House of Commons, London

Disease and Medicine

Charles Kingsley, the writer, told his wife on 24th October, 1849: "I was yesterday . . . over the cholera districts of Bermondsey; and, oh God! what I saw! People having no water to drink – hundreds of them – but the water of the common sewer which stagnates full [of] dead fish, cats and dogs, under their windows." The lack of pure water had long been a blight on London life. One of the River Thames' tributaries, the Fleet, was especially notorious, and in the eighteenth century had been condemned as an "open sewer". Now, most of this "ditch" had been built over, but running underground it still carried an almost unbelievable trail of filth into the Thames, including infected matter disgorged by the slaughter houses in Lambeth and Whitechapel. Consequently, the River Thames itself, the main source of water for London (82 million gallons per day), was in a state of emergency. Sydney Smith claimed on 19th November, 1834, that there were "a million insects in every drop". *Punch* produced a famous cartoon to this effect in 1850.

"A million insects in every drop", a London cartoonist's impression of London water (1850)

A crisis was reached in 1855, known to contemporaries as the year of the "Great Stink". In that hot summer, unsoftened by rainfall, even Parliament in session at Westminster by the River Thames felt obliged to screen its windows with curtains drenched in chloride of lime, to permit Members to breathe. Desperate measures were proposed, for example, to move the Law Courts out of London to Oxford or St. Albans, to seal up the 369 sewer openings along the River Thames between Putney and Blackwall, and build tall chimneyed gas furnaces instead, and to tax all smoking fireplaces. One obstacle was that London's water supply was controlled by nine independent water companies; they strenuously resisted Edwin Chadwick's proposal to liquidate them, and bring water from several miles further upstream (Richmond, Farnham and Bagshot Heath) at a weekly charge of two-pence to every London household. But despite the "Great Stink" of 1855, most Londoners remained apathetic and cynical, and looked upon it as a joke rather than an urgent problem. Not until the creation of the Metropolitan Water Board in 1903 did matters really improve.

But Edwin Chadwick, a barrister and assistant Poor Law commissioner, had already been forcefully directing attention to London's sanitary problems in the 1840s. In 1842 he had published his famous *Sanitary Report*, and the following year his *Report on Interment in Towns*. In the second he pointed out the great health hazard created by the city of London's overflowing cemeteries. Some 50,000 people were buried each year (over half were young people) in the same 218 acres, and the gravediggers had to resort to "dreadful expedients" to cope with this task. Throughout its history, London had periodically fallen victim to cholera and other epidemics, and in times of crisis hundreds of people were hastily buried by relatives in shallow graves. Strong passions were aroused by this public health issue; hundreds of small independent churches and chapels refused to allow incursions into their freeholds or their independence.

The worst of the epidemics which visited the Victorian towns was

Smallpox and fever were a serious health hazard everywhere

"HAPPY HAMPSTEAD!"

undoubtedly cholera. No one understood the causes of this fearful disease. Edwin Chadwick and many others believed in the "pythogenic theory" which held that cholera, typhus, and other diseases were in some way present in the atmosphere. The nature of infection was hardly understood. In 1849, London experienced a terrible cholera epidemic. One Gideon Mantell wrote in his *Journal* (1852) that during September between 200 and 400 people perished from cholera every day. Basement cesspools, overcrowded tenements, open sewers, lack of personal hygiene – all these contributed to the disaster. On 5th July, 1849, as the epidemic was nearing its height, the following agonized – if illiterate – letter was published in *The Times* above fifty-four signatures: "Sur, May we beg and beseech your proteckshion and power. We are Sur, as it may be, livin in a Wilderniss, so far as the rest of London knows anything of us, or as the rich and great people care about. We live in muck and filthe. We aint got no privez, no dust bins, no drains, no water splies, and no drain or suer in the whole place. The Suer Company, in Greek Street, Soho Square, all great, rich and powerfool men, take no notice watsomedever of our complaints. The Stenche of a Gully-hole is disgustin. We al of us suffur, and numbers are ill, and if the Colera comes Lord help us."

In the days before any kind of national health service existed, the poor could scarcely ever hope to afford the services of a private doctor, unlike the more affluent middle classes. The poor put their trust either in folk cures or in God. Having had a rather disreputable name in the eighteenth century, surgeons and physicians were beginning to improve their image; advances were made in medical science, and in standards of medical training in the new teaching hospitals. But the medical profession was still more or less unregulated, and medical practitioners would often advertise their services in newspaper columns: "To the Nervous and Paralysed – Brighton. Mr. Harry Lobb, Surgeon and Electrician, having a vacancy at his house, 2, Old Steine, offerd to Patients the comforts of a Home, Sea Air, and the professional employment of the latest discoveries in Medical Electricity." Medical men with special qualifications would not neglect to list them: "A. Eskell, Surgeon Dentist, Author of *Dental Surgery, Pure Dentistry, Painless Tooth Extraction, etc.*, may be consulted Daily, at his only residence, 8, Grosvenor Street, Bond Street." (*Illustrated London News*, 15th December, 1868).

The hypochondriac (and the merely careful) spent a good deal of money on pseudo-medical preparations, ointments, pills and potions, with grand-sounding names such as the Universal Pill, or Parr's Life Pills (said to increase the beauty of women), Elixirs of Life in every shape and form. In the city of Exeter, "a young man was effectively cured in a single night of insanity by swallowing the whole contents of a thirteen penny-halfpenny box of Number Two Pills which had been inadvertently left in the bedroom."

Many pills contained nothing more than compressed vegetables and animal fats, but however quackish their contents the manufacturer never failed to sell his product in the finest technical-sounding phrases and even threats: "The coldness of the winter renders torpid the acrimonious fluids of the body and in this state of inactivity their evil to the system is not perceived; but at the spring these are aroused, and if not checked, mix up and circulate in the blood, and thus the whole system is contaminated." For many people, it was far cheaper to invest a few pence in a box of health pills than to consult a doctor in private practice. The pill-manufacturer Thomas Beecham achieved great success with his slogan: "Worth a guinea a box."

The poorer classes might not have been able to afford items such as those, but they might qualify for admission to a charitable hospital. A number of these had been founded before 1800 to care for the sick. They varied a good deal in their standards of medical care and skill. In the nineteenth century, dozens of specialist hospitals were founded in London and elsewhere, and did much to foster specialist medical studies. Some of the better known were:

A ward in Guy's hospital, London (1887)

    1802 The London Fever Hospital
    1805 Moorfields Eye Hospital (London)
    1814 Royal Hospital for Diseases of the Chest (London)
    1835 St. Mark's Hospital for Cancer
    1838 Metropolitan Ear, Nose and Throat Hospital
    1840 Kensington Children's Hospital
    1849 London Homoeopathic Hospital
    1850 London Smallpox Hospital
    1852 Great Ormond Street Hospital for Children (London)
    1858 Royal Dental Hospital (London)
    1859 National Hospital for Paralysis and Epilepsy
    1887 London Skin Hospital

More than seventy specialist hospitals were founded between 1800 and 1860. But inside most of them the lack of real medical knowledge worked against the proper treatment and segregation of patients. In the London Fever Hospital, for example, victims of typhus, cholera and scarlet fever were housed in the same wards, and indeed often in the same wards as sufferers of non-infectious diseases. In her *Notes on Hospitals* (1859) Florence Nightingale (1820–1910) acidly wrote: "The first requirement of a hospital [is] that it should do the sick no harm." And a year later she wrote in her *Notes on Nursing* that "if a patient is cold, if a patient is feverish, if a patient is faint, if he is sick after taking food, if he has a bed sore, it is generally the fault not of the disease, but of the nursing." The nature of infection was still barely understood in the early years of the century.

Despite the growth of hospital building, some classes of the community were still hardly cared for at all. These included young children, of whom more than 20,000 died in London alone each year; and sufferers of incurable diseases whom the hospitals would not accept (at least until the foundation of the Royal Hospital and Home for the Incurable at Putney, London).

In the early 1800s hospital treatment was primitive. Doctors still used leeches for a wide number of ailments, in the hope of drawing off "bad" blood. St. Bartholomew's Hospital in London actually used more and more leeches as time went on: 25,000 in 1821, and 96,000 by 1837. One reason was that bleeding made a patient unconscious, and

Poor people queuing for medical help

Top Florence Nightingale. *Above* Gathering leeches for medical purposes. *Below* Joseph Lister, later Lord Lister

so acted as a kind of primitive anaesthetic, enabling the doctors to carry out an amputation or replace a dislocated limb.

Many operations, however, were performed without any kind of anaesthetic. A patient at one hospital described how he underwent an operation for the removal of a stone from the bladder in 1811. So keyed-up was he, that "the first incision did not even make me wince ... the forcing up of the [surgeon's] staff prior to the introduction of the gorget gave me the first real pain, but this instantly subsided after the incision of the bladder was made, the rush of the urine appeared to relieve it and soothe the wound. When the forceps were introduced the pain was again very considerable, and every movement of the instrument in endeavouring to find the stone increased it." The stone was not found at the first attempt, but only at the second, and the patient was becoming deeply dispirited after his initial resolve. "When the necessary force was applied to withdraw the stone the sensation was such as I cannot find words to describe. In addition to the positive pain there was something peculiar in the feel. The bladder embraced the stone as firmly as the stone was itself grasped by the forceps; it seemed as if the whole organ was about to be torn out. . . ." Then, after the terrible moment had passed, he felt a "fulness of heart which can only be conceived."

Humphry Davy had experimented on himself with nitrous oxide in 1800 and discovered its anaesthetic effects, and Michael Faraday had discovered similar properties in ether in 1818; but anaesthetics were not generally used until 1846. In that year the American William T. G. Morton (1819–68) began to use ether vapour for dental extractions, and a year later the Scottish physician James Simpson (1811–70) began to use chloroform. Local anaesthetics were used from 1898. Both ether and chloroform had unpleasant after effects in nausea and headaches, but they did allow surgeons to attempt many more operations than had been possible before. Unfortunately, the death rate on the operating table was still very high, roughly between a quarter and a third: so many wounds turned septic, making the patients die of blood-poisoning. Although the word "antiseptic" had been in use since the eighteenth century, no one yet understood that it was infection that made wounds septic. Surgeons still operated in their ordinary working clothes; the value of cleansing was not appreciated; wounds were sewn up with horse hair hanging from hooks in the theatre; visitors (including food and drink pedlars) were allowed to wander freely about the wards; bed sheets and bandages were often no more than torn rags donated as charity as a result of advertisements posted by hospitals like the Radcliffe Infirmary, Oxford, as late as 1869. Some surgeons were extremely wary of operating in such conditions, and one wrote to *The Times* (1829): "In every case of dangerous operation or one of questionable expediency, the principal surgeons and consulting surgeons [should] hold a conference in the presence of their pupils, and determine by a majority of the votes of such surgeons the measures to be adopted."

By about 1865 the Professor of Surgery at Glasgow University (Joseph Lister) had begun to suspect that it was germs in the air that

Doctors using a carbolic spray to prevent infection during an operation

caused wounds to fester and turn septic. He devised a chemical weapon to destroy germs, in the shape of a carbolic acid spray (or dressing) which reduced the mortality in his surgical operations by a considerable amount. Lister's methods were widely adopted by surgeons in the next twenty years, but by this time Lister himself was becoming more interested in the idea of absolute cleanliness in surgical conditions, the ideal being sterilization of all equipment, and the covering of the surgeon and his assistants in specially designed coats, gloves and masks, to prevent their own germs infecting the patient.

Crime

Below Sir Robert Peel. *Bottom* A Victorian policeman

In the first half of the nineteenth century crime presented a grave social problem. Matters were made worse by widespread poverty, and the want of proper law enforcement. Some 250 felonies ranging from theft to murder were punishable by death, and there was a grim reality in the phrase, "better be hung for a sheep than a lamb". Pickpockets and other petty criminals were liable to be transported for life, at least until the 1840s when native opinion in Australia and elsewhere grew up against it. For some time penal reformers like Samuel Romilly (1757–1818) and James Mackintosh (1765–1832) had been campaigning for a reduction in these brutal penalties. At last, when Sir Robert Peel became Home Secretary in 1825 something was done. Peel argued that a certain punishment was far better than a brutal one, and set about founding a properly organized police system. Most towns had their caped night watchmen, with warning bells and rattles, and the magistrate Henry Fielding had originated a pioneer detective force in London in the eighteenth century, the Bow Street runners; but Peel was the first man (in 1829) to institute a police force in the modern sense of the term. The example made in London was quickly followed by magistrates in other parts of the country, and in 1856 it was made compulsory for every town to have a police force. To avoid looking too military, the constables were dressed in quasi-civilian blue serge uniforms and armed only with whistles and wooden truncheons. They were nicknamed "bobbies" or "peelers" after Sir Robert Peel. At the same time, Peel managed to abolish the death penalty from more than 200 offences. The orgy of crime which many people had gloomily predicted failed to materialize, and Peel's policy was vindicated; although the "bobbies" remained rather unpopular with the general public for some years.

Although the number of capital crimes had been steadily cut back

A coiner at work

in the first decades of the nineteenth century, hanging continued to be held in public right up to 1868. In 1801 the *Aberdeen Journal* carried this advertisement: "Wanted, an executioner for the City of Aberdeen. Such persons as may wish to be appointed to the office are desired immediately to apply to George Turiff, Dean of Guild's Officer, who will give information respecting the salary and emoluments, which are considerable, besides a free house."

Charles Dickens, like many of his contemporaries, was appalled at the barbaric practice of public executions, which seemed to express the very worst side of human nature. "The horrors of the gibbet and of the crime which brought the wretched murderers to it, faded from my mind before the atrocious bearing, looks and language of the assembled spectators. When I came upon the scene at midnight, the shrillness of the cries and howls that were raised from time to time, denoting that they came from a concourse of boys and girls already assembled in the best places, made my blood run cold." He added, "When the two miserable creatures who attracted all this ghastly sight about them were turned quivering into the air, there was no more emotion, no more pity, no more thought that two immortal souls had gone to judgement, no more restraint in any of the previous obscenities, than if the name of Christ had never been heard in this world."

Public opinion had undergone a considerable change since 1783; Dr. Johnson had dourly remarked then, on hearing that the processions to the place of public execution at Tyburn were to be ended, "The public was gratified by a procession, the criminal was supported by it. Why is all this to be swept away?" This great Englishman of the eighteenth century would have found himself uncomfortably out of place in the reforming atmosphere of the nineteenth.

One of the most authentic pictures of criminal life in England is to be found in the writings of Henry Mayhew, who recorded hundreds of interviews with rogues of every kind. Illegal coining was fairly common in the city centres, and Mayhew described the methods which the ingenious coiner used. A shilling piece or other coin was well-scoured with soap and water, and allowed to dry. It was then greased with suet or tallow, which was later partly wiped off. The prepared coin was then impressed in plaster of Paris to make an accurate cast of its two sides, and the two casts were fitted together as the mould, and dried out. A small hole was made in one side through which cheap molten

A public execution in London

metal was poured, and when this dried and solidified, the small piece in the entry-hole, known as the "gat", was carefully trimmed off with a pair of scissors, and the coin was then ready for coating. "You get a galvanic battery with nitric acid and sulphuric acid, a mixture of each diluted in water to a certain strength," one coiner told Mayhew. "You then get some cyanide and attach a copper wire to a screw of the battery. Immerse that in the cyanide of silver when the process of electro-plating commences. The coin has to pass through another process. Get a little lampblack and oil, and make it into a sort of composition, 'slumming' the coin with it. This takes the bright colour away and makes it fit for circulation. Then wrap the coins up separately in paper so as to prevent them from rubbing. When coiners are going to circulate them, they take them up and rub each piece separately. The counterfeit coin will then have the greatest resemblance to a genuine coin, if well manufactured."

London pickpockets

Mayhew added that at least two people were needed to undertake coining properly. Often one person acted as "crow" or lookout "in case the officers of justice should make their appearance and detect them in the act." Police raids often led to some violence. "On such occasions, the men endeavour to destroy the mould, while the women throw the counterfeit coin into the fire, or into the melted metal, which effectually injures it. This is done to prevent the officers getting these articles into their possession as evidence against them. The coiners," he added, "frequently throw the hot metal at the officers, or the acids they use in their coining processes, or they attempt to strike them with a chair or stool, or other weapon that comes their way."

According to Henry Mayhew, a huge trade was carried on in the sale of stolen goods. Often the receivers were disreputable pawn-brokers, who generally paid the thief about a quarter of the stolen object's value. Even stolen banknotes were received by some pawn-brokers, for a poorly-dressed thief might find it troublesome to dispose of a high-value banknote. The larger the value of the note, the smaller the sum paid by the receiver; a £5 note might fetch £4 or £4. 10s., but a £50 note would only fetch about £35. Mayhew listed a number of prevailing prices of stolen property. "Silks and satins are generally sold to the fence at a shilling a yard, whatever the quality of the fabric. Silk handkerchiefs of excellent quality are sold at one shilling each; good broadcloths from four to five shillings a yard, possibly worth from a guinea to four pounds five shillings. Neckties, sold in the shop from one shilling and sixpence to two shillings are given away for four-pence to sixpence each; kid-gloves, worth from two shillings to three and sixpence are sold at sixpence a pair; and women's boots, worth from six and six to one and six are given for two shillings."

Crime and vice flourished at night, and in London thieves, pick-pockets and footpads mingled with the evening crowds, the poor with the rich. The Haymarket in London, linking Trafalgar Square with Piccadilly, was thought to have been one of the most scandalous scenes of London night life. One observer wrote in *Household Words* (1857): "About the top of this thoroughfare is diffused, every night, a very large part of what is blackguard, ruffianly, and deeply dangerous

A disturbance of the peace at London's Haymarket at night

in London. If Piccadilly may be termed an artery of the metropolis, most assuredly that strip of pavement between the top of the Haymarket and the Regent Circus is one of its ulcers. . . . It is always an offensive place to pass, even in the daytime; but at night it is absolutely hideous, with its sparring snobs, and flashing satins and sporting gents, and painted cheeks, and brandy-sparkling eyes, and bad tobacco, and hoarse horse-laughs, and loud indecency. . . . From an extensive continental experience of cities, I can take personally an example from three quarters of the globe; but I have never anywhere witnessed such open ruffianism and wretched profligacy as rings along those Piccadilly flagstones any time after the gas is lighted.''

Another critic, in *London in the Sixties*, wrote that the Haymarket "literally blazed with light from such temples as the Blue Post, Barnes's, The Burmese, and Barron's Oyster Rooms . . . the decorous Panton Street of today was another very sink of iniquity. Night-houses abounded, and Rose Burton's and Jack Percival's were sandwiched between hot baths of questionable respectability, and abominations of every kind."

The Haymarket was the focal point of prostitution in London. Henry Mayhew found many French, German and Belgian street walkers, in addition to native born ones. Many of them promenaded at dusk, if not before, decked out in silk *paletots* and wide skirts extended by ample crinolines, looking "almost like a pyramid". At the apex of the pyramid was set a black or white satin bonnet, "trimmed with waving ribbons and gay flowers". Mayhew found them strolling up and down Regent Street and the Haymarket, often singly, or sometimes arm in arm with some gallant whom they have picked up, calling at the wine vaults or restaurants to drink a glass of wine or gin. At other times they might frequent the glittering coffee-rooms, hung about with large mirrors, to drink a cup of good "bohea" or coffee. "Others of higher style proceed to the Alhambra Music Hall, or to the Argyle Rooms, rustling in splendid dresses, to spend the time till midnight, when they accompany the gentlemen they have met there to the expensive supper rooms and night houses which abound in the neighbourhood." Many of the small streets leading off the Haymarket – Panton Street, Oxenden Street and James Street – contained "houses of accommodation" where the prostitutes could rent rooms by the hour instead of returning to their seedy lodgings. Some of the girls cohabited with "bullies" or "fancy-men" for convenience or protection.

Most London prostitutes gained an extremely uncertain living. "At one time they are in splendid dress," wrote Mayhew, "and at another time in the humblest attire. Occasionally they are assisted by men who are interested in them, and restored to their former position, when they get their clothes out of the hands of the pawnbrokers. Their living is very precarious. . . . They are frequently treated to splendid suppers in the Haymarket and its vicinity, where they sit surrounded with splendour, partaking of costly *viands* amid lascivious smiles. But the scene is changed when you follow them to their own apartments in Soho or Chelsea, where you find them during the day, lolling drowsily on their beds, in tawdry dress and in sad *deshabillé*, with dishevelled hair, seedy-looking countenance, and muddy dreary eyes – their voices frequently hoarse with bad humour and misery." The upper echelons of London prostitution were smoothly and efficiently organized; the fees were usually half a guinea to a guinea. Most prostitutes conducted themselves with care, for to run foul of the law would easily ruin their livelihood; the careful middle-class Victorian patron dreaded the prospect of public scandal.

The dark alleys and streets of London and other cities were frequented by those prostitutes who had grown old, or who had fallen upon harder times. Most of them lived by begging or stealing, and forced themselves on their younger and more successful counterparts. "Many of the poor girls are glad to pay her a sixpence occasionally to get rid of her company, as gentlemen are often scared away from them by the intrusion of this shameless hag, with her thick lips, sable black skin, leering countenance and obscene disgusting tongue, resembling a lewd spirit of darkness from the nether world." Something was done to curb the worst aspects of prostitution by the Criminal Law Amendment Act (1885) which raised the age of consent from thirteen to sixteen and of abduction from sixteen to eighteen.

In *London's Underworld* (1862), Henry Mayhew wrote that picking pockets could be a highly lucrative profession. Boys who had once lived "by a felon's hearth" might be seen fifteen or twenty years later "dressed in the highest style of fashion . . . glittering in gold chains, studs and rings . . . step by step they have emerged from their rags and squalor to a higher position of physical comfort, and have risen to higher dexterity and accomplishment in their base and ignoble profession."

Mayhew found that young pickpockets generally sprang from the poorest and roughest areas of London, often where their own family were thieves by trade – Whitechapel, Shoreditch, Spitalfields, Lambeth, the Borough, Clerkenwell, Drury Lane and other localities. Many of them were the children of Irish parents, costermongers, bricklayers' workmen and others. "They often begin to steal at six or seven years of age, sometimes as early as five years, and commit petty sneaking thefts, as well as pick handkerchieves from gentlemen's pockets." Many of these "ragged urchins" were taught to steal by their companions in the penny lodging houses where they lived; others were taught by professional "trainers of thieves" like Dickens' Fagin. "They are learned to be expert in this way: a coat is suspended on the wall with a bell attached to it, and the boy attempts to take the handkerchief from the pocket without the bell ringing. Until he is able to do this with proficiency he is not considered well trained." There was another method too, with which Oliver Twist was familiar. The trainer "walks up and down the room with a handkerchief in the tail of his coat, and the ragged boys amuse themselves abstracting it until they learn to do it in an adroit manner."

The pickpockets would often work in a small team. One police officer reported a case at Cremorne, a London park, where he had seen three persons, a man and a boy and a woman, whom he suspected to be picking pockets. The man was about twenty-eight, and rather less than average height; the woman at his side, who was very good-looking,

A London ragamuffin

was about twenty-four, dressed in a green gown, a Paisley shawl, and straw bonnet trimmed with red velvet and red flowers. The man was dressed in a black frock coat, brown trousers and black hat. The boy, who was fourteen, and the man's brother, was dressed in a brown shooting coat, corduroy trousers and black cap with peak. The boy had "an engaging countenance, with sharp features and smart manner". The officer then observed "the man touch the boy on the shoulder, and point him towards an old lady. The boy placed himself on her right side, and the man and woman kept behind. The former put his left hand into the pocket of the lady's gown and drew nothing from it; then left her and went about two yards further; there he placed himself by two other ladies, tried both their pockets and left them again. He followed another lady and succeeded in picking her pocket of a small sum of money and a handkerchief. The officer took them all to the police station with the assistance of another detective officer, when they were committed for trial at Clerkenwell sessions. The man was sentenced to ten years' penal servitude, the boy to two months' hard labour and three months in a reformatory, and the woman was sentenced to two years' imprisonment, with hard labour, in the House of Correction at Westminster."

An important figure in the pickpocket's life was the fence. Often, this was the "trainer", and "these base wretches buy the stolen handkerchiefs from the boys at a paltry sum." Fagin in *Oliver Twist* was one such. At other times, they might take their booty to "some low receiving house, where wretches encourage them in stealing; sometimes to low coffee houses, low hairdressers or tailors, who act as middlemen to dispose of the property, generally giving them but a small part of the value." Henry Mayhew was impressed by the extraordinary dexterity of some pickpockets. Some would accost a gentleman in the street, and while asking the way or enquiring after a fictitious acquaintance, would quietly slip their hand into his waistcoat pocket and steal his watch. The really accomplished pickpockets generally worked alone, with no partners or lookouts, and changed their haunts frequently. Mayhew gave an example of a young lady, who was standing by a shop window admiring a fine engraving. "Meantime, a handsomely dressed young man, with gold chain and moustache, also takes his station at the window beside her, apparently admiring the same engraving. The young lady stands gazing on the beautiful picture, with her countenance glowing with sentiment, which may be enhanced by the sympathetic presence of the nice-looking young man by her side; and while her bosom is thus throbbing with romantic emotion, her purse, meanwhile, is being quietly transferred to the pocket of this elegantly attired young man, whom she might find in the evening dressed as a rough coster-monger, mingling among the low ruffians at the Seven Dials or White-chapel, or possibly lounging in some low beer shop in the Borough."

One of the scandals of city life in Victorian times was the large numbers of small children forced by poverty to live off the streets, variously begging and stealing. Henry Mayhew remembered that in the New Cut market at Lambeth, the young thieves used to wait until dusk before venturing out. "In the evening, when the lamps are lit,

A den of thieves

they steal forth from their haunts, with keen roguish eye, looking out for booty. We then see them loitering about the stalls or mingling among the throng of people in the street, looking wistfully on the tempting fruit displayed on the stalls."

Mayhew was shocked by the extreme youth of some of them. These "young Arabs of the city" had a strange and motley appearance; many of them were only six or seven years old, others eight or ten. Some of them had no jacket, cap or shoes, and wandered about the streets of London with their ragged trousers hanging by a single brace. Some wore old tattered coats, threadbare, and much too large for them, with no shoes or stockings on their feet, and – for some unexplained reason – one trouser leg rolled up to the knee. Others of these ragged urchins wore ancient greasy caps pulled low over their faces, old cast-off jackets, usually torn at the elbows and with strips of lining hanging down behind.

The urchins used to congregate at street corners, often with shoe black boxes slung over their shoulders. "We may occasionally see them running alongside of omnibuses, cabs and hansoms, nimbly turning somersaults on the pavement as they scamper along, and occasionally walking on their hands, with their feet in the air, to the merriment of the passers-by." Most of them, according to Mayhew, were "Irish cockneys" which could be discovered in their features and in their accents. They were generally very astute and quick-witted, and "have a knowing twinkle in their eye which exhibits the precocity of their minds."

Venturing forth at nightfall, the urchins kept a sharp lookout for "bobbies" or "peelers" proceeding on their rounds, as well as the detectives in their "quiet and cautious movements". Apparently, the urchins seldom stole from the barrows of costermongers; perhaps the risk of being caught was too great. But they often stole from old women's stalls. "One will push an old woman off her seat – perhaps a bushel basket – while the others will steal her fruit or the few coppers lying on her stall. This is done by day as well as by night, but chiefly in the dusk of the evening."

The thieves generally went about the street in parties of three or four, and sometimes as many as eight. Watching for their chance, they would suddenly snatch at apples and pears, or oranges and nuts or walnuts, and then run off with the cry of "Stop thief!" ringing in their ears. Mayhew felt that these petty thefts were often carried out "from a love of mischief rather than from a desire for plunder." Given the social conditions of the time, whichever motive prompted these children, they could have had little or no awareness of honesty or dishonesty. Indeed, if they were arrested in the street by a police officer, the youngsters were capable of making an extreme commotion, screaming "Let me go!" and stubbornly lying down in the gutter, until a crowd of angry bystanders would assemble and demand that the policeman cease his bullying. Many of these children used to visit the gallery of the Victorian Theatre in London, to watch popular melo-dramas of burglaries, robberies or murders.

Another class of theft, commonly carried out by small boys, was the rifling of shop tills. This was generally done by two or three boys together, in a time-honoured manner: one of the boys would toss his cap through the door of a greengrocer or other small dealer, if the shop seemed to be empty. Then another boy would creep in on his hands and knees to fetch it, covered by a third boy keeping "crow" at the door. Any passer-by seeing the cap thrown in would take no particular notice, assuming that it was just some thoughtless prank. In the meantime, the boy would creep round and rifle the till. If caught, he would say: "Let me go! I've done nothing! That boy who is standing outside, and has just run away, threw in my bonnet, and I came to fetch it!" The shop-keeper would then let the boy go, and not find out his loss until too late.

Education

England owes her modern system of education to the nineteenth century. At a time when many children had to do a full day's work, one of the first ideas was that of the Sunday School, pioneered in 1780 by Robert Raikes (1735–1811). These schools, which undertook secular and religious education, grew under the auspices of the Church of England National Society and the Nonconformist British and Foreign Society. Founded earlier in the century, these two organizations were awarded a public grant of £20,000 in 1833 to build more schools, and six years later government inspectors were appointed to report their progress. In their early reports, the inspectors found too great an emphasis upon religious instruction, and too little upon other subjects. In a Report of 1847–48 they found that "the want of fit and proper books on secular subjects may be considered amongst the chief obstacles to the progress of education in our National Schools." The Report added that: "The entire want of useful apparatus had been a great hindrance to the advancement of science." The lack even of simple blackboards, the study of arithmetic, of linear drawing and of singing had been hindered, and the absence of maps and globes had produced "an almost incredible extent of ignorance in geography both local and general."

A nineteenth-century school-master

Owing to the want of teachers, some schools operated a monitor system, where the older children instructed the younger; only one or two teachers were needed for general supervision, and to instruct the older pupils. One of the early users of the monitor system was Joseph Lancaster (1778–1838), who introduced it at a south London school in 1801. Some children, though not many in relation to the whole population, attended fee-paying dames' schools, where matrons with some education taught the rudiments of reading, writing and arithmetic. One of the first schools inspectors, the Reverend Allen, found some of these places "oppressive and disagreeable". He found one in the rear of a shop, in a small area measuring ten feet by twelve, in which it was almost impossible to stand upright. The mistress who was paid to teach was usually busy serving customers in the shop, and had left a baby-bearing girl to look after the children.

In most schools, there was no idea that learning should be an

A schoolroom in Regent's Park, London (1870)

enjoyable process. According to the educational reformer James Kay-Shuttleworth, most teachers believed that "education will be best promoted by coercion", and that "knowledge is in itself repulsive". He added: "I think the great majority of such schoolmasters would conceive that they deserted their duty if they treated the children kindly." The cane and the dunce's cap could be found in every school-room, on whose walls hung tracts of an improving nature.

Reports of the Education Committee listed frequent cases of physical violence by school masters and mistresses against their pupils. One Report commented that "if the village schoolmaster be worse paid than the village carpenter or blacksmith, what hope is there of finding any but the most incompetent person in the former situation?" A Report of 1861 added that none were too old, poor, ignorant, feeble, sickly or unqualified to be regarded as unfit for teaching.

The Secretary of the Education Committee was James Kay-Shuttleworth, who had previously been an Assistant Poor Law Commissioner, where he had spent some of his time visiting workhouse schools. A prominent educational reformer, he worked hard to improve conditions in the state-aided schools under his care. For example, in 1846 he brought in a scheme to replace the old inefficient and abused monitorial system by a new system of apprentice-schoolmasters. To encourage these five-year apprenticeships, both the pupil-teacher and the headmaster or headmistress were paid. The teacher apprentices had to be at least thirteen years old, and had to be able to read "with fluency, ease and expression", write neatly and accurately, be familiar with the tables of weights and measures, and understand the basic rules of arithmetic. If their school were governed by the Church of England or another religious body, they would also have to be able to recite the Catechism, and would be in part examined by a priest. At the end of his apprenticeship, the pupil-teacher could enter a teacher training college, or normal college, by taking the Queen's Scholarship Examination. The earliest teacher training colleges included the Borough Road College, founded in Southwark in 1798 by Joseph Lancaster, the Glasgow Normal Seminary founded by David Stow in 1827, and Battersea College, founded on a government grant by Dr. Phillips-Kay (later Sir James Kay-Shuttleworth) in 1840. Dozens more opened from the 1840s. In this way, a start was made to improving the poor social status of the teacher.

Since the first government grants had been awarded in 1833, more and more money was being spent each year on schools, for example in proficiency payments to qualified teachers. By 1851 government spending on education was more than £150,000 per year, and by 1857 it had risen to more than £540,000. Indeed, by this time the government was becoming alarmed at the rising costs of education, and a Royal Commission under the Duke of Newcastle was set up to evaluate the results of this expenditure. In 1861 the Newcastle Commission reported itself generally satisfied with progress, but deplored the fact that work levels were low, and that attendance was irregular. At this time, of course, many children still did not attend school at all. Not until 1870 was the milestone of the Education Act reached, which made elementary education compulsory for all.

This Act was passed within three years of another Reform Bill (1867), which was to give the electoral vote to a much wider section of the community than hitherto. By this time, radicals and reformers in some of the larger industrial towns had begun to prepare the way for educational reform. In Birmingham, for instance, the National Education League was founded in 1869. The 1870 Education Act firmly placed education on a local basis, creating elective school boards which could make elementary education in their areas mandatory between the ages of five and thirteen. Fees might have to be paid by the parents under a means test, and not until 1918 were fees entirely abolished in the elementary schools. Had public apathy been less, and had not the future of English education been for so long disputed by the Church of England and Nonconformists, faster progress might have been made. School attendance was enforced – not always successfully – by the local school board officers. Most of the schools founded as a result of the 1870 Act were not ready to take their first pupils until 1872. In 1876 attendance was made generally compulsory, unless the parents could show that the child was receiving adequate education elsewhere. These measures did much to make child employment a thing of the past, even if they did not entirely end it. In 1902, another major Education Act was passed. This abolished the old school boards, which had served for a generation, and firmly integrated education with a reformed system of local government. The 1902 Act also made the first provisions for secondary education up to the age of sixteen, although free places were limited to those who won entrance scholarships.

The independent, privately endowed public schools attained a peak of power and prestige in the nineteenth century. The best known ones included Eton, Winchester, Westminster, Charterhouse, St. Paul's, Merchant Taylors', Harrow, Shrewsbury, and Rugby (the scene of *Tom Brown's Schooldays*). Marlborough (1843) and Wellington (1843) were among the new Victorian foundations. Here, the sons of the gentry and the wealthy lived together in semi-monastic and authoritarian conditions, studying Latin and Greek languages, literature and grammar. Under the more reforming and liberal leadership of men like Dr. Thomas Arnold of Rugby and Samuel Butler at Shrewsbury, they might also learn some mathematics, modern languages and natural sciences. Even the best known public schools were still small foundations in the earlier part of the century. Indeed, many of them were in a state of decline owing to the rising costs of keeping boys there. In 1828 Harrow had only 128 boys, and by 1844 even this tiny number had shrunk to 69. Rugby School had only 123 boys when Dr. Arnold became its headmaster in 1827.

Harrow school

In the earlier part of the nineteenth century, the 300-odd public schools were severely criticized for their primitive living conditions, and for their lax discipline. Cases of bullying and brutality were fairly common. One junior Westminster schoolboy, Dacres Adams, described a typical day at Westminster School in 1820: "In winter I get up at half-past seven, excepting every fourth day, when I get up at six. At eight I carry my master's book into school. I am in school till nine, excepting the times I am sent about messages. From nine to half-past I go into the birch room and there I make rods. I cannot do more than half a one, it is such hard work. From half-past nine to ten I go to breakfast, and at ten I go into school to lesson, and there stand all the time. I do nothing in the way of learning. At eleven I go to my seat, where I sit, unless I am sent about messages. I am obliged, every time I go into school, to bring three pens, three quaterns, and a dip [ink-well] and a knife. At twelve I go into the green and play at hockey. I may be sent away from play if anyone chuses.

"At one I go to dinner, where I have to mash some potatoes for my master [senior boy], and brown them before the fire, and to toast his meat. After I have done that I may sit down to dinner, if there is time, for I have only half an hour to do everything. I am not allowed to help myself till all are helped, and then I may cut off from what is left what I chuse. It takes me only four or five minutes to eat my dinner, and sometimes I have not time for it – so sometimes I go without – not more than once. The seniors have all the potatoes, so we have only bread and meat to eat, and that takes us less time." The boy also had to clean candlesticks, pots, pans and gridirons and other domestic equipment belonging to the "master" for whom he fagged.

Eton College

In response to public pressure a small number of headmasters began to initiate reforms. Their schools gained reputations for defending orthodox religion, for working hard, for promoting unquestioning loyalty and national pride, and for producing young men who were well equipped to enter British government or foreign service. In the middle part of the century interest in the public schools grew. A Royal Commission was appointed in 1864 to investigate a handful of leading schools. It reported that more emphasis should be placed upon the natural sciences, mathematics, music and modern languages. But it was in the main a vindication of the public schools, which it described as "the chief nurseries of our statesmen". (*Clarendon Report.*)

The Report was followed by the Public Schools Act (1868) which reformed certain aspects of public school government. The Taunton Report, which also began hearing evidence in 1864, dealt with several hundred smaller private schools of all descriptions, and made various recommendations, most of which had little practical effect. It was estimated that there were some 10,000 schools in England run for

Girton College, Cambridge

private profit in the 1860s; they were collectively known as "private adventure schools". These continued to play a central part in the educational life of the nation until well after the end of the century.

Formal education for women had been pioneered by the Misses Buss and Beale; Frances Mary Buss founded the North London Collegiate School for girls in 1850, and the famous Cheltenham Ladies College was founded eight years later, with Dorothea Beale as its first head-mistress. The universities, too, were yielding to pressure from women. Bedford College in London was opened in 1849; Girton College, founded at Hitchin in 1869, had moved into Cambridge four years later under Miss Emily Davies, followed by Newnham College in 1875. At Oxford, Lady Margaret Hall and Somerville Hall were founded in 1879, a year after the University of London had begun to award degrees to women students. But women were not to be given the vote until after the First World War (1918), eighteen years after their counterparts in the United States of America.

Formal scientific and technical training had been more or less non-existent in England before the 1870s. Cambridge University did not create a Natural Science Tripos until 1848, nor Oxford its Honours School of Natural Science until 1853. London University did not open a Science Department until 1858. But by the 1870s, politicians and businessmen were becoming alarmed at the new levels of technical excellence elsewhere in Europe, notably in Germany. True, the Great Exhibition of 1851 had seemed to prove Britain's superiority, but the British entry at the Paris Exhibition of 1867 was generally reckoned to be disappointing. The experience of 1867 led to the calling of a Royal Commission on Scientific Instruction and the Advancement of Science (one of whose members was the scientist T. H. Huxley, 1825–95). The ensuing Devonshire Report, completed in 1875, demanded that for every 200 schoolboys there should be at least one science teacher. The value would be "not merely in imparting the facts of science, but in habituating the pupil to observe for himself on what he observes, and to check the conclusions at which he arrives by further observation or experiment." But neither the Devonshire Report nor the Samuelson and Bryce Reports which followed it, had much immediate practical effect. Technical education was not really developed until after 1900.

Women's Rights

Queen Victoria, the greatest woman of her age, was herself vehemently opposed to the advance of "women's rights". She wrote to Theodore Martin: "The Queen is most anxious to enlist everyone who can speak or write in checking this mad, wicked folly of 'women's rights' with all its attendant horrors, on which her poor feeble sex is bent, forgetting every sense of womanly feeling and propriety. . . . It is a subject which makes the Queen so furious that she cannot contain herself. Woman would become the most hateful, heartless and disgusting of human beings were she allowed to unsex herself; and where would be the protection which man was intended to give the weaker sex?" Gladstone, too, feared for the purity of womanhood: "I have no fear lest the woman should encroach upon the power of the man. The fear I have is, lest we should invite her unwittingly to trespass upon her own nature, which are the present sources of its power."

The *Sphere* in 1900 bemoaned the lack of true feminine spirit in maids of the time: "The servant who takes interest in her work seems no longer to exist, and in return for high wages we get but superficial service. Where is the maid to be found who takes pride in the brilliance of the glass used upon the table, or remembers of her own initiative to darn the damask? Every sort of contrivance now lessens labour – carpet sweepers, knife machines, bathrooms, lifts – in spite of these the life of a housewife is one long wrestle and failure to establish order."

Many critics of the "modern woman" ridiculed them for their conduct. A musical comedy *Gentleman Joe* (1895) had the lines:

A lady cyclist complete with bloomers

> *My eye! Here's a lady bicyclist!*
> *Look at her! Look at her! Look at her! Look at her!*
> *Hi! Hi! Hi!*
> *She's put her petticoats up the spout,*
> *And now she has to go without;*
> *She hopes her mother won't find out,*
> *And thinks they won't be missed.*
> *Oh my! Hi! Hi!*
> *Keep your eye on the lady bi-*
> *The lady bicyclist!*

Advanced women were also ridiculed for their mannish dress. In 1899 Lady Harburton actually brought a law suit against a hotel which had refused to allow her entry while she was wearing "bloomers". "Mark this!" she declared when the case was over, "short skirts for walking gear will be a boon that ought to be easily attained and, once attained, cherished like Magna Carta in the British constitution."

Many of the women who disdained public opinion and went their own way were regarded as bores, interested more in intellectual matters and other male preserves, rather than in proper feminine activities. *Punch* published these lines at the turn of the century:

> *There is a New Woman and what do you think,*
> *She lives upon nothing but foolscap and ink!*
> *But, though foolscap and ink are the whole of her diet,*
> *This nagging New Woman can never be quiet!*

Not surprisingly, the professions were slow to admit women members. Among the first women allowed to practise as doctors was Elizabeth Garrett Anderson (1836–1917), who was also the first woman to be elected a mayor. Elizabeth Anderson was involved in a hard struggle before she was allowed to enter medical practice, having been refused a degree by the University of London, and having been banned from work in English hospitals. Many years passed before women began to infiltrate the other learned professions: the first woman barrister was not called to the bar until 1921.

Reforms for Seamen

For as long as anyone could remember, the life of seamen, whether in the Royal or Merchant Navy, had been a harsh and neglected one. But from 1850 the merchant service was placed under the general eye of the Board of Trade. From this date, ship's officers had to pass naval examinations and hold certificates of good service. The seamen were given guaranteed standards of food and quartering, and were given more security of employment. In the latter part of the century, a Member of Parliament called Samuel Plimsoll (1824–98), led a famous campaign to defend the interests of the ordinary seaman. After vigorous efforts he managed to have a Merchant Shipping Act passed in 1876 to prevent ships being dangerously overloaded to the peril of their crews. Every ship had to be painted with a white watermark, or "Plimsoll line", to gauge its maximum cargo. Safety at sea had also been helped by the foundation of the Royal Lifeboat Institution in 1824, and by the incorporation of the great marine insurance company, Lloyds, whose professional vigilance helped to reduce naval disasters and negligence, for example by use of the telegraph.

Religious Minorities

A major social reform of the nineteenth century was the virtual ending of discrimination against religious minorities, in other words those who did not belong to the Church of England. When the century opened, Church of England members had many exclusive privileges: they alone could sit as Members of Parliament, hold official public posts, and attend the universities of Oxford and Cambridge. These privileges were denied to Catholics, Jews, and to Protestant Nonconformists such as Methodists, Congregationalists and Baptists. The first steps towards religious emancipation took place in the late 1820s, with the Catholic Emancipation Act of 1829. This Act was passed to reduce the threat of civil war in Catholic Ireland, which had hitherto only been allowed to return Protestant Members of Parliament to Westminster. Another landmark was the repeal of a number of Test Acts which had stopped dissenters from taking a full part in public affairs. The Jews did not receive the same equality until 1858, when they were finally allowed to enter Parliament. Benjamin Disraeli, who became Tory Prime Minister, was the most prominent member of this group.

5   *Family Life and Pleasures*

THE NINETEENTH CENTURY was a great age of English family life. The relationships between the different members of the family were strongly defined, and for the most part easily accepted. The father was the head of the household, and as his natural right expected the unquestioning obedience, not only of his children, but of his wife, whose promise to "honour and obey" him was literally meant. In return, the wife managed all domestic matters and was responsible for the day to day care of the children. The children were expected to be dutiful, and to follow the examples of good conduct set by their parents, to take pride in the family name, and to look upon their childhood as a preparation for adulthood. Middle-class Victorian family life has sometimes been presented with rather a gloomy aspect, which was not always merited. True, the children may sometimes have felt weighed down by the obligations laid upon them by their parents, but this is not to say that they did not generally lead happy lives. Indeed, the busy community life of a large middle-class family, with perhaps eight or nine children and three or four servants, was in many ways more healthy and less confining than the smaller and more isolated family units of modern urban life.

Marriage

Marriage in the middle class was looked upon as a matter of general family concern, in which due thought had to be given to social and financial matters. A close eye was kept upon the family's young unmarried daughters. Elaborate steps were taken to see that they only met male friends who were socially acceptable, and under proper supervision. A resourceful couple could always find time to themselves, but much of their time had to be spent together at family tea parties, dinners, dances, outings and other social occasions. A daughter suspected of forming an undesirable attachment would be taken to task by her father and reminded of her duty. A persistently unruly daughter might be sent away to stay with relatives in the country until she had "recovered" herself.

In middle- and upper-class sections of society, at least, sex was a more or less taboo subject, outwardly regarded as distasteful to God and man alike. There was widespread ignorance about the subject in both its physical and psychological aspects. But the conventions of the time seem to have worked well enough for most contemporaries, and there was certainly no lack of romance.

A man who wished to marry a woman had to ask her father for her hand, and indeed might do so against the wishes of the daughter her-

A wedding group (1890s)

self. In practice, however, parentally arranged marriages grew less common; they could easily be sabotaged by a determined party. In any case, few parents were willing to see their daughters unhappily married.

In an age when girls were carefully chaperoned wherever they went, it is perhaps not surprising to find the "agony" columns of the newspapers filled with romantic messages from anonymous lovers: "To A: if humanity has not entirely fled from your breast, return, oh! return ere it is too late, write, tell her, oh! tell her where you are that she may follow you, her own, her all, and die! See her once more." (*The Times*, 1850).

It behoved young ladies to be careful, and to avoid shark-infested waters such as the *Morning Herald* (1827): "A private gentleman aged 24, entirely independent. . . . To any female of respectability who would study for domestic comfort, and willing to confide her future happiness in one in every way qualified to render the marriage state desirable, as the advertiser is in affluence. The lady must have the power of some property. . . ." Such advertisements had to be regarded with caution, for as one J. Curtis observed, "an upright, prudent and moral man would hardly, we conceive, make his desires in matrimony known through the medium of a newspaper."

"£15,000 a year", a cartoonist's idea of the attractive woman

When the marriage was arranged, the bride-to-be would begin the elaborate preparation of her *trousseau* in readiness for the wedding day. (Marriage was always celebrated in church.) When at last the great day came, and both families were assembled in the church, the bride – dressed in white and assisted by bridesmaids – would pass from daughter to wife, exchanging one unequal status for another. The English wife in Victorian times and before enjoyed little shelter from her husband under the common law. Until the passing of the Married Women's Property Act the husband's marriage vow, "With all my worldly goods I thee endow," was ironic. In fact the reverse happened. A newly-wed husband legally acquired all his wife's real and personal property, and he could dispose of it exactly as he thought fit. Not every husband approved of this state of affairs. The economist John Stuart Mill voluntarily gave up his marital rights on his own wedding day. As he pointed out in *The Subjection of Woman* (1869), if the wife "leaves her husband she can take nothing with her, neither her children nor anything which is rightfully her own." Only if a wife obtained a court decree, which seldom happened, would she be entitled "to live apart, without being forced back into the custody of an exasperated jailer." On the other hand, a husband did have the enforceable duty to maintain his wife and the children.

The actress Sarah Siddons was one married woman to suffer hardship. She handed over all her considerable earnings to her manager-husband, only to be sent on a long and tedious tour of Ireland in order to recoup £10,000 which he had lost in unwise speculation.

It was certainly true of marriage that there was one law for the rich and another for the poor. The rich, who could afford expensive legal advice, could invoke the special help of the Court of Equity; and in this way a rich married woman was able to protect the marriage settlement made by her father on the wedding day.

Left A Victorian interior.
Right A Victorian sitting room
of 1895 crowded with ornaments
and photographs

House and Home

What kind of a house would the new middle-class housewife come to?
First of all it would be very dark. The windows might be fairly long and
tall, but they would generally be obscured by heavy curtains and
pelmets, made perhaps of dark red or blue velvet; the walls would be
covered in dark heavily patterned wallpaper. Yet until the start of the
nineteenth century the only form of domestic lighting had been
candles. But from 1800, the first lamps were lit with coal gas; and in
1809 it was first used for street lighting in Pall Mall, London. Gas
lamps were lit by tapers and from 1834 by patented lucifer matches,
tipped with an odorous and dangerous mixture of sulphur and phos-
phorus. The safety match was invented later: this could only be lit by
striking against a strip of phosphorized paper. The domestic gas lamp
remained much the same throughout the century, although gas
brackets, hanging lamps ("gaseliers") and glass globes were of many
different kinds. In 1886 a Viennese chemist called Karl von Welsbach
invented the gas mantle. This consisted of a network of special metals
which glowed brilliant incandescent white when fired by the gas flame.
But candles were still commonly used throughout the century, and in
middle-class homes it was the custom to leave a candlestick in the hall
at night for the benefit of those retiring upstairs to bed. Candles were
made of beeswax or tallow, which gave an irregular and smoky flame,
and from the middle of the century, paraffin wax. By this time, wicks
were better made, and the candles burned more reliably. Oil lamps
were used in the home, too, and were much improved by fitting little
glass chimneys over the burning wicks to concentrate their brightness.

   The second feature of the Victorian home, which would be most
striking to a modern visitor, would have been the way in which the
living rooms were crowded with ornaments of every kind. The curtains
and wallpaper would be heavily patterned; gilt and silver framed
water-colours, cameos, and later in the century, photographs would be
hung on the walls, and placed on flat surfaces such as tables, dressers
and pianos (which were themselves covered in lace cloths). Occasional
tables, stools, sewing baskets, canterburys, davenports, armchairs, and
many other items of furniture would fill the room, making it seemingly
impossible to walk about in safety. The furniture in the dining room

would be heavily carved in mahogany or oak, in a neo-Jacobean, or perhaps an oriental style; it was hard work to polish and keep clean.

Sanitation was seen to be of more importance in the nineteenth century than in the eighteenth. Toward the end of the century many houses were equipped with bathrooms. In the earlier years, however, and for less affluent families, baths were taken in a hip bath filled with pitchers of hot water and placed before the hearth. Some homes contained a portable Turkish bath, such as manufactured by Messrs. Foot of New Bond Street, London: "The delight of bathing by the Turkish or Roman method – of steaming the impurities from your system – of absorbing healthful medicated atmosphere, can be enjoyed at home as well as in a public establishment. The Home Turko-Russian (Self Purifying) Folding Bath Cabinets: enables you to take Dry Steam, Vapour, Oxygen, Medicated or Perfumed bathing privately, economically, and with the assurance of perfect cleanliness. A new and perfect Principle of Bathing. A cure for colds, pneumonia, gout, rheumatism, nervous diseases, kidney and liver troubles, *etc*." (From an advertisement of Messrs. Foot & Co.)

An enormous range of new toiletries and dressings appeared on the market in the nineteenth century: Odonto (a dentifrice), Cerelaum for headaches, Kalydor – "an Oriental botanical preparation" – for redness and pimples, Essence of Tyre for dyeing the hair, macassar hair oil, Cantharides Oil for stimulating hair growth, "aromatic regenerators" for the hair and skin, "pulmonic wafers" for the chest, creams and other preparations with pseudo-scientific and quasi-classical names like Aethereal Oleine, Elmes's Arcanum, Winn's Anticardium, Olden's Eukeirogenion, and Rypophagon Soap, to name but a few. Those who manufactured or sold them sometimes described themselves as "hygiests".

As in the eighteenth century and before, the lady of the house constantly supervised the efficient running of her household, and instructed her daughters in good household management, perhaps with the aid of Mrs. Beeton's famous book *Household Management*. Most middle-class families kept at least one maid, but even so much of the day's housework had to be carried out by the girls. In the days before electricity and modern household gadgets, housework was hard and tedious – carrying coals to light the fires in each room, carrying pitchers

Many new temptations appeared in the nineteenth century

of water to make baths, scrubbing the stone passages and kitchen and scullery floors, polishing the heavily carved furniture.

The kitchen, which was usually in the basement, was a large and fairly comfortable room, with a couple of armchairs in which the cooks could rest. Coal was relatively cheap, and every middle-class kitchen was equipped with an enormous cooking range, over which rows of copper-bottomed pans were hung. The kitchen was filled with every conceivable type of pot, pan and other cooking utensils from skillets to aspic dishes. Most of the food was home-made (canned food was available, but was not much liked or trusted) – bread, cakes, jellies, preserves, pickles, and many other items.

An important part of the housewife's job was shopping for household essentials, and for the various items which could not be made or prepared at home. Sometimes she would have her purchases delivered by local tradesmen, or later in the century she might use catalogues or answer newspaper advertisements. But for everyday items she would visit one of the local markets which were a part of town life throughout the country. London, as today, had many markets, which were the focus of local community life. Whitechapel market, which still exists today in the East End of London, was described by Henry Mayhew in *London's Underworld* (1862). Along the Whitechapel Road were ranged on either side scores of market stalls. Various kinds of merchandise were on sale: there were stalls for fruit, vegetables and oysters, and there were stalls where fancy goods were on sale – combs, brushes, chimney ornaments, children's toys, and common articles of jewellery. Middle-aged women stood about, or walked slowly up and down, carrying baskets of chopped firewood, and "Cheap Johns" (bargain sellers) selling all kinds of Sheffield cutlery, stationery and plated goods.

Another popular market was held at New Cut in Lambeth on the south bank of the River Thames. Mayhew remembered seeing an old Irish woman, with a tray of apples and pears set on top of a barrel, behind which she sat, placidly smoking a clay pipe. "In another place you see a costermonger's barrow, with large green and yellow piles of fruit of better quality than the others, and a group of boys and girls assembled around him as he smartly disposes of pennyworths to the persons passing along the street." Some tradesmen and pedlars pre-

A lady of fashion

Below left A confectioner's shop in London. *Right* Covent Garden fruit and vegetable market (1820)

ferred to stand outside public houses or "beer shops", where people were constantly entering and coming out. "Outside a public house you see a young man, humpbacked, with a basket of herrings and haddocks standing on the pavement, called 'Yarmouth herrings – three-a-penny!' and at the door of a beershop with the sign of the *Pear Tree* we find a miserable looking old woman selling [water] cresses, seated on a stool with her feet in an old basket."

The Victorian housewife would have visited shops which were still open-fronted, having a large flat surface built into the window, where the goods were displayed. Henry Mayhew found many such shops in New Cut, with "a heterogeneous assortment of household furniture, tables, chairs, looking glasses, plain and ornamental, cupboards, fire screens, *etc.*, ranged along the broad pavement; while on tables are stores of carpenters' tools in great variety, copper kettles, brushes, and bright tin pannikins, and other articles." Grocers displayed their food uncovered in the open air, with little thought for hygiene. One grocer stood before his door, "with blue apron, hailing the passer-by to make a purchase. On either side of his shop door were stands, piled high with unwrapped rashers of bacon, ticketed: 'Of fine flavour', or 'Very Mild'."

The housewife might buy something for herself on a shopping expedition. She might visit a milliner, seated beneath an awning in front of her door, busily knitting. Black and white straw bonnets and crinolines would swing from iron and wooden rods suspended on each side of her doorway; and on the tables set before her would be boxes of brightly coloured feathers and flowers, and shirt fronts of various styles with stacks of gown pieces of different patterns.

A covered market in Whitechapel

Family Entertainment

A family Bible reading

The Victorians had a great capacity for entertaining themselves within the family, and most families set aside time for some sort of regular family entertainment. Sometimes, in the evening, the family would gather around the piano, while the father sang ballads and the mother played; or they would recite poems, or read stories to one another; often the subject matter was chosen for its "improving" nature (a regular part of life for many families was the reading of passages from the family Bible). Parties would be held for the children; and the more serious-minded members of the family might play a game of chess, draughts or mah-jong. The middle of the nineteenth century saw a rapid proliferation of ingenious toys for the children of the middle classes. These toys were often designed to show off the technical prowess of their inventors, as much as to amuse the children. For example: "The Wonderful Electric Toy. The Merry Mountebanks go through their Grotesque Gambols without the aid of strings, wire or Springs, the Motive Power being Electricity. Price 1s. 6d. Carriage free for thirty stamps. H. G. Clarke & Co., 2, Garrick Street, Covent Garden." (*Illustrated London News*, 15th December, 1868).

The Victorians had an insatiable appetite for the curious and the exotic. A popular figure was the showman with a dancing bear and monkey, who made his living wandering about the towns and villages. Little thought was spared for the poor bear. A cockney chimney sweep who helped one of these showmen told the writer Henry Mayhew how the keeper treated his bear, called Jenny. "He was not to say roughish to her unless she was obstrepelous [*sic*]. If she were, he showed her the large mop stick and beat her with it, sometimes hard, especially when she wouldn't let the monkey get on top of her head, for that was a part of the performance. The monkey was dressed the same as a soldier, but the bear had no dress but for her muzzle and chain." Jenny fed on an invariable diet of bread, water, potatoes and carrots; meat would have

A Lancashire working man and family at home

made her savage. The monkey seems to have fared better, being fed with nuts, apples, ginger-bread, and titbits proffered by the gaping bystanders.

Although the troupe preferred to work in country towns such as Cheltenham and Gloucester, the local magistrates would often not allow them in; as a result the troupe spent most of its time in London, where Jenny was eventually shot by order of the magistrates, and her carcass sold to a hair-dresser. The assistant keeper told Mayhew: "I couldn't stay to see her shot, and had to go into an alehouse on the road. I don't know what her carcass sold for. It wasn't very fat." After the bear's execution, the assistant keeper evidently fell on hard times. Sometimes he found work in other troupes. But "I do other jobs, when I can get 'em, at other times; I delivers bills, carries boards, and 'elps at funerals."

Another entertainer found more success with Chinese shades. This was a shadow show whose basic items of equipment were a white sheet, a lantern, and cut-out paper characters. One of the most popular productions was *The Woodchopper's Frolic*. The woodchopper's daughter Kitty, steals her father's mutton supper. The showman explained: "Then the mother falls down, and calls out, 'I shall faint! I shall faint! Oh, bring me a pail of gin!' . . . Then comes the correction scene. Kitty comes to her, and her mother says, 'Where have you been?' and Kitty says, 'Playing at shuttlecock, mummy,' and then the mother says, 'I'll give you some shuttlecock with the gridiron,' and exeunt, and comes back with the gridiron; and then you see her with the child on her knee correcting her." The scene closed with a battle between the wood-chopper and his wife, and the daring theft of the fireplace and mutton-pot by a goblin, Spring-heeled Jack. The showman added that the per-formance contained elements of danger, as a real fire was used behind the sheet which might easily catch alight. The spirited violence of the dialogue in these shows has much in common with the more horrific English nursery rhymes.

Some entertainers went to considerable lengths to impress their gullible audiences. One man made a fair living by visiting respectable taverns in and around London, and performing fire-eating feats. He had many variations of these. But one "trick is with the brimstone. I have a plate of lighted sulphur, and first inhale the fumes, and then devour it with a fork and swallow it. As a costermonger said to me when he saw me do it, 'I say, old boy, your game ain't all brandy!' There is a kind of acid, nasty, sour taste in this feat, and at first it used to make me feel sick; but now I'm used to it and it don't. When I puts it in my mouth it clings just like sealing-wax and forms a kind of dead ash. Of a morning, if I haven't got my breakfast by a certain time, there's a kind of retching in my stomach, and that's the only inconvenience I feel from swallowing the sulphur for that there feat." If the fire-eater is to be believed, he once became so short of money that a betting man persuaded him to challenge a dog in killing rats in a rat pit. The dog killed twenty rats in seventeen minutes, and the fire-eater bit the same number of rats to death in thirteen. He emerged with a five-shilling purse and a festering rat bite on his shoulder.

Street performers on stilts, an illustration from *Mayhew's London*

A shooting picnic (1896)

Out and About

In the nineteenth century, more than ever before, people began to seek pleasure outside their own homes and their own towns. Railways, newspapers, and later on the telegraph, were all helping to widen people's horizons, and to interest them more actively in people and places outside their own immediate localities. On a public holiday, such as Easter Monday, the working population were for a few hours able to escape from the drabness and poverty of their urban surroundings, and find the fresh and wholesome air of the nearby countryside. On Easter Monday, thousands of working people of London would make their way south of the River Thames into Greenwich fields for fresh air and recreation. Charles Dickens wrote that the "road to

Saint Monday or the working-man's holiday – the pleasure van for Hampton Court

A picnic

Greenwich during the whole of Easter Monday is in a perpetual state of bustle and noise". Cabs, hackney coaches, "shay" carts, coal wagons, stage-coaches, omnibuses, sociables, gigs, donkey chaises, every imaginable form of wheeled transport was crammed with people, and the dust flew in clouds.

In Dickens's time more and more people were beginning to discover the delights of the seaside, following the fashion set by the Prince Regent at Brighton – formerly Brighthelmstone – in the early years of the century. A writer in the *Observer* (1856) was very struck by the holiday scene on the beach at Ramsgate, one of the new seaside resorts which was rapidly becoming a popular place of visit for town dwellers. The bathing machines were in use from about ten in the morning until one or two o'clock in the afternoon, and the beach was so crowded with ladies and gentlemen that it was difficult to pick one's way through the throng, especially at high tide when there was less room on the beach. The water, he added, was black with bathers. "Should the sea be rather rough, the females do not venture beyond the surf, and lay themselves on their backs, waiting for the coming waves." According to the writer, the waves carried the ladies' bathing dresses up over their heads, "so that as far as decency is concerned they might as well be without any dresses at all." The gentlemen, he added, were there equipped with glasses as if attending the opera. A sign of the times, it seemed, was that the ladies stared back without so much as a blush or a giggle. "How is it that ladies, who are so very delicate in London, should, when they arrive at Ramsgate, throw off all pretensions to modesty and decency, as they do with their shawls and wrappers?"

> *I'm afloat, I'm afloat, what matters it where?*
> *So the devils don't know my address, I don't care.*
> *Of London I'm sick, I've come down to the sea,*
> *And let who will make up next week's number for me!*

Seaside fun at Scarborough on the Yorkshire coast (1857)

The Victorian age was not an age of dramatists, but was a great age of theatrical personalities. It was the age of the great actor-managers, men like the first theatrical knight Sir Henry Irving (1838–1905) at the Lyceum Theatre and Herbert Beerbohm Tree (1852–1917), at Her Majesty's. In his great partnership with the actress Ellen

The Haymarket theatre

Above H. Beerbohm Tree
Below Miss Ellen Terry

Terry (1848–1928), Irving produced and appeared in costume plays at the Lyceum for more than thirty years. In the age of Irving and Tree, there was a premium upon the lavish production and the costly presentation: costumes were rich, the casts enormous: George Sanger's production of *The Fall of Khartoum and Death of General Gordon* contained a hundred camels, 200 Arab horses and two military bands, all appearing nightly: it was little wonder that Sanger lost £10,000 on the production, even though it ran to packed audiences for 280 performances. The style of the stage tended to be melodramatic and sentimental, whether the production were of Shakespeare or Sheridan or of a new play by J. M. Barrie, Oscar Wilde or George Bernard Shaw. The actors and actresses who played at the Duke of York's, the Gaiety, the Lyric, Royalty or Strand, all seemed to be larger than life – Mrs. Patrick Campbell, Charles Hawtrey, Marie Tempest and others.

The later nineteenth century saw the heyday of the music hall. Even outside London, the larger provincial cities often had several music halls. Nottingham, for example, had two by 1867, and its third, the old Malt Cross hall, opened ten years later. By the end of the century Birmingham had six music halls, Liverpool six, Manchester four, Sheffield five, and Glasgow six. London alone had fifty, from the Alhambra to the Victoria Coffee Palace. The music halls afforded work to a huge band of itinerant performers of all kinds, many comedians (notably Marie Lloyd, who was born in 1870), and singers, dancers, acrobats, ventriloquists, magicians, impersonators, animal trainers and others. A large number of London's music halls were built in the 1860s, for example the South London (1860), the Metropolitan (1864) and Gatti's (1865). These and many others attracted enormous crowds, who were often curious to see not only the great comedians but sensational guest performers such as the first Channel swimmer, Captain Matthew Webb, or Charles Blondin who had crossed the Niagara Falls on a tightrope.

The music hall was the perfect mirror of the times, of political as well as of social matters. For example, this famous song was first sung at the London Pavilion in 1877, at a time of great popular fear that Russia was planning to challenge control of the Mediterranean by seizing Constantinople:

> *We don't want to fight, but by Jingo if we do*
> *We've got the ships, we've got the men, we've got the money too;*
> *We've fought the bear before,*
> *And while Britons shall be true,*
> *The Russians shall not have Constantinople.*

And the start of the South African War in 1899 prompted the Australian baritone Hamilton Hill to sing:

> *Goodbye Dolly, I must leave you,*
> *Though it breaks my heart to go.*
> *Something tells me I am needed*
> *At the front to fight the foe.*

The nation's feelings of patriotism were grandly stirred by songs like *The Army of Today's All Right*, *The Union Jack of Dear Old England*, or *Soldiers of the Queen*.

Magic lanterns had been in use since at least the sixteenth century, and became very popular in Victorian times, both for amusement in the home, and for instruction in village halls and the new working men's clubs. In the late 1880s, the American George Eastman, who founded the Kodak Company, discovered a way of using sensitized celluloid film instead of the glass plates and papers used before. In the early 1890s, many people helped to develop the technique of moving pictures, where a succession of frames was projected in front of a lamp, separated by the movements of a shutter. On 20th February, 1896, the brothers August and Louis Lumiere of Paris staged a performance of their *Cinematographie* in Regent Street, London, in which three short films were projected. One was a scene of the Lumiere factory at Lyons, another showed the mail packet arriving at Folkestone, the third was a comic feature entitled *Teasing the Gardener*. Another cinematographer, Robert W. Paul, was at the same time demonstrating his Theatrograph, which made use of hand-painted moving pictures.

In the early days of film, there was no idea of the film as an art form. Victorian audiences were fascinated by the invention's sheer novelty, and eagerly devoured everything that was served before them – unedited comic incidents, tricks and "magic", shots of a roaring lion in a zoo, romantic shots of rivers and waterfalls, and other familiar scenes of everyday life. The people who appeared before the cameras were usually anonymous friends of the cameraman, and had nothing to do with the theatre. Until about 1910 most films ran between one and fifteen minutes, rarely any longer. When Queen Victoria watched a film of part of her Diamond Jubilee Procession of 1897, she remarked: "Very tiring to the eyes, but worth a headache to have seen such a marvel."

In 1896 Robert Paul filmed the Derby at Epsom, which in that year was won by the Prince of Wales' horse, Persimmon. Paul brought the film to the Alhambra in Leicester Square, London, where he showed it over and over again in the same programme, to satisfy the enormous curiosity of his audience. He recalled, "They went crazy . . . I had to rewind the film and show it over and over again. They stood on the seats and cheered it every time. Then they sang *God bless the Prince of Wales*. I remember that some of the artists on the bill were a little jealous." Then the profit potential of the film suddenly struck him: "I suddenly realized while I was rewinding between one of the many repetitions of the film that, apart from the hire of the wagonette (on which the camera had been mounted) the picture had only cost me fifteen shillings to make. People came to see it night after night, and I showed it at other halls, and I was receiving a pound a minute for showing it, every time it went on the screen." Robert Paul's business boomed, and many other people began to realize the commercial possibilities of this amazing novelty.

Another important figure in these infant years of the cinema in England was Cecil M. Hepworth, who filmed the Oxford and Cambridge Universities' boat race in 1898, the Henley Regatta of 1900, and other eventful public occasions which his public were eager to see, including those of serious importance such as the departure of troops for the South African War in 1899. Other leading cinematographers included Arthur Collins, the Drury Lane impresario and representative of the French Gaumont Company, G. A. Smith and J. A. Williamson.

Lumiere's cinematograph

The *Brighton Herald* declared in December 1900: "It is astonishing how soon one grows accustomed to new wonders. Otherwise the exhibition of animated photographs now on view at the West Street concert hall would be nothing short of sensational. As it is, we have been trained within a very brief space of time to accept photographic records of events, showing all the life and movement and excitement of a scene, almost as much a matter of course as a newspaper record. The Biograph has speedily taken a place in our life as a supplemental chronicler of the more notable events of the day in all quarters of the world, and a highly interesting chronicler it is, enabling us to realize the spirit of scenes with an actuality and vividness hitherto unattainable. This week, at the West Pier concert hall, scenes of this kind of the highest interest are brought before the eyes of the spectators with impressive interest, the medium being the American Biograph, identical with that shown at the Palace Theatre, London." The films on this occasion were mainly news items concerning the South African War, linked together by concert music to allow the projectionists time to change the reels of film. Admission to the hall was popularly priced at threepence.

High Society

In a time when income tax was still only a few pence in the pound, there were enormous disparities of wealth in English society. As late as 1900, for example, there were still more than a million men and women in domestic service in Britain, for the most part poorly paid and half-starved, with their living quarters in draughty attics. Many of them came from poor country districts, or from Ireland. A maid-servant seldom earned more than five shillings a week plus her keep. The household of a prominent noble family could be large indeed; the kitchen staff under the Steward would comprise one or more butlers, grooms, footmen, page boys, chefs, bakers; kitchen, vegetable, scullery and stillroom maids, porter, helpers, and "odd men". The head house-keeper would be in charge of personal valets and maids, as well as tutors and governesses. A really large household would employ a full staff of resident maintenance men – engineers, carpenters, firemen, telephonists, telegraphers and nightwatchmen. The stable, run by the head coachman, would have under-coachmen, grooms, strappers and "helpers", and in houses of more modern outlook, chauffeurs and car-washers. The Duke and Duchess of Portland also had a chaplain, organist, librarian, clerk, and stud groom and fifteen assistants for their racing stable, about a hundred gardeners and roadmen, a head instructor and Japanese trainer in their private gymnasium, a head greensman and ten helpers on their private golf course, and laundress and twelve assistant launderers, and three full-time window cleaners. The Duke of Portland owned an estate of some 100,000 acres, and had an income of several million pounds a year, mostly derived from his coal-mining interests.

The Earl of Lonsdale was another example of aristocratic affluence. When welcoming the German Kaiser as a house guest in 1895, the fifth Lord Lonsdale attended him with a squadron of yeomanry, liveried outriders, and ten carriages, to escort him from the entrance to the estate along the eight miles drive to Lowther House itself. Like many of his peers, Lonsdale was more than ready to accept responsi-bilities in proportion to his wealth. In 1900, he offered to supply the War Office with 208 officers and men, three maxim guns, four ambu-lances, a squad of trained nurses and 280 carts from his estate, to help fight in the South African War. This was a strong echo of medieval times, when the great territorial magnates were feudally bound to help their king in time of war. The wealth accumulated by some of the English peerage by the late nineteenth century was legendary: the Duke of Sutherland was apparently in the habit of pinning £1,000 notes to the pillow of his sleeping wife.

Many of those who were elevated to the peerage in Victoria's reign – and there were hundreds – owed their social success to commerce. Many a great landowner found that his estates could be profitably turned into iron or coal mines, for example in Nottinghamshire and

Top A Victorian butler and his master (1879). *Centre* Footmen and butler below stairs. *Above* Cook, footmen and housemaid below stairs (1847)

Derbyshire; or perhaps he could sell or lease his land to the wealthy railway companies, many of whom were ambitious to expand regardless of cost. Dukes, earls and barons often became skilled financiers and industrial managers, directors of railway companies and banks, ruling commercial empires as once they had ruled landed ones. In 1899, Lord and Lady Warwick showed a sign of the changing times by converting their estates into a limited liability company, Warwick Estates Limited, with a registered share capital of £120,000. The practice was followed by many others.

In the nineteenth century many new country houses were built by the rich, often under the personal supervision of the buyer, and executed by prominent architects such as Norman Shaw, Philip Webb, George Devey, and perhaps most notably Sir Edward Lutyens. To be able to have one's own house built was a mark of social distinction, and firm views were held as to taste and style. Many such country houses were built in the neo-Gothic manner, with patterned brick walls, turrets, battlements and pointed arches. Victorian architects drew heavily on the past as well as on exotic foreign influences in their domestic designs. The style of the late Elizabethan and Jacobean period was very popular, too. To most modern eyes, houses like these may seem too heavily ornamented, lacking functionality and simplicity of design; to their owners, they were highly romantic individual castles or palaces in miniature. The houses built by Lutyens, C. F. A. Voysey and Webb did, however, display more grace and character while keeping their roots in the varied traditions of the English countryside.

The cook and her gentleman caller

The rich divided their time each year between their country homes and London. Country house parties and rural pursuits were generally given up in favour of the London Season, with its round of dinners, dances and other social engagements. Lady St. Helier wrote: "Society now runs mad after anyone who can get himself talked of. . . . To have a good cook, to be the smartest dressed woman, to give the most magnificent entertainments where a fortune is spent on flowers and decorations, to be the most favoured guest of Royalty, or to have sailed as near to the wind of social disaster as is compatible with not being shipwrecked, are a few of the features which characterize some of the smartest people in London society. It must be admitted that these qualifications are not high or difficult to attain to, while the training ground is large and well-studded with instructors."

For the daughters of upper-class families, it was essential to be presented at Court. *The Harmsworth Magazine* (1900) declared: "It is an epoch in a woman's life not easily forgotten. To a young girl it signifies the transition from girlhood to womanhood; from the obscurity of the schoolroom to the brilliancy of society life, in which at-homes, dinners, balls, garden parties, operas and theatres follow each other in a continuous whirl. The smile of her Queen had transformed the little homely grub into a gay butterfly."

The presentations were made at St. James's Palace, and had to be effected through an introduction by someone who had in their turn already been presented. By the end of the century, members of the

A young girl smuggles in a secret visitor

"A morning" at Holland House, London (1872)

most exclusive sets were complaining that almost anyone, even "in trade", could get in. The rules of the presentation were strict, as the *Harmsworth Magazine* pointed out: "For a *débutante* the dress *must* be white, but coloured flowers are permissible and shower bouquets have recently been much in favour. The bodice is cut in a round *décolletage*, showing the shoulders, and with short sleeves." If through ill health a bodice could not be worn, special permission had to be obtained from the Queen (through the Lord Chamberlain's office) to wear High Court dress. This implied a bodice cut square or V-shaped, and filled in either with transparent or with thick white material, and elbow sleeves to match. An unmarried lady must wear two white ostrich feathers in her hair, and a married lady three. The plumes had to be so arranged in front that Her Majesty could clearly see them when the *débutantes* approached. White gloves had to be worn. Cassell's *Etiquette of Good Society* explained that when the lady's name had been read out by the Lord Chamberlain, she must advance before the Queen, curtsy very low – almost as if kneeling. If the lady were the daughter of a peer or peeress, the Queen would kiss her forehead; otherwise, the Queen would extend her hand to be kissed. "The lady then rises, and making a curtsy to any member of the Royal Family who may be present, passes on, keeping her face towards the Queen, until she has passed out of the door appointed for those leaving the Presence Chamber."

Queen Victoria and Prince Albert

Opposite top Ladies and gentlemen with their four-in-hands by the Serpentine in Hyde Park, London. *Below* An outing to the rowing regatta at Henley on the River Thames (1886)

Débutantes after being presented at court at the turn of the century

A contemporary wrote in the later years of the century that: "English ladies of the nineteenth century are not expected to milk cows and feed pigs, but if circumstances oblige them to do these or any similar acts of labour, what we impress is that they would not necessarily cease to be 'ladies' in the proper sense of the word. The constant use of the word 'lady' and the term 'lady friend' is also objectionable. It is to be presumed that all your female acquaintances are 'ladies'. A writer sarcastically observes: 'There is scarce one *woman* to be met with; the sex consists almost entirely of *ladies*.' "

The "New Woman"

The "New Woman" of the 1890s was indulging in new fashions, but she was doing so rather cautiously. If long skirts were plain black or grey, blouses and bodices were often as feminine as they had ever been. A large range of ready-made garments could be purchased, both home-manufactured brands, and imported German and other European designs. Woman wore high-necked bodices, which lay outside their skirts, rather in the manner of Eton jackets. Women of the middle class changed their dress for the different times of the day – tea gowns and walking gowns, afternoon and evening dresses in various styles. There was another rather uncertain and curious contrast, too, between the masses of fine lace with which their clothes were styled, and the rather small and squat trilby-shaped hats which were worn perched on top of the head. Many accessories were used – mufflers, fans, gloves, chain purses, hair pieces, parasols. To avoid the risks of a high wind, some women took to weighting down their skirts with gun shot, a nice mixture of modesty and mechanical ingenuity with which to enter the twentieth century.

Epilogue:
The Death of a Queen

Two royal jubilees were celebrated in the nineteenth century. The first was that of the sick George III in 1809, the second Queen Victoria's in June 1887. The second date seemed to mark the zenith of British wealth, imperial power and prestige. Tributes and homage of the most magnificent kind arrived from every corner of the globe – India, Canada, Australia, Africa, America, Europe. On 21st June, 1887, a massive royal pageant wound its way from Buckingham Palace to Westminster Abbey. The heads of Europe's royal families rode in fifteen closed carriages, followed by the representatives of the British Empire and of the armed forces, and a guard of honour which included no less than sixteen princes related to the Queen, three of them her own sons. Some of the music played at the jubilee service in West-minster Abbey had been composed by Albert, the late Prince Consort whose death the Queen still mourned. Even greater were the festivities ten years later, when the nation celebrated the Queen's occupation of the throne for more than sixty years. After a great Diamond Jubilee banquet at Buckingham Palace, a vast royal and colonial procession made its way through the streets of London, which were filled with more than a million and a half cheering onlookers. Never in British history had any monarch seemed more to express in the royal person the spirit of the people.

But Queen Victoria was growing old. During the whole of 1900 she suffered from fatigue. She celebrated her eighty-first birthday in May 1900, and by the following January her general health had begun to deteriorate. She was world weary. On 19th January, 1901, an official bulletin from her residence at Osborne announced that her condition was causing anxiety. Three days later at half past six in the evening she died, surrounded by her closest relatives and supported by the Kaiser of Germany.

When the news of her death was made public, all England went into mourning. The old Queen had reigned for more than sixty-three years, more than the entire lifetime of most of her subjects. For many her death naturally marked the end of an era. On the morning following her death the *Daily Telegraph* sorrowfully declared: "The golden reign is closed. The supreme woman of the world, best of the highest, greatest of the good, is gone. The Victorian age is over. Never, never was loss like this, so inward and profound that only the slow years can reveal

Queen Victoria

its true reality. The Queen is dead." The *Observer* noted: "Victoria, the Queen, has gone, and the world is poorer for her loss. From savages in South Africa who say they will now look out at night for a new star in their heavens, to monarchs on their thrones who will miss the sympathy of which a modern throne needs so much, all feel they have lost a friend." Victoria had only been out of her long mourning for Prince Albert for six months.

The Queen's body was taken by royal yacht to the mainland and escorted via London to Windsor, ready for burial in the royal mausoleum at Frogmore. The pioneer film maker Cecil Hepworth filmed the procession in his *Funeral of Queen Victoria*. He recalled: "I had a wonderful position just inside the railings of Grosvenor Gardens opposite Victoria Station. My camera was the coffin-like construction which had been made some time before for taking the *Phantom Rides* (a railway film). When it was used on the front of an engine I did not realize, or care, how much noise it made. In the great silence and hush of the most solemn funeral in history it was a very different matter. That silence was a thing that closed in everything like an almost palpable curtain, not broken, but only accentuated, by the muted strains of the funeral march. Then at the moment of greatest tension I started to turn my camera, and the silence was shattered! If I could have had my deepest wish then the ground would certainly have opened at my feet and swallowed me and my beastly machine. But the noise had one curious effect. It caught the attention, as it must certainly have done, of the new King, Edward VII, and I believe that is why he halted the procession so that posterity might have the advantage of the cinematograph record." Even at a moment such as this, the new King was not unaware of the possible value of the medium in capturing for everyone the atmosphere.

The Duke of Cambridge, and a cousin of the late Queen, remembered that "The crowds were very enormous, but their demeanour magnificent, solemn and silent." The whole nation went into mourning, and many ordinary English families continued to wear black for many months afterwards.

Table of Dates

1799   Combination Act bans unions of working people
1801   First official population census
1803   Opening of the horse-drawn Surrey Iron Railway
1806   Installation of the first steam-operated loom: Manchester
1812   Charles Dickens born
1815   End of the French Wars and defeat of Napoleon at Waterloo
1820   Death of George III, accession of George IV
1824   Repeal of the Combination Act allows limited unions
1825   Opening of the Stockton & Darlington Railway, the first passenger line
1829   Sir Robert Peel creates England's first true police force, the "bobbies" or "peelers"
1830   Publication of William Cobbett's *Rural Rides*
        Opening of the Liverpool & Manchester Railway
1832   The Great Parliamentary Reform Act
1833   First Factory Act passed
        First government grants for education
1837   Accession of the young Queen Victoria
1838   The *Sirius* makes the first trans-Atlantic steam-ship crossing
        The Chartists present their first petition
1840   Rowland Hill introduces the penny post
1842   The *Coal Commission Report* published
        Charles Dickens publishes his *American Notes*
        Health reformer Edwin Chadwick publishes the famous *Sanitary Report*
        Children's Employment Commission Report published
1846   The Government repeals the Corn Laws
1849   London suffers a cholera epidemic
1851   The Great Exhibition
1855   The year of London's "great stink"
1860   Florence Nightingale publishes her *Notes on Nursing*
1864   Foundation of the Wholesale Co-operative Society
1867   Passing of the second Parliamentary Reform Act
1869   Foundation of the Trades Union Congress
1870   Death of Charles Dickens
        The Education Act makes elementary education compulsory for all
1874   Trade Unions acquire a legal right to strike
1884   Passing of the third Parliamentary Reform Act
1887   Queen Victoria's first Jubilee
1896   Motorists hold the first London–Brighton car rally
1897   Queen Victoria's Diamond Jubilee
1901   Death of Queen Victoria and accession of Edward VII

Glossary

CENSUS   An official, periodic count of a population, including such information as sex, age and occupation.

CHARTIST   A member of the Chartism movement, whose demands included payment of members of Parliament, equal electoral districts, annual Parliaments, voting by ballot and abolition of property qualifications for members of Parliament.

CLIPPER   A fast sailing ship.

COLLECTIVE BARGAINING   Negotiation between a trade union and an employer on the incomes and working conditions of the employees.

COMMODITIES   Units of wealth, such as any consumer good or service, which can be exchanged.

CONSUMPTION   A condition where body tissues waste away, especially as seen in tuberculosis of the lungs.

DECOLLETAGE   A low cut neckline or a piece of women's clothing with a low neckline.

DESHABILLE   Partly or carelessly dressed.

DETERRENT   A means of discouraging or preventing something.

EMOLUMENTS   Profits arising from employment, usually in the form of fees or wages.

FAG   A young public schoolboy who performs menial tasks for an older boy or prefect.

FOOTPAD   A robber or highwayman, on foot rather than horseback.

GENTRY   People of high birth or social standing; just below nobility in social rank.

IMMURE   To imprison, or shut oneself away from society.

INCURSION   Sudden penetration or attack.

INIQUITY   An injustice or wicked act.

LEECH   A worm that feeds on blood and which was used as a medical treatment.

LEVIATHAN   Any huge, powerful thing.

LITANY   A form of prayer.

LONDON SEASON   The period of the year when the rich would leave their country houses to stay in London, so they could attend the fashionable social engagements.

MANDATORY   Compulsory.

NON-CONFORMIST   A member of a Protestant group which disagrees with an established church, especially the Church of England.

OBFUSCATE   To obscure or bewilder.

OSIER   The branches of willow trees used for making baskets.

PALETOT   A woman's fitted coat often worn over a crinoline or bustle.

PERQUISITES   Benefits received in addition to a regular income (eg, today, the use of a company car).

PHAETON   A four-wheeled, two-seater horse-drawn carriage.

PHILANTHROPY   The practice of performing charitable or benevolent actions.

REPEAL   To officially revoke, or withdraw.

UNIONIST   A supporter of unionism.

VIANDS   Delicacies.

WORKHOUSE   An institution maintained at public expense where poor, able-bodied people did unpaid work in return for food and accommodation.

Further Reading

MODERN WORKS

Carl Benz and the Motor Car, D. Nye (Wayland, 1973)

England in the Nineteenth Century, D. Thomson (Pelican History of England)

English Costume of the Nineteenth Century, I. Brook (A. & C. Black)

Everyday Life in the Nineteenth Century, E. R. Chamberlain (Macdonald)

Gladstone and Disraeli, P. Rooke (Wayland, 1987)

The Great Exhibition of 1851: A Commemorative Album (H.M.S.O.)

Radicals, Railways and Reform – Britain 1815–51, R. Tames (Batsford)

Spotlight on the Victorians, S. Ross (Wayland, 1985)

The Stephensons and Steam Railways, C. C. Dorman (Wayland, 1975)

Victorian Engineering, L. T. C. Rolt (Penguin, 1970)

Victorian England: Portrait of an Age, G. M. Young (OUP, 1964)

Victorian People, S. Margetson (Batsford, 1977)

CONTEMPORARY WORKS

The Coal Commission Report (1842)

London Labour and the London Poor, Henry Mayhew (1851)

The Manufacturing Population of England, Peter Gaskell (1833)

Mary Barton, Elizabeth Gaskell (1848)

Notes of Nursing, Florence Nightingale (1860)

Oliver Twist, Charles Dickens (1838)

Rural Rides, William Cobbett (1830)

Tom Brown's Schooldays, Thomas Hughes (1857)

All The Year Round (periodical)

The Graphic (periodical)

Household Words (periodical)

The Illustrated London News (periodical)

Punch (periodical)

Index

The Complete
Ninja Foodi
2-Basket Air Fryer
Cookbook

1200 Days
Quick, Healthy and Affordable Recipes
for Enjoy Everyday Homemade Meals

Winifred Marchetti

Table of Contents

Chapter 5 : Poultry Recipes _____ 38

Chapter 6 : Beef, Pork, And Lamb Recipes _____ 53

Chapter 7 : Vegetables And Sides Recipes _____ 68

Chapter 1 : Introduction

What the Ninja Foodi Dual Zone Air Fryer is

The Ninja Foodi Dual Zone Air Fryer is the next revolutionary appliance coming from the awesome folks working at Ninja Kitchen! No matter how unbelievable the concept might sound, Ninja Kitchen has put on countless hours of engineering into crafting this meticulously designed appliance that takes the Air Frying game to a whole different level.

At its heart, the Ninja Foodi Dual Zone Air Fryer is a simple and exceedingly effective Air Fryer that gives you all the basic functions that you would expect from an Air Fryer. With this appliance, you can Air Frye, Bake, Broil, Dehydrate, Air Crisp, and more! You know, the usual Air Fryer stuffs.

However, what makes this unique is the super cool "Dual Zone" technology that completely flips the game in the Air Frying market.

If you are looking to cut down your cooking to half, or you want to make two different meals at the same time. The same appliance, then the Ninja Foodi Dual Zone Air Fryer is exactly what you need!

Simply put, the Dual Zone technology allows the

appliance to be put on either single cook mode or multi cook mode. Single cook mode works as usual; you cook using just a single basket. However, with the Dual Cook mode, you can seamlessly set the different timer, mode, and temperature for both of the zones individually and cook the meals you require. Alternatively, you may give the same settings to both of the zones and cook the same meal in a doubled portion without spending any more time than you would need when making just a single portion.

While handling two Air Fryer baskets might sound a little bit complicated at first, the way how Ninja Kitchen has engineered this appliance has made it extremely accessible and easy to handle.

Ninja Dual Zone Air Fryer Processes

The Ninja Dual Zone Air Fryer operates similarly to other air fryers in that it circulates hot air around food to produce a texture that is akin to deep frying—crisp and brown—while using only about 15 milliliters of cooking oil. This Air Fryer also features two distinct cooking baskets that let you cook a variety of dishes at once, even at various temperatures. Its dual baskets may be used to their full potential thanks to some clever features like advanced cooking presets, "sync," and "match" buttons.

The Ninja Air Fryer deserves a spot on your countertop due to its dual cooking controls that will ravish you. Its adaptability will quickly win you over. Using the sync button will allow you to simultaneously create two meals at different temperatures, with both meals being finished at the same time. Additionally, if you're cooking a large quantity of the same food, you can use the match button to automatically change the temperature and cooking time for both baskets.

Added advantage? With its sophisticated presets, you can maximize crisping, roasting, baking, reheating, dehydrating, and air-frying while saving up to 75% on your energy costs.

Ninja Dual Zone Air Fryer Cooking Tips

Remember these nifty tips whenever you are cooking with your new air fryer.

1. Pressing the Start/Pause button while using the Smart Finish will pause the cooking process on both zones. Press the same button to resume cooking.

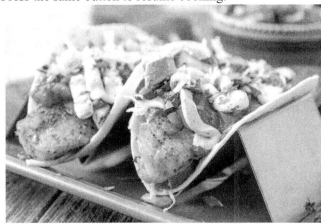

2. If at any time you need to pause the cooking process in one of the baskets, first select the zone, then the Start/Pause button.

3. To stop or end the cooking process, select the zone, then set the time to zero using the arrow down button. The display should show End after a few seconds, and the cooking process in this zone will stop.

4. You can adjust the temperature and time in each zone at any time during the cooking process. Select the zone, then adjust the setting using the arrow buttons.

5. Place a single layer of food and avoid stacking whenever possible.

6. To get the best results, toss or shake the food at least twice within the cooking cycle, especially for foods that overlap, like French fries. This will produce a more even cooking throughout.

7. When cooking fresh vegetables, add at least one tablespoon of cooking oil. More oil can be added to create a crispier texture.

8. Use the crisper plates when you want your food to become crunchy. Note that the crisper plates will slightly elevate your food to allow hot air to permeate the bottom and result in a crispier texture.

9. Follow the correct breading technique for wet battered food. Coat the food with flour first, then with egg, and finally with bread crumbs. Press the crumbs into the food to avoid it from flying around when air frying.

10. It is best to regularly check the progress to avoid overcooking.

11. A food-safe temperature must be reached to avoid any foodborne illness. Use a thermometer to check for doneness, especially when cooking raw meat. Instant-read thermometers are your best choice for this. Once cooking time is up or when the desired browning is achieved, promptly remove the food from the unit.

12. Do not use metal cutleries or tools that can damage the non-stick coating. Dump the food directly on a plate or use silicon-tipped tongs.

13. Small bits of food may be blown away while cooking. You can avoid this by securing pieces of food with toothpicks.

14. To cook recipes intended for traditional ovens, simply reduce the temperature by 25 °F and regularly check for doneness.

15. Do not let food touch the heating elements.

16. Never overload the baskets. Not only will this result in uneven cooking, but it may also cause the appliance to malfunction as well.

Care and Cleaning

● Clean often. If substances are stuck on the Ninja, cleaning them sooner or later can save you some headaches.

● Remember, the drawer and racks are machine washable, so popping them in the dishwasher can save you some headaches when all else fails. That said, hand washing the drawer can extend its lifespan, depending on your dishwasher and how gentle it is with cleaning.

● Wipe down the air fryer with a damp cloth every so often, particularly if food gets on it.

● Never immerse the air fryer outside the drawers and racks in water. You should know why.

● When wiping it down, be sure that you unplug before doing so.

● If there's food stuck in the drawer, submerge it in warm, soapy water for an hour or two.

Chapter 2 : Measurement Conversions

BASIC KITCHEN CONVERSIONS & EQUIVALENTS

DRY MEASUREMENTS CONVERSION CHART
3 TEASPOONS = 1 TABLESPOON = 1/16 CUP
6 TEASPOONS = 2 TABLESPOONS = 1/8 CUP
12 TEASPOONS = 4 TABLESPOONS = 1/4 CUP
24 TEASPOONS = 8 TABLESPOONS = 1/2 CUP
36 TEASPOONS = 12 TABLESPOONS = 3/4 CUP
48 TEASPOONS = 16 TABLESPOONS = 1 CUP

METRIC TO US COOKING CONVERSIONS
OVEN TEMPERATURES
120 °C = 250 °F
160 °C = 320 °F
180° C = 360 °F
205 °C = 400 °F
220 °C = 425 °F

LIQUID MEASUREMENTS CONVERSION CHART
8 FLUID OUNCES = 1 CUP = 1/2 PINT = 1/4 QUART
16 FLUID OUNCES = 2 CUPS = 1 PINT = 1/2 QUART
32 FLUID OUNCES = 4 CUPS = 2 PINTS = 1 QUART = 1/4 GALLON
128 FLUID OUNCES = 16 CUPS = 8 PINTS = 4 QUARTS = 1 GALLON

BAKING IN GRAMS
1 CUP FLOUR = 140 GRAMS
1 CUP SUGAR = 150 GRAMS
1 CUP POWDERED SUGAR = 160 GRAMS
1 CUP HEAVY CREAM = 235 GRAMS

VOLUME
1 MILLILITER = 1/5 TEASPOON
5 ML = 1 TEASPOON
15 ML = 1 TABLESPOON
240 ML = 1 CUP OR 8 FLUID OUNCES
1 LITER = 34 FL. OUNCES

WEIGHT
1 GRAM = .035 OUNCES

100 GRAMS = 3.5 OUNCES
500 GRAMS = 1.1 POUNDS
1 KILOGRAM = 35 OUNCES

US TO METRIC COOKING CONVERSIONS
1/5 TSP = 1 ML
1 TSP = 5 ML
1 TBSP = 15 ML
1 FL OUNCE = 30 ML
1 CUP = 237 ML
1 PINT (2 CUPS) = 473 ML
1 QUART (4 CUPS) = .95 LITER
1 GALLON (16 CUPS) = 3.8 LITERS
1 OZ = 28 GRAMS
1 POUND = 454 GRAMS

BUTTER
1 CUP BUTTER = 2 STICKS = 8 OUNCES = 230 GRAMS = 8 TABLESPOONS

WHAT DOES 1 CUP EQUAL
1 CUP = 8 FLUID OUNCES
1 CUP = 16 TABLESPOONS
1 CUP = 48 TEASPOONS
1 CUP = 1/2 PINT
1 CUP = 1/4 QUART
1 CUP = 1/16 GALLON
1 CUP = 240 ML

BAKING PAN CONVERSIONS
1 CUP ALL-PURPOSE FLOUR = 4.5 OZ
1 CUP ROLLED OATS = 3 OZ 1 LARGE EGG = 1.7 OZ
1 CUP BUTTER = 8 OZ 1 CUP MILK = 8 OZ
1 CUP HEAVY CREAM = 8.4 OZ
1 CUP GRANULATED SUGAR = 7.1 OZ
1 CUP PACKED BROWN SUGAR = 7.75 OZ
1 CUP VEGETABLE OIL = 7.7 OZ
1 CUP UNSIFTED POWDERED SUGAR = 4.4 OZ

BAKING PAN CONVERSIONS
9-INCH ROUND CAKE PAN = 12 CUPS
10-INCH TUBE PAN =16 CUPS
11-INCH BUNDT PAN = 12 CUPS
9-INCH SPRINGFORM PAN = 10 CUPS
9 X 5 INCH LOAF PAN = 8 CUPS
9-INCH SQUARE PAN = 8 CUPS

Chapter 3 : **Breakfast Recipes**

Salmon Quiche

Servings: 4
Cooking Time: 20 Minutes
Ingredients:

- 275g salmon fillets, chopped
- Salt and ground black pepper, as required
- 1 tablespoon fresh lemon juice
- 2 egg yolks
- 7 tablespoons chilled butter
- 165g flour
- 2 tablespoons cold water
- 4 eggs
- 6 tablespoons whipping cream
- 2 spring onions, chopped

Directions:

1. In a bowl, mix together the salmon, salt, black pepper and lemon juice. Set aside.
2. In another bowl, add egg yolk, butter, flour and water and mix until a dough forms.
3. Divide the dough into 2 portions.
4. Place each dough onto a floured smooth surface and roll into about 17.5cm round.
5. Place each rolled dough into a quiche pan and press firmly in the bottom and along the edges.
6. Then trim the excess edges.
7. In a small bowl, add the eggs, cream, salt and black pepper and beat until well combined.
8. Place the cream mixture over each crust evenly and top with the salmon, followed by the spring onion.
9. Press either "Zone 1" or "Zone 2" of Ninja Foodi 2-Basket Air Fryer and then rotate the knob for each zone to select "Air Fry".
10. Set the temperature to 180 degrees C and then set the time for 5 minutes to preheat.
11. After preheating, arrange 1 quiche pan into the basket of each zone.
12. Slide the basket into the Air Fryer and set the time for 20 minutes.
13. After cooking time is completed, remove the quiche pans from Air Fryer.
14. Cut each quiche in 2 portions and serve hot.

Banana And Raisins Muffins

Servings:2
Cooking Time:16
Ingredients:

- Salt, pinch
- 2 eggs, whisked
- 1/3 cup butter, melted
- 4 tablespoons of almond milk
- ¼ teaspoon of vanilla extract
- ½ teaspoon of baking powder
- 1-1/2 cup all-purpose flour
- 1 cup mashed bananas
- 2 tablespoons of raisins

Directions:

1. Take about 4 large (one-cup sized) ramekins and layer them with muffin papers.
2. Crack eggs in a large bowl, and whisk it all well and start adding vanilla extract, almond milk, baking powder, and melted butter
3. Whisk the ingredients very well.
4. Take a separate bowl and add the all-purpose flour, and salt.
5. Now, combine the add dry ingredients with the wet ingredients.
6. Now, pour mashed bananas and raisins into this batter
7. Mix it well to make a batter for the muffins.
8. Now pour the batter into four ramekins and divided the ramekins in the air fryer zones.
9. Set the timer for zone 1 to 16 minutes at 350 degrees F.
10. Select the MATCH button for the zone 2 basket.
11. Check if not done, and let it AIR FRY for one more minute.
12. Once it is done, serve.

Nutrition:

- (Per serving) Calories 727| Fat 43.1g| Sodium366 mg | Carbs 74.4g | Fiber 4.7g | Sugar 16.1g | Protein 14.1g

Parmesan Sausage Egg Muffins

Servings: 4
Cooking Time: 20 Minutes
Ingredients:

- 170 g Italian-seasoned sausage, sliced
- 6 eggs
- 30 ml double cream
- Salt and ground black pepper, to taste
- 85 g Parmesan cheese, grated

Directions:
1. Preheat the air fryer to 176ºC. Grease a muffin pan.
2. Put the sliced sausage in the muffin pan.
3. Beat the eggs with the cream in a bowl and season with salt and pepper.
4. Pour half of the mixture over the sausages in the pan.
5. Sprinkle with cheese and the remaining egg mixture.
6. Bake in the preheated air fryer for 20 minutes or until set.
7. Serve immediately.

Baked Mushroom And Mozzarella Frittata With Breakfast Potatoes

Servings:4
Cooking Time: 35 Minutes
Ingredients:

- FOR THE FRITTATA
- 8 large eggs
- ⅓ cup whole milk
- 1 teaspoon kosher salt
- ½ teaspoon freshly ground black pepper
- 1 cup sliced cremini mushrooms (about 2 ounces)
- 1 teaspoon olive oil
- 2 ounces part-skim mozzarella cheese, cut into ½-inch cubes
- FOR THE POTATOES
- 2 russet potatoes, cut into ½-inch cubes
- 1 tablespoon olive oil
- ½ teaspoon garlic powder
- ¼ teaspoon kosher salt
- ¼ teaspoon freshly ground black pepper

Directions:
1. To prep the frittata: In a large bowl, whisk together the eggs, milk, salt, and pepper. Stir in the mushrooms.
2. To prep the potatoes: In a large bowl, combine the potatoes, olive oil, garlic powder, salt, and black pepper.
3. To cook the frittata and potatoes: Brush the bottom of the Zone 1 basket with 1 teaspoon of olive oil. Add the egg mixture to the basket, top with the mozzarella cubes, and insert the basket in the unit. Install a crisper plate in the Zone 2 basket. Place the potatoes in the basket and insert the basket in the unit.
4. Select Zone 1, select BAKE, set the temperature to 350°F, and set the time to 30 minutes.
5. Select Zone 2, select AIR FRY, set the temperature to 400°F, and set the time to 35 minutes. Select SMART FINISH.
6. Press START/PAUSE to begin cooking.
7. When the Zone 2 timer reads 15 minutes, press START/PAUSE. Remove the basket and shake the potatoes for 10 seconds. Reinsert the basket and press START/PAUSE to resume cooking.
8. When cooking is complete, the frittata will pull away from the edges of the basket and the potatoes will be golden brown. Transfer the frittata to a cutting board and cut into 4 portions. Serve with the potatoes.
Nutrition:

- (Per serving) Calories: 307; Total fat: 17g; Saturated fat: 5.5g; Carbohydrates: 18g; Fiber: 1g; Protein: 19g; Sodium: 600mg

Double-dipped Mini Cinnamon Biscuits

Servings: 8 Biscuits
Cooking Time: 13 Minutes
Ingredients:

- 475 ml blanched almond flour
- 120 ml liquid or powdered sweetener
- 1 teaspoon baking powder
- ½ teaspoon fine sea salt
- 60 ml plus 2 tablespoons (¾ stick) very cold unsalted butter
- 60 ml unsweetened, unflavoured almond milk
- 1 large egg
- 1 teaspoon vanilla extract
- 3 teaspoons ground cinnamon
- Glaze:
- 120 ml powdered sweetener
- 60 ml double cream or unsweetened, unflavoured almond milk

Directions:

1. Preheat the air fryer to 175ºC. Line a pie pan that fits into your air fryer with parchment paper. 2. In a medium-sized bowl, mix together the almond flour, sweetener , baking powder, and salt. Cut the butter into ½-inch squares, then use a hand mixer to work the butter into the dry ingredients. When you are done, the mixture should still have chunks of butter. 3. In a small bowl, whisk together the almond milk, egg, and vanilla extract until blended. Using a fork, stir the wet ingredients into the dry ingredients until large clumps form. Add the cinnamon and use your hands to swirl it into the dough. 4. Form the dough into sixteen 1-inch balls and place them on the prepared pan, spacing them about ½ inch apart. Bake in the zone 1 air fryer basket until golden, 10 to 13 minutes. Remove from the air fryer and let cool on the pan for at least 5 minutes. 5. While the biscuits bake, make the glaze: Place the powdered sweetener in a small bowl and slowly stir in the heavy cream with a fork. 6. When the biscuits have cooled somewhat, dip the tops into the glaze, allow it to dry a bit, and then dip again for a thick glaze. 7. Serve warm or at room temperature. Store unglazed biscuits in an airtight container in the refrigerator for up to 3 days or in the freezer for up to a month. Reheat in a preheated 175ºC air fryer for 5 minutes, or until warmed through, and dip in the glaze as instructed above.

Air Fried Sausage

Servings: 4
Cooking Time: 13 Minutes.
Ingredients:
- 4 sausage links, raw and uncooked
Directions:
1. Divide the sausages in the two crisper plates.
2. Return the crisper plate to the Ninja Foodi Dual Zone Air Fryer.
3. Choose the Air Fry mode for Zone 1 and set the temperature to 390 degrees F and set the time to 13 minutes.
4. Select the "MATCH" button to copy the settings for Zone 2.
5. Initiate cooking by pressing the START/STOP button.
6. Serve warm and fresh.
Nutrition:
- (Per serving) Calories 267 | Fat 12g |Sodium 165mg | Carbs 39g | Fiber 1.4g | Sugar 22g | Protein 3.3g

Donuts

Servings: 6
Cooking Time: 15 Minutes
Ingredients:
- 1 cup granulated sugar
- 2 tablespoons ground cinnamon
- 1 can refrigerated flaky buttermilk biscuits
- ¼ cup unsalted butter, melted
Directions:
1. Combine the sugar and cinnamon in a small shallow bowl and set aside.
2. Remove the biscuits from the can and put them on a chopping board, separated. Cut holes in the center of each biscuit with a 1-inch round biscuit cutter (or a similarly sized bottle cap).
3. Place a crisper plate in each drawer. In each drawer, place 4 biscuits in a single layer. Insert the drawers into the unit.
4. Select zone 1, then AIR FRY, then set the temperature to 360 degrees F/ 180 degrees C with a 10-minute timer. To match zone 2 settings to zone 1, choose MATCH. To begin cooking, select START/STOP.
5. Remove the donuts from the drawers after the timer has finished.
Nutrition:
- (Per serving) Calories 223 | Fat 8g | Sodium 150mg | Carbs 40g | Fiber 1.4g | Sugar 34.2g | Protein 0.8g

Sausage Breakfast Casserole

Servings: 4
Cooking Time: 10 Minutes
Ingredients:
- 455g hash browns
- 455g ground breakfast sausage
- 1 green capsicum diced
- 1 red capsicum diced
- 1 yellow capsicum diced
- ¼ cup sweet onion diced
- 4 eggs
Directions:
1. Layer each air fryer basket with parchment paper.
2. Place the hash browns in both the baskets.
3. Spread sausage, onion and peppers over the hash brown.

4. Return the air fryer basket 1 to Zone 1, and basket 2 to Zone 2 of the Ninja Foodi 2-Basket Air Fryer.
5. Choose the "Air Fry" mode for Zone 1 at 355 degrees F temperature and 10 minutes of cooking time.
6. Select the "MATCH COOK" option to copy the settings for Zone 2.
7. Initiate cooking by pressing the START/PAUSE BUTTON.
8. Beat eggs in a bowl and pour over the air fried veggies.
9. Continue air frying for 10 minutes.
10. Garnish with salt and black pepper.
11. Serve warm.

Nutrition:
- (Per serving) Calories 267 | Fat 12g |Sodium 165mg | Carbs 39g | Fiber 1.4g | Sugar 22g | Protein 3.3g

Cinnamon Rolls

Servings: 12 Rolls
Cooking Time: 20 Minutes

Ingredients:
- 600 ml shredded Mozzarella cheese
- 60 g cream cheese, softened
- 235 ml blanched finely ground almond flour
- ½ teaspoon vanilla extract
- 120 ml icing sugar-style sweetener
- 1 tablespoon ground cinnamon

Directions:
1. In a large microwave-safe bowl, combine Mozzarella cheese, cream cheese, and flour. Microwave the mixture on high 90 seconds until cheese is melted.
2. Add vanilla extract and sweetener, and mix 2 minutes until a dough forms.
3. Once the dough is cool enough to work with your hands, about 2 minutes, spread it out into a 12 × 4-inch rectangle on ungreased parchment paper. Evenly sprinkle dough with cinnamon.
4. Starting at the long side of the dough, roll lengthwise to form a log. Slice the log into twelve even pieces.
5. Divide rolls between two ungreased round nonstick baking dishes. Place the dishes into the two air fryer drawers. Adjust the temperature to 192°C and bake for 10 minutes.
6. Cinnamon rolls will be done when golden around the edges and mostly firm. Allow rolls to cool in dishes 10 minutes before serving.

Egg And Bacon Muffins

Servings: 1
Cooking Time: 15 Minutes

Ingredients:
- 2 eggs
- Salt and ground black pepper, to taste
- 1 tablespoon green pesto
- 85 g shredded Cheddar cheese
- 140 g cooked bacon
- 1 spring onion, chopped

Directions:
1. Line a cupcake tin with parchment paper. Beat the eggs with pepper, salt, and pesto in a bowl. Mix in the cheese.
2. Pour the eggs into the cupcake tin and top with the bacon and spring onion.
3. Place the cupcake tin into the zone 1 drawer and bake at 180°C for 15 minutes, or until the egg is set. Serve immediately.

Honey-apricot Granola With Greek Yoghurt

Servings: 6
Cooking Time: 30 Minutes

Ingredients:
- 235 ml rolled oats
- 60 ml dried apricots, diced
- 60 ml almond slivers
- 60 ml walnuts, chopped
- 60 ml pumpkin seeds
- 60 to 80 ml honey, plus more for drizzling
- 1 tablespoon olive oil
- 1 teaspoon ground cinnamon
- ¼ teaspoon ground nutmeg
- ¼ teaspoon salt
- 2 tablespoons sugar-free dark chocolate chips (optional)
- 700 ml fat-free plain Greek yoghurt

Directions:

1.   Line the zone 1 and zone 2 drawer with two parchment papers. In a large bowl, combine the oats, apricots, almonds, walnuts, pumpkin seeds, honey, olive oil, cinnamon, nutmeg, and salt, mixing so that the honey, oil, and spices are well distributed. Pour the mixture onto the parchment papers and spread it into an even layer.

2.   Bake at 130ºC for 10 minutes, then shake or stir and spread back out into an even layer. Continue baking for 10 minutes more, then repeat the process of shaking or stirring the mixture.

3.   Bake for an additional 10 minutes before removing from the air fryer. Allow the granola to cool completely before stirring in the chocolate chips and pouring into an airtight container for storage. For each serving, top 120 ml Greek yoghurt with 80 ml granola and a drizzle of honey, if needed.

Egg In Bread Hole

Servings: 1
Cooking Time: 8 Minutes
Ingredients:
- 1 tablespoon butter, softened
- 2 eggs
- 2 slices of bread
- Salt and black pepper, to taste

Directions:
1.   Line either basket of "Zone 1" and "Zone 2" with a greased piece of foil.
2.   Press your chosen zone - "Zone 1" or "Zone 2" and then rotate the knob to select "Air Fryer".
3.   Set the temperature to 160 degrees C, and then set the time for 3 minutes to preheat.
4.   After preheating, place the butter on both sides of the bread. Cut a hole in the centre of the bread and crack the egg.
5.   Slide the basket into the Air Fryer and set the time for 6 minutes.
6.   After cooking time is completed, transfer the bread to a serving plate and serve.

Sausage & Butternut Squash

Servings: 2
Cooking Time: 20 Minutes
Ingredients:
- 450g butternut squash, diced
- 70g kielbasa, diced
- ¼ onion, diced
- ¼ tsp garlic powder
- ½ tbsp olive oil
- Pepper
- Salt

Directions:
1.   In a bowl, toss butternut squash with garlic powder, oil, onion, kielbasa, pepper, and salt.
2.   Insert a crisper plate in the Ninja Foodi air fryer baskets.
3.   Add sausage and butternut squash mixture in both baskets.
4.   Select zone 1, then select "air fry" mode and set the temperature to 375 degrees F for 20 minutes. Press "match" to match zone 2 settings to zone 1. Press "start/stop" to begin. Stir halfway through.

Nutrition:
- (Per serving) Calories 68 | Fat 3.6g |Sodium 81mg | Carbs 9.7g | Fiber 1.7g | Sugar 2.2g | Protein 0.9g

Mushroom-and-tomato Stuffed Hash Browns

Servings: 4
Cooking Time: 20 Minutes
Ingredients:
- Olive oil cooking spray
- 1 tablespoon plus 2 teaspoons olive oil, divided
- 110 g baby mushrooms, diced
- 1 spring onion, white parts and green parts, diced
- 1 garlic clove, minced
- 475 ml shredded potatoes
- ½ teaspoon salt
- ¼ teaspoon black pepper
- 1 plum tomato, diced
- 120 ml shredded mozzarella

Directions:
1.   Lightly coat the inside of a 6-inch cake pan with olive oil cooking spray. In a small skillet, heat 2 teaspoons olive oil over medium heat. Add the mushrooms, spring onion, and garlic, and cook for 4 to 5 minutes, or until they have softened and are beginning to show some color.
2.   Remove from heat. Meanwhile, in a large bowl, combine the potatoes, salt, pepper, and the remaining tablespoon olive oil. Toss until all potatoes are well coated. Pour half of the potatoes into the bottom of the cake pan.
3.   Top with the mushroom mixture, tomato, and mozzarella. Spread the remaining potatoes over the top. Place the cake pan into the zone 1 drawer.
4.   Select Bake button and adjust temperature to 190ºC, set time to 12 to 15 minutes and press Start. Until the top is golden brown, remove from the air fryer and allow to cool for 5 minutes before slicing and serving.

Cinnamon Toast

Servings: 6
Cooking Time: 5 Minutes
Ingredients:

- 12 slices bread
- 115g butter, at room temperature
- 100g white sugar
- 1½ teaspoons ground cinnamon
- 1½ teaspoons pure vanilla extract
- 1 pinch of salt

Directions:
1. Softened butter is mashed with a fork or the back of a spoon, and then sugar, cinnamon, vanilla, and salt are added.
2. Stir everything together thoroughly.
3. Spread one-sixth of the mixture onto each slice of bread, covering the entire surface.
4. Press your chosen zone - "Zone 1" or "Zone 2" and then rotate the knob to select "Air Fryer".
5. Set the temperature to 200 degrees C, and then set the time for 3 minutes to preheat.
6. After preheating, arrange bread into the basket of each zone.
7. Slide the basket into the Air Fryer and set the time for 5 minutes.
8. After cooking time is completed, remove both baskets from Air Fryer.
9. Cut bread slices diagonally and serve.

Parmesan Ranch Risotto And Oat And Chia Porridge

Servings: 6
Cooking Time: 30 Minutes
Ingredients:

- Parmesan Ranch Risotto:
- 1 tablespoon olive oil
- 1 clove garlic, minced
- 1 tablespoon unsalted butter
- 1 onion, diced
- 180 ml Arborio rice
- 475 ml chicken stock, boiling
- 120 ml Parmesan cheese, grated
- Oat and Chia Porridge:
- 2 tablespoons peanut butter
- 4 tablespoons honey
- 1 tablespoon butter, melted
- 1 L milk
- 475 ml oats
- 235 ml chia seeds

Directions:
1. Make the Parmesan Ranch Risotto :
2. Preheat the air fryer to 200ºC.
3. Grease a round baking tin with olive oil and stir in the garlic, butter, and onion.
4. Transfer the tin to the zone 1 air fryer basket and bake for 4 minutes. Add the rice and bake for 4 more minutes.
5. Turn the air fryer to 160ºC and pour in the chicken stock. Cover and bake for 22 minutes.
6. Scatter with cheese and serve.
7. Make the Oat and Chia Porridge :
8. Preheat the air fryer to 200ºC.
9. Put the peanut butter, honey, butter, and milk in a bowl and stir to mix. Add the oats and chia seeds and stir.
10. Transfer the mixture to a bowl and bake in the zone 2 air fryer basket for 5 minutes. Give another stir before serving.

Strawberry Baked Oats Chocolate Peanut Butter Baked Oats

Servings:12
Cooking Time: 15 Minutes
Ingredients:

- FOR THE STRAWBERRY OATS
- 1 cup whole milk
- 1 cup heavy (whipping) cream
- ½ cup maple syrup
- 2 teaspoons vanilla extract
- 2 large eggs
- 2 cups old-fashioned oats
- 2 teaspoons baking powder
- ½ teaspoon ground cinnamon
- ¼ teaspoon kosher salt
- 1½ cups diced strawberries
- FOR THE CHOCOLATE PEANUT BUTTER OATS
- 2 very ripe bananas
- ½ cup maple syrup
- ¼ cup unsweetened cocoa powder
- 2 teaspoons vanilla extract
- 2 teaspoons baking powder
- 2 large eggs
- ½ teaspoon kosher salt
- 2 cups old-fashioned oats
- 2 tablespoons peanut butter

Directions:

1. To prep the strawberry oats: In a large bowl, combine the milk, cream, maple syrup, vanilla, and eggs. Stir in the oats, baking powder, cinnamon, and salt until fully combined. Fold in the strawberries.
2. To prep the chocolate peanut butter oats: In a large bowl, mash the banana with a fork. Stir in the maple syrup, cocoa powder, vanilla, baking powder, and salt until smooth. Beat in the eggs. Stir in the oats until everything is combined.
3. To bake the oats: Place the strawberry oatmeal in the Zone 1 basket and insert the basket in the unit. Place the chocolate peanut butter oatmeal in the Zone 2 basket. Add ½ teaspoon dollops of peanut butter on top and insert the basket in the unit.
4. Select Zone 1, select BAKE, set the temperature to 320°F, and set the time to 15 minutes. Select MATCH COOK to match Zone 2 settings to Zone 1.
5. Press START/PAUSE to begin cooking.
6. When cooking is complete, serve each oatmeal in a shallow bowl.

Nutrition:
*   (Per serving) Calories: 367; Total fat: 19g; Saturated fat: 11g; Carbohydrates: 42g; Fiber: 3.5g; Protein: 8g; Sodium: 102mg

Bacon-and-eggs Avocado And Simple Scotch Eggs

Servings: 5
Cooking Time: 25 Minutes
Ingredients:
*   Bacon-and-Eggs Avocado:
*   1 large egg
*   1 avocado, halved, peeled, and pitted
*   2 slices bacon
*   Fresh parsley, for serving (optional)
*   Sea salt flakes, for garnish (optional)
*   Simple Scotch Eggs:
*   4 large hard boiled eggs
*   1 (340 g) package pork sausage meat
*   8 slices thick-cut bacon
*   4 wooden toothpicks, soaked in water for at least 30 minutes

Directions:
1. Make the Bacon-and-Eggs Avocado :
2. 1. Spray the zone 1 air fryer basket with avocado oil. Preheat the air fryer to 160ºC. Fill a small bowl with cool water. Soft-boil the egg: Place the egg in the zone 1 air fryer basket. Air fry for 6 minutes for a soft yolk or 7 minutes for a cooked yolk. Transfer the egg to the bowl of cool water and let sit for 2 minutes. Peel and set aside. 3. Use a spoon to carve out extra space in the center of the avocado halves until the cavities are big enough to fit the soft-boiled egg. Place the soft-boiled egg in the center of one half of the avocado and replace the other half of the avocado on top, so the avocado appears whole on the outside. 4. Starting at one end of the avocado, wrap the bacon around the avocado to completely cover it. Use toothpicks to hold the bacon in place. 5. Place the bacon-wrapped avocado in the zone 1 air fryer basket and air fry for 5 minutes. Flip the avocado over and air fry for another 5 minutes, or until the bacon is cooked to your liking. Serve on a bed of fresh parsley, if desired, and sprinkle with salt flakes, if desired. 6. Best served fresh. Store extras in an airtight container in the fridge for up to 4 days. Reheat in a preheated 160ºC air fryer for 4 minutes, or until heated through.
3. Make the Simple Scotch Eggs :
4. Slice the sausage meat into four parts and place each part into a large circle.
5. Put an egg into each circle and wrap it in the sausage. Put in the refrigerator for 1 hour.
6. Preheat the air fryer to 235ºC.
7. Make a cross with two pieces of thick-cut bacon. Put a wrapped egg in the center, fold the bacon over top of the egg, and secure with a toothpick.
8. Air fry in the preheated zone 2 air fryer basket for 25 minutes.
9. Serve immediately.

Easy Sausage Pizza

Servings: 4
Cooking Time: 6 Minutes
Ingredients:
*   2 tablespoons ketchup
*   1 pitta bread
*   80 ml sausage meat
*   230 g Mozzarella cheese
*   1 teaspoon garlic powder
*   1 tablespoon olive oil

Directions:
1. Preheat the air fryer to 170ºC.
2. Spread the ketchup over the pitta bread.
3. Top with the sausage meat and cheese. Sprinkle with the garlic powder and olive oil.
4. Put the pizza in the zone 1 air fryer basket and bake for 6 minutes.
5. Serve warm.

Tomato And Mozzarella Bruschetta And Portobello Eggs Benedict

Servings: 3
Cooking Time: 10 To 14 Minutes
Ingredients:

- Tomato and Mozzarella Bruschetta:
- 6 small loaf slices
- 120 ml tomatoes, finely chopped
- 85 g Mozzarella cheese, grated
- 1 tablespoon fresh basil, chopped
- 1 tablespoon olive oil
- Portobello Eggs Benedict:
- 1 tablespoon olive oil
- 2 cloves garlic, minced
- ¼ teaspoon dried thyme
- 2 portobello mushrooms, stems removed and gills scraped out
- 2 plum tomatoes, halved lengthwise
- Salt and freshly ground black pepper, to taste
- 2 large eggs
- 2 tablespoons grated Pecorino Romano cheese
- 1 tablespoon chopped fresh parsley, for garnish
- 1 teaspoon truffle oil (optional)

Directions:
1. Make the Tomato and Mozzarella Bruschetta :
2. Preheat the air fryer to 175°C.
3. Put the loaf slices inside the zone 1 air fryer basket and air fry for about 3 minutes.
4. Add the tomato, Mozzarella, basil, and olive oil on top.
5. Air fry for an additional minute before serving.
6. Make the Portobello Eggs Benedict :
7. Preheat the air fryer to 205°C.
8. In a small bowl, combine the olive oil, garlic, and thyme. Brush the mixture over the mushrooms and tomatoes until thoroughly coated. Season to taste with salt and freshly ground black pepper.
9. Arrange the vegetables, cut side up, in the zone 2 air fryer basket. Crack an egg into the center of each mushroom and sprinkle with cheese. Air fry for 10 to 14 minutes until the vegetables are tender and the whites are firm. When cool enough to handle, coarsely chop the tomatoes and place on top of the eggs. Scatter parsley on top and drizzle with truffle oil, if desired, just before serving.

Sweet Potato Hash

Servings: 4
Cooking Time: 15 Minutes
Ingredients:

- 3 sweet potatoes, peel & cut into ½-inch pieces
- ½ tsp cinnamon
- 2 tbsp olive oil
- 1 bell pepper, cut into ½-inch pieces
- ½ tsp dried thyme
- ½ tsp nutmeg
- 1 medium onion, cut into ½-inch pieces
- Pepper
- Salt

Directions:
1. In a bowl, toss sweet potatoes with the remaining ingredients.
2. Insert a crisper plate in Ninja Foodi air fryer baskets.
3. Add potato mixture in both baskets.
4. Select zone 1 then select "air fry" mode and set the temperature to 355 degrees F for 15 minutes. Press "match" to match zone 2 settings to zone 1. Press "start/stop" to begin.

Nutrition:
- (Per serving) Calories 167 | Fat 7.3g |Sodium 94mg | Carbs 24.9g | Fiber 4.2g | Sugar 6.8g | Protein 2.2g

Banana Bread

Servings: 8
Cooking Time: 35 Minutes
Ingredients:

- 95g flour
- 1 teaspoon ground cinnamon
- ¼ teaspoon ground nutmeg
- ½ teaspoon salt
- ¼ teaspoon baking soda
- 2 medium-sized ripe bananas mashed
- 2 large eggs lightly beaten
- 100g granulated sugar
- 2 tablespoons whole milk
- 1 tablespoon plain nonfat yoghurt
- 2 tablespoons vegetable oil
- 1 teaspoon vanilla

- 2 tablespoons walnuts roughly chopped

Directions:
1. Combine flour, cinnamon, nutmeg, baking soda, and salt in a large mixing basin.
2. Mash the banana in a separate dish before adding the eggs, sugar, milk, yoghurt, oil, and vanilla extract.
3. Combine the wet and dry ingredients in a mixing bowl and stir until just incorporated.
4. Pour the batter into the loaf pan and top with chopped walnuts.
5. Press either "Zone 1" and "Zone 2" and then rotate the knob select "Air Fryer".
6. Set the temperature to 155 degrees C, and then set the time for 3 minutes to preheat.
7. After preheating, arrange 1 loaf pan into the basket.
8. Slide basket into Air Fryer and set the time for 35 minutes.
9. After cooking time is completed, remove pan from Air Fryer.
10. Place the loaf pan onto a wire rack to cool for about 10 minutes.
11. Carefully invert the bread onto a wire rack to cool completely before slicing
12. Cut the bread into desired-sized slices and serve.

Egg White Muffins

Servings: 8
Cooking Time: 10 Minutes
Ingredients:
- 4 slices center-cut bacon, cut into strips
- 4 ounces baby bella mushrooms, roughly chopped
- 2 ounces sun-dried tomatoes
- 2 tablespoon sliced black olives
- 2 tablespoons grated or shredded parmesan
- 2 tablespoons shredded mozzarella
- ¼ teaspoon black pepper
- ¾ cup liquid egg whites
- 2 tablespoons liquid egg whites

Directions:
1. Heat a saucepan with a little oil, add the bacon and mushrooms and cook until fully cooked and crispy, about 6–8 minutes.
2. While the bacon and mushrooms cook, mix the ¾ cup liquid egg whites, sun-dried tomato, olives, parmesan, mozzarella, and black pepper together in a large bowl.
3. Add the cooked bacon and mushrooms to the tomato and olive mixture, stirring everything together.
4. Spoon the mixture into muffin molds, followed by 2 tablespoons of egg whites over the top.
5. Place half the muffins mold in zone 1 and half in zone 2, then insert the drawers into the unit.
6. Select zone 1, select AIR FRY, set temperature to 390 degrees F/ 200 degrees C, and set time to 22 minutes.
7. Select MATCH to match zone 2 settings to zone 1. Press the START/STOP button to begin cooking.
8. When cooking is complete, remove the molds and enjoy!

Nutrition:
- (Per serving) Calories 104 | Fat 5.6g | Sodium 269mg | Carbs 3.5g | Fiber 0.8g | Sugar 0.3g | Protein 10.3g

Crispy Hash Browns

Servings: 4
Cooking Time: 13 Minutes.
Ingredients:
- 3 russet potatoes
- ¼ cup chopped green peppers
- ¼ cup chopped red peppers
- ¼ cup chopped onions
- 2 garlic cloves chopped
- 1 teaspoon paprika
- Salt and black pepper, to taste
- 2 teaspoons olive oil

Directions:
1. Peel and grate all the potatoes with the help of a cheese grater.
2. Add potato shreds to a bowl filled with cold water and leave it soaked for 25 minutes.
3. Drain the water and place the potato shreds on a plate lined with a paper towel.
4. Transfer the shreds to a dry bowl and add olive oil, paprika, garlic, and black pepper.
5. Make four flat patties out of the potato mixture and place two into each of the crisper plate.
6. Return the crisper plate to the Ninja Foodi Dual Zone Air Fryer.
7. Choose the Air Fry mode for Zone 1 and set the temperature to 390 degrees F and set the time to 13 minutes.
8. Select the "MATCH" button to copy the settings for Zone 2.
9. Initiate cooking by pressing the START/STOP button.
10. Flip the potato hash browns once cooked halfway through, then resume cooking.
11. Once done, serve warm.

Nutrition:
- (Per serving) Calories 190 | Fat 18g |Sodium 150mg | Carbs 0.6g | Fiber 0.4g | Sugar 0.4g | Protein 7.2g

Sausage Hash And Baked Eggs

Servings:4
Cooking Time: 30 Minutes

Ingredients:
- FOR THE HASH
- 2 yellow potatoes (about 1 pound), cut into ½-inch pieces
- 4 garlic cloves, minced
- 1 teaspoon kosher salt
- ¼ teaspoon freshly ground black pepper
- 2 tablespoons olive oil
- ½ pound pork breakfast sausage meat
- 1 small yellow onion, diced
- 1 red bell pepper, diced
- 1 teaspoon Italian seasoning
- FOR THE EGGS
- Nonstick cooking spray
- 4 large eggs
- 4 tablespoons water

Directions:
1. To prep the hash: In a large bowl, combine the potatoes, garlic, salt, black pepper, and olive oil and toss to coat. Crumble in the sausage and mix until combined.
2. To prep the eggs: Mist 4 silicone muffin cups with cooking spray. Crack 1 egg into each muffin cup. Top each egg with 1 tablespoon of water.
3. To cook the hash and eggs: Install a crisper plate in the Zone 1 basket. Place the sausage and potato mixture in the Zone 1 basket and insert the basket in the unit. Place the egg cups in the Zone 2 basket and insert the basket in the unit.
4. Select Zone 1, select AIR FRY, set the temperature to 400°F, and set the time to 30 minutes.
5. Select Zone 2, select BAKE, set the temperature to 325°F, and set the time to 12 minutes. Select SMART FINISH.
6. Press START/PAUSE to begin cooking.
7. When the Zone 1 timer reads 20 minutes, press START/PAUSE. Remove the basket and add the onion, bell pepper, and Italian seasoning to the hash. Mix until combined, breaking up any large pieces of sausage. Reinsert the basket and press START/PAUSE to resume cooking.
8. When cooking is complete, serve the hash topped with an egg.

Nutrition:
- (Per serving) Calories: 400; Total fat: 23g; Saturated fat: 5.5g; Carbohydrates: 31g; Fiber: 2g; Protein: 19g; Sodium: 750mg

Sesame Bagels

Servings: 4
Cooking Time: 15 Minutes

Ingredients:
- 125g self-rising flour
- 240g non-fat plain Greek yoghurt
- 1 beaten egg
- 30g sesame seeds

Directions:
1. Combine the self-rising flour and Greek yoghurt in a medium mixing bowl using a wooden spoon.
2. Knead the dough for about 5 minutes on a lightly floured board.
3. Divide the dough into four equal pieces and roll each into a thin rope, securing the ends to form a bagel shape. Sprinkle the sesame seeds on it.
4. Press either "Zone 1" or "Zone 2" and then rotate the knob to select "Air Fryer".
5. Set the temperature to 140 degrees C, and then set the time for 3 minutes to preheat.
6. After preheating, arrange bagels into the basket.
7. Slide basket into Air Fryer and set the time for 15 minutes.
8. After cooking time is completed, remove both pans from Air Fryer.
9. Place the bagels onto a wire rack to cool for about 10 minutes and serve.

Bacon Cheese Egg With Avocado And Potato Nuggets

Servings: 8
Cooking Time: 20 Minutes

Ingredients:
- Bacon Cheese Egg with Avocado:
- 6 large eggs
- 60 ml double cream
- 350 ml chopped cauliflower
- 235 ml shredded medium Cheddar cheese
- 1 medium avocado, peeled and pitted
- 8 tablespoons full-fat sour cream
- 2 spring onions, sliced on the bias
- 12 slices bacon, cooked and crumbled
- Potato Nuggets:

- 1 teaspoon extra virgin olive oil
- 1 clove garlic, minced
- 1 L kale, rinsed and chopped
- 475 ml potatoes, boiled and mashed
- 30 ml milk
- Salt and ground black pepper, to taste
- Cooking spray

Directions:
1. Make the Bacon Cheese Egg with Avocado :
2. In a medium bowl, whisk eggs and cream together. Pour into a round baking dish.
3. Add cauliflower and mix, then top with Cheddar. Place dish into the zone 1 air fryer drawer.
4. Adjust the temperature to 160ºC and set the timer for 20 minutes.
5. When completely cooked, eggs will be firm and cheese will be browned. Slice into four pieces.
6. Slice avocado and divide evenly among pieces. Top each piece with 2 tablespoons sour cream, sliced spring onions, and crumbled bacon.
7. Make the Potato Nuggets :
8. Preheat the zone 2 air fryer drawer to 200ºC.
9. In a skillet over medium heat, sauté the garlic in the olive oil, until it turns golden brown. Sauté with the kale for an additional 3 minutes and remove from the heat.
10. Mix the mashed potatoes, kale and garlic in a bowl. Pour in the milk and sprinkle with salt and pepper.
11. Shape the mixture into nuggets and spritz with cooking spray.
12. Put in the zone 2 air fryer drawer and air fry for 15 minutes, flip the nuggets halfway through cooking to make sure the nuggets fry evenly.
13. Serve immediately.

Potatoes Lyonnaise

Servings: 4
Cooking Time: 31 Minutes
Ingredients:
- 1 sweet/mild onion, sliced
- 1 teaspoon butter, melted
- 1 teaspoon brown sugar
- 2 large white potatoes (about 450 g in total), sliced ½-inch thick
- 1 tablespoon vegetable oil
- Salt and freshly ground black pepper, to taste

Directions:
1. Preheat the air fryer to 188ºC.
2. Toss the sliced onions, melted butter and brown sugar together in the zone 1 air fryer drawer. Air fry for 8 minutes, shaking the drawer occasionally to help the onions cook evenly.
3. While the onions are cooking, bring a saucepan of salted water to a boil on the stovetop. Par-cook the potatoes in boiling water for 3 minutes. Drain the potatoes and pat them dry with a clean kitchen towel.
4. Add the potatoes to the onions in the zone 1 air fryer drawer and drizzle with vegetable oil. Toss to coat the potatoes with the oil and season with salt and freshly ground black pepper.
5. Increase the air fryer temperature to 204ºC and air fry for 20 minutes, tossing the vegetables a few times during the cooking time to help the potatoes brown evenly.
6. Season with salt and freshly ground black pepper and serve warm.

Pork Sausage Eggs With Mustard Sauce

Servings: 8
Cooking Time: 12 Minutes
Ingredients:
- 450 g pork sausage meat
- 8 soft-boiled or hard-boiled eggs, peeled
- 1 large egg
- 2 tablespoons milk
- 235 ml crushed pork scratchings
- Smoky Mustard Sauce:
- 60 ml mayonnaise
- 2 tablespoons sour cream
- 1 tablespoon Dijon mustard
- 1 teaspoon chipotle hot sauce

Directions:
1. Divide the sausage into 8 portions. Take each portion of sausage, pat it down into a patty, and place 1 egg in the middle, gently wrapping the sausage around the egg until the egg is completely covered.
2. Repeat with the remaining eggs and sausage. In a small shallow bowl, whisk the egg and milk until frothy. In another shallow bowl, place the crushed pork scratchings. Working one at a time, dip a sausage-wrapped egg into the beaten egg and then into the pork scratchings, gently rolling to coat evenly. Repeat with the remaining sausage-wrapped eggs.

3. Put them half in zone 1, the remaining in zone 2. Lightly spray with olive oil. In zone 1 , select Air fry button, adjust temperature to 200ºC, set time to 10 to 12 minutes. In zone 2, select Match Cook and press Start. Pause halfway through the baking time to turn the eggs, until the eggs are hot and the sausage is cooked through.
4. To make the sauce:
5. In a small bowl, combine the mayonnaise, sour cream, Dijon, and hot sauce. Whisk until thoroughly combined. Serve with the Scotch eggs.

Bacon And Egg Omelet

Servings:2
Cooking Time:10
Ingredients:
- 2 eggs, whisked
- ½ teaspoon of chopped tomatoes
- Sea Salt and black pepper, to taste
- 2 teaspoons of almond milk
- 1 teaspoon of cilantro, chopped
- 1 small green chili, chopped
- 4 slices of bacon

Directions:
1. Take a bowl and whisk eggs in it.
2. Then add green chili salt, black pepper, cilantro, almond milk, and chopped tomatoes.
3. Oil greases the ramekins.
4. Pour this into ramekins.
5. Put the bacon in the zone 1 basket and ramekins in zone 2 basket of the Ninja Foodie 2-Basket Air Fryer.
6. Now for zone 1, set it to AIR FRY mode at 400 degrees F for 10 minutes
7. And for zone 2, set it 350 degrees for 10 minutes in AIR FRY mode.
8. Press the Smart finish button and press start, it will finish both at the same time.
9. Once done, serve and enjoy.

Nutrition:
- (Per serving) Calories 285| Fat 21.5g| Sodium1000 mg | Carbs 2.2g | Fiber 0.1g| Sugar1 g | Protein 19.7g

Cajun Breakfast Sausage

Servings: 8
Cooking Time: 15 To 20 Minutes
Ingredients:
- 680 g 85% lean turkey mince
- 3 cloves garlic, finely chopped
- ¼ onion, grated
- 1 teaspoon Tabasco sauce
- 1 teaspoon Cajun seasoning
- 1 teaspoon dried thyme
- ½ teaspoon paprika
- ½ teaspoon cayenne

Directions:
1. Preheat the air fryer to 188ºC.
2. In a large bowl, combine the turkey, garlic, onion, Tabasco, Cajun seasoning, thyme, paprika, and cayenne. Mix with clean hands until thoroughly combined. Shape into 16 patties, about ½ inch thick.
3. Arrange the patties in a single layer in the two air fryer drawers. Pausing halfway through the cooking time to flip the patties, air fry for 15 to 20 minutes until a thermometer inserted into the thickest portion registers 74ºC.

Air Fryer Sausage Patties

Servings: 12
Cooking Time: 10 Minutes
Ingredients:
- 1-pound pork sausage or ready-made patties
- Fennel seeds or preferred seasonings

Directions:
1. Prepare the sausage by slicing it into patties, then flavor it with fennel seed or your favorite seasonings.
2. Install a crisper plate in both drawers. Place half the patties in zone 1 and half in zone 2, then insert the drawers into the unit.
3. Select zone 1, select AIR FRY, set temperature to 390 degrees F/ 200 degrees C, and set time to 10 minutes.
4. Select MATCH to match zone 2 settings to zone 1.
5. Press the START/STOP button to begin cooking.
6. When cooking is complete, remove the patties from the unit and serve with sauce or make a burger.

Nutrition:
- (Per serving) Calories 130 | Fat 10.5g | Sodium 284mg | Carbs 0.3g | Fiber 0.2g | Sugar 0g | Protein 7.4g

Sausage And Cheese Balls

Servings: 16 Balls
Cooking Time: 12 Minutes
Ingredients:
- 450 g pork sausage meat, removed from casings
- 120 ml shredded Cheddar cheese
- 30 g full-fat cream cheese, softened
- 1 large egg

Directions:
1. Mix all ingredients in a large bowl. Form into sixteen balls. Place the balls into the two air fryer drawers.
2. Adjust the temperature to 204°C and air fry for 12 minutes.
3. Shake the drawers two or three times during cooking. Sausage balls will be browned on the outside and have an internal temperature of at least 64°C when completely cooked.
4. Serve warm.

Breakfast Pitta

Servings: 2
Cooking Time: 6 Minutes
Ingredients:
- 1 wholemeal pitta
- 2 teaspoons olive oil
- ½ shallot, diced
- ¼ teaspoon garlic, minced
- 1 large egg
- ¼ teaspoon dried oregano
- ¼ teaspoon dried thyme
- ⅛ teaspoon salt
- 2 tablespoons shredded Parmesan cheese

Directions:
1. Brush the top of the pitta with olive oil, then spread the diced shallot and minced garlic over the pitta. Crack the egg into a small bowl or ramekin, and season it with oregano, thyme, and salt.
2. Place the pitta into the zone 1 drawer, and gently pour the egg onto the top of the pitta. Sprinkle with cheese over the top.
3. Select Bake button and adjust temperature to 190°C, set time to 6 minutes and press Start. After the end, allow to cool for 5 minutes before cutting into pieces for serving.

Cheesy Baked Eggs

Servings: 4
Cooking Time: 16 Minutes
Ingredients:
- 4 large eggs
- 57g smoked gouda, shredded
- Everything bagel seasoning, to taste
- Salt and pepper to taste

Directions:
1. Crack one egg in each ramekin.
2. Top the egg with bagel seasoning, black pepper, salt and gouda.
3. Place 2 ramekins in each air fryer basket.
4. Return the air fryer basket 1 to Zone 1, and basket 2 to Zone 2 of the Ninja Foodi 2-Basket Air Fryer.
5. Choose the "Air Fry" mode for Zone 1 and set the temperature to 400 degrees F and 16 minutes of cooking time.
6. Select the "MATCH COOK" option to copy the settings for Zone 2.
7. Initiate cooking by pressing the START/PAUSE BUTTON.
8. Serve warm.

Nutrition:
- (Per serving) Calories 190 | Fat 18g |Sodium 150mg | Carbs 0.6g | Fiber 0.4g | Sugar 0.4g | Protein 7.2g

Chapter 4 : **Fish And Seafood Recipes**

Spicy Fish Fillet With Onion Rings

Servings:1
Cooking Time:12
Ingredients:

- 300 grams of onion rings, frozen and packed
- 1 codfish fillet, 8 ounces
- Salt and black pepper, to taste
- 1 teaspoon of lemon juice
- oil spray, for greasing

Directions:

1. Put the frozen onion rings in zone 1 basket of the air fryer.
2. Next pat dry the fish fillets with a paper towel and season them with salt, black pepper, and lemon juice.
3. Grease the fillet with oil spray.
4. Put the fish in zone 2 basket.
5. Use MAX crisp for zone 1 at 240 degrees for 9 minutes.
6. Use MAX crisp for zone 2 basket and set it to 210 degrees for 12 minutes.
7. Press sync and press start.
8. Once done, serve hot.

Nutrition:

- (Per serving) Calories 666| Fat23.5g| Sodium 911mg | Carbs 82g | Fiber 8.8g | Sugar 17.4g | Protein 30.4g

Salmon With Fennel Salad

Servings: 4
Cooking Time: 17 Minutes.
Ingredients:

- 2 teaspoons fresh parsley, chopped
- 1 teaspoon fresh thyme, chopped
- 1 teaspoon salt
- 4 (6-oz) skinless center-cut salmon fillets
- 2 tablespoons olive oil
- 4 cups fennel, sliced
- ⅔ cup Greek yogurt
- 1 garlic clove, grated
- 2 tablespoons orange juice
- 1 teaspoon lemon juice
- 2 tablespoons fresh dill, chopped

Directions:

1. Preheat your Ninja Foodi Dual Zone Air Fryer to 200 degrees F.
2. Mix ½ teaspoon of salt, thyme, and parsley in a small bowl.
3. Brush the salmon with oil first, then rub liberally rub the herb mixture.
4. Place 2 salmon fillets in each of the crisper plate.
5. Return the crisper plate to the Ninja Foodi Dual Zone Air Fryer.
6. Choose the Air Fry mode for Zone 1 and set the temperature to 390 degrees F and the time to 17 minutes.
7. Select the "MATCH" button to copy the settings for Zone 2.
8. Initiate cooking by pressing the START/STOP button.
9. Meanwhile, mix fennel with garlic, yogurt, lemon juice, orange juice, remaining salt, and dill in a mixing bowl.
10. Serve the air fried salmon fillets with fennel salad.
11. Enjoy.

Nutrition:

- (Per serving) Calories 305 | Fat 15g |Sodium 482mg | Carbs 17g | Fiber 3g | Sugar 2g | Protein 35g

Fried Lobster Tails

Servings: 4
Cooking Time: 18 Minutes.
Ingredients:

- 4 (4-oz) lobster tails
- 8 tablespoons butter, melted
- 2 teaspoons lemon zest
- 2 garlic cloves, grated
- Salt and black pepper, ground to taste
- 2 teaspoons fresh parsley, chopped
- 4 wedges lemon

Directions:

1. Spread the lobster tails into Butterfly, slit the top to expose the lobster meat while keeping the tail intact.
2. Place two lobster tails in each of the crisper plate with their lobster meat facing up.
3. Mix melted butter with lemon zest and garlic in a bowl.
4. Brush the butter mixture on top of the lobster tails.

5. And drizzle salt and black pepper on top.
6. Return the crisper plate to the Ninja Foodi Dual Zone Air Fryer.
7. Choose the Air Fry mode for Zone 1 and set the temperature to 390 degrees F and the time to 18 minutes.
8. Select the "MATCH" button to copy the settings for Zone 2.
9. Initiate cooking by pressing the START/STOP button.
10. Garnish with parsley and lemon wedges.
11. Serve warm.
Nutrition:
- (Per serving) Calories 257 | Fat 10.4g |Sodium 431mg | Carbs 20g | Fiber 0g | Sugar 1.6g | Protein 21g

Tuna Patties

Servings: 6
Cooking Time: 10 Minutes
Ingredients:
- For the tuna patties:
- 1 tablespoon extra-virgin olive oil
- 1 tablespoon butter
- ½ cup chopped onion
- ½ red bell pepper, chopped
- 1 teaspoon minced garlic
- 2 (7-ounce) cans or 3 (5-ounce) cans albacore tuna fish in water, drained
- 1 tablespoon lime juice
- 1 celery stalk, chopped
- ¼ cup chopped fresh parsley
- 3 tablespoons grated parmesan cheese
- ½ teaspoon dried oregano
- ¼ teaspoon salt
- Black pepper, to taste
- 1 teaspoon sriracha
- ½ cup panko crumbs
- 2 whisked eggs
- For the crumb coating:
- ½ cup panko crumbs
- ¼ cup parmesan cheese
- Non-stick spray

Directions:
1. In a skillet, heat the oil and butter over medium-high heat.
2. Sauté the onions, red bell pepper, and garlic for 5 to 7 minutes.
3. Drain the tuna from the cans thoroughly. Put the tuna in a large mixing bowl. Add the lime juice.
4. Add the sautéed vegetables to the mixing bowl.
5. Add the celery, parsley, and cheese. Combine well.
6. Add the oregano, salt, and pepper to taste. Mix well.
7. Add a dash of sriracha for a spicy kick and mix well.
8. Add the panko crumbs and mix well.
9. Mix in the eggs until the mixture is well combined. You can add an extra egg if necessary, but the tuna is usually wet enough that it isn't required. Form 6 patties from the mixture.
10. Refrigerate for 30 to 60 minutes (or even overnight).
11. Remove from refrigerator and coat with a mixture of the ½ cup of panko crumbs and ¼ cup of parmesan cheese.
12. Spray the tops of the coated patties with some non-stick cooking spray.
13. Place a crisper place in each drawer. Put 3 patties in each drawer. Insert the drawers into the unit.
14. Select zone 1, then AIR FRY, then set the temperature to 390 degrees F/ 200 degrees C with a 10-minute timer. To match zone 2 settings to zone 1, choose MATCH. To begin, select START/STOP.
15. Remove and garnish with chopped parsley.
Nutrition:
- (Per serving) Calories 381 | Fat 16g | Sodium 1007mg | Carbs 23g | Fiber 2g | Sugar 4g | Protein 38g

Broiled Teriyaki Salmon With Eggplant In Stir-fry Sauce

Servings:4
Cooking Time: 25 Minutes
Ingredients:
- FOR THE TERIYAKI SALMON
- 4 salmon fillets (6 ounces each)
- ½ cup teriyaki sauce
- 3 scallions, sliced
- FOR THE EGGPLANT
- ¼ cup reduced-sodium soy sauce
- ¼ cup packed light brown sugar
- 1 tablespoon minced fresh ginger
- 1 tablespoon minced garlic
- 2 teaspoons sesame oil
- ¼ teaspoon red pepper flakes
- 1 eggplant, peeled and cut into bite-size cubes
- Nonstick cooking spray

Directions:
1. To prep the teriyaki salmon: Brush the top of each salmon fillet with the teriyaki sauce.
2. To prep the eggplant: In a small bowl, whisk together the soy sauce, brown sugar, ginger, garlic, sesame oil, and red pepper flakes. Set the stir-fry sauce aside.
3. Spritz the eggplant cubes with cooking spray.
4. To cook the salmon and eggplant: Install a crisper plate in each of the two baskets. Place the salmon in a single layer in the Zone 1 basket and insert the basket in the unit. Place the eggplant in the Zone 2 basket and insert the basket in the unit.
5. Select Zone 1, select AIR BROIL, set the temperature to 450°F, and set the time to 8 minutes.
6. Select Zone 2, select AIR FRY, set the temperature to 390°F, and set the time to 25 minutes. Select SMART FINISH.
7. Press START/PAUSE to begin cooking.
8. When the Zone 2 timer reads 5 minutes, press START/PAUSE. Remove the basket and pour the stir-fry sauce evenly over the eggplant. Shake or stir to coat the eggplant cubes in the sauce. Reinsert the basket and press START/PAUSE to resume cooking.
9. When cooking is complete, the salmon should be cooked to your liking and the eggplant tender and slightly caramelized. Serve hot.

Nutrition:
- (Per serving) Calories: 499; Total fat: 22g; Saturated fat: 2g; Carbohydrates: 36g; Fiber: 3.5g; Protein: 42g; Sodium: 1,024mg

Lemon-pepper Trout

Servings: 4
Cooking Time: 15 Minutes
Ingredients:
- 4 trout fillets
- 2 tablespoons olive oil
- ½ teaspoon salt
- 1 teaspoon black pepper
- 2 garlic cloves, sliced
- 1 lemon, sliced, plus additional wedges for serving

Directions:
1. Preheat the air fryer to 190ºC.
2. Brush each fillet with olive oil on both sides and season with salt and pepper. Place the fillets in an even layer in the two air fryer baskets.
3. Place the sliced garlic over the tops of the trout fillets, then top the garlic with lemon slices and roast for 12 to 15 minutes, or until it has reached an internal temperature of 65ºC.
4. Serve with fresh lemon wedges.

Chilean Sea Bass With Olive Relish And Snapper With Tomato

Servings: 4
Cooking Time: 15 Minutes
Ingredients:
- Chilean Sea Bass with Olive Relish:
- Olive oil spray
- 2 (170 g) Chilean sea bass fillets or other firm-fleshed white fish
- 3 tablespoons extra-virgin olive oil
- ½ teaspoon ground cumin
- ½ teaspoon kosher or coarse sea salt
- ½ teaspoon black pepper
- 60 g pitted green olives, diced
- 10 g finely diced onion
- 1 teaspoon chopped capers
- Snapper with Tomato:
- 2 snapper fillets
- 1 shallot, peeled and sliced
- 2 garlic cloves, halved
- 1 bell pepper, sliced
- 1 small-sized serrano pepper, sliced
- 1 tomato, sliced
- 1 tablespoon olive oil
- ¼ teaspoon freshly ground black pepper
- ½ teaspoon paprika
- Sea salt, to taste
- 2 bay leaves

Directions:
1. Make the Chilean Sea Bass with Olive Relish :
2. Spray the zone 1 air fryer drawer with the olive oil spray. Drizzle the fillets with the olive oil and sprinkle with the cumin, salt, and pepper. Place the fish in the zone 1 air fryer drawer. Set the air fryer to 164ºC for 10 minutes, or until the fish flakes easily with a fork.
3. Meanwhile, in a small bowl, stir together the olives, onion, and capers.

4. Serve the fish topped with the relish.
5. Make the Snapper with Tomato :
6. Place two baking paper sheets on a working surface. Place the fish in the center of one side of the baking paper.
7. Top with the shallot, garlic, peppers, and tomato. Drizzle olive oil over the fish and vegetables. Season with black pepper, paprika, and salt. Add the bay leaves.
8. Fold over the other half of the baking paper. Now, fold the paper around the edges tightly and create a half moon shape, sealing the fish inside.
9. Cook in the zone 2 air fryer drawer at 200ºC for 15 minutes. Serve warm.

Italian Baked Cod

Servings: 4
Cooking Time: 12 Minutes
Ingredients:
- 4 cod fillets, 170 g each
- 2 tablespoons salted butter, melted
- 1 teaspoon Italian seasoning
- ¼ teaspoon salt
- 120 ml tomato-based pasta sauce

Directions:
1. Place cod into an ungreased round nonstick baking dish. Pour butter over cod and sprinkle with Italian seasoning and salt. Top with pasta sauce.
2. Place dish into the two air fryer drawers. Adjust the temperature to 176ºC and bake for 12 minutes. Fillets will be lightly browned, easily flake, and have an internal temperature of at least 64ºC when done. Serve warm.

Herb Lemon Mussels

Servings: 6
Cooking Time: 10 Minutes
Ingredients:
- 1kg mussels, steamed & half shell
- 1 tbsp thyme, chopped
- 1 tbsp parsley, chopped
- 1 tsp dried parsley
- 1 tsp garlic, minced
- 60ml olive oil
- 45ml lemon juice
- Pepper
- Salt

Directions:
1. In a bowl, mix mussels with the remaining ingredients.
2. Insert a crisper plate in the Ninja Foodi air fryer baskets.
3. Add the mussels to both baskets.
4. Select zone 1 then select "air fry" mode and set the temperature to 360 degrees F for 10 minutes. Press "match" to match zone 2 settings to zone 1. Press "start/stop" to begin.
Nutrition:
- (Per serving) Calories 206 | Fat 11.9g |Sodium 462mg | Carbs 6.3g | Fiber 0.3g | Sugar 0.2g | Protein 18.2g

Beer Battered Fish Fillet

Servings:2
Cooking Time:14
Ingredients:
- 1 cup all-purpose flour
- 4 tablespoons cornstarch
- 1 teaspoon baking soda
- 8 ounces beer
- 2 egg beaten
- ½ cup all-purpose flour
- 1 teaspoon smoked paprika
- 1 teaspoon salt
- 1/4 teaspoon freshly ground black pepper
- ¼ teaspoon of cayenne pepper
- 2 cod fillets, 1½-inches thick, cut into 4 pieces
- Oil spray, for greasing

Directions:
1. Take a large bowl and combine flour, baking soda, corn starch, and salt
2. In a separate bowl beat eggs along with the beer.
3. In a shallow dish mix paprika, salt, pepper, and cayenne pepper.
4. Dry the codfish fillets with a paper towel.
5. Dip the fish into the eggs and coat it with seasoned flour.
6. Then dip it in the seasoning.
7. Grease the fillet with oil spray.
8. Divide the fillet between both zones.

9. Set zone 1 to AIR FRY mode at 400 degrees F for 14 minutes.
10. Select MACTH button for zone 2 basket.
11. Press start and let the AIR fry do its magic.
12. Once cooking is done, serve the fish.
13. Enjoy it hot.

Nutrition:
- (Per serving) Calories 1691| Fat 6.1g| Sodium 3976mg | Carbs105.1 g | Fiber 3.4g | Sugar15.6 g | Protein 270g

Lemony Prawns And Courgette

Servings: 4
Cooking Time: 7 To 8 Minutes
Ingredients:
- 570 g extra-large raw prawns, peeled and deveined
- 2 medium courgettes (about 230 g each), halved lengthwise and cut into ½-inch-thick slices
- 1½ tablespoons olive oil
- ½ teaspoon garlic salt
- 1½ teaspoons dried oregano
- ⅛ teaspoon crushed red pepper flakes (optional)
- Juice of ½ lemon
- 1 tablespoon chopped fresh mint
- 1 tablespoon chopped fresh dill

Directions:
1. Preheat the air fryer to 176ºC.
2. In a large bowl, combine the prawns, courgette, oil, garlic salt, oregano, and pepper flakes and toss to coat.
3. Arrange a single layer of the prawns and courgette in the two air fryer drawers. Air fry for 7 to 8 minutes, shaking the drawer halfway, until the courgette is golden and the prawns are cooked through.
4. Transfer to a serving dish and tent with foil while you air fry the remaining prawns and courgette.
5. Top with the lemon juice, mint, and dill and serve.

Southwestern Fish Fillets

Servings: 4
Cooking Time: 16 Minutes
Ingredients:
- 455g trout fillets
- 1 tsp garlic powder
- 29g breadcrumbs
- 15ml olive oil
- 1 tsp chilli powder
- 1 tsp onion powder

Directions:
1. In a small bowl, mix breadcrumbs, garlic powder, onion powder, and chilli powder.
2. Brush fish fillets with oil and coat with breadcrumbs.
3. Insert a crisper plate in the Ninja Foodi air fryer baskets.
4. Place coated fish fillets in both baskets.
5. Select zone 1 then select "air fry" mode and set the temperature to 375 degrees F for 16 minutes. Press "match" and "start/stop" to begin.

Nutrition:
- (Per serving) Calories 272 | Fat 13.5g |Sodium 120mg | Carbs 5g | Fiber 0.6g | Sugar 0.7g | Protein 31.1g

Lemon Pepper Fish Fillets

Servings: 4
Cooking Time: 10 Minutes
Ingredients:
- 4 tilapia fillets
- 30ml olive oil
- 2 tbsp lemon zest
- ⅛ tsp paprika
- 1 tsp garlic, minced
- 1 ½ tsp ground peppercorns
- Pepper
- Salt

Directions:
1. In a small bowl, mix oil, peppercorns, paprika, garlic, lemon zest, pepper, and salt.
2. Brush the fish fillets with oil mixture.
3. Insert a crisper plate in the Ninja Foodi air fryer baskets.
4. Place fish fillets in both baskets.
5. Select zone 1 then select "air fry" mode and set the temperature to 390 degrees F for 10 minutes. Press "match" to match zone 2 settings to zone 1. Press "start/stop" to begin.

Nutrition:
- (Per serving) Calories 203 | Fat 9g |Sodium 99mg | Carbs 0.9g | Fiber 0.2g | Sugar 0.2g | Protein 32.1g

Snapper With Fruit

Servings: 4
Cooking Time: 9 To 13 Minutes
Ingredients:

- 4 red snapper fillets, 100 g each
- 2 teaspoons olive oil
- 3 nectarines, halved and pitted
- 3 plums, halved and pitted
- 150 g red grapes
- 1 tablespoon freshly squeezed lemon juice
- 1 tablespoon honey
- ½ teaspoon dried thyme

Directions:
1. Put the red snapper in the two air fryer baskets and drizzle with the olive oil. Air fry at 200ºC for 4 minutes.
2. Remove the baskets and add the nectarines and plums. Scatter the grapes over all.
3. Drizzle with the lemon juice and honey and sprinkle with the thyme.
4. Return the baskets to the air fryer and air fry for 5 to 9 minutes more, or until the fish flakes when tested with a fork and the fruit is tender. Serve immediately.

Panko-crusted Fish Sticks

Servings: 4
Cooking Time: 15 Minutes
Ingredients:

- Tartar Sauce:
- 470 ml mayonnaise
- 2 tablespoons dill pickle relish
- 1 tablespoon dried minced onions
- Fish Sticks:
- Olive or vegetable oil, for spraying
- 455 g tilapia fillets
- 75 g plain flour
- 120 g panko bread crumbs
- 2 tablespoons Creole seasoning
- 2 teaspoons garlic granules
- 1 teaspoon onion powder
- ½ teaspoon salt
- ¼ teaspoon freshly ground black pepper
- 1 large egg

Directions:
1. Make the Tartar Sauce: In a small bowl, whisk together the mayonnaise, pickle relish, and onions. Cover with plastic wrap and refrigerate until ready to serve. You can make this sauce ahead of time; the flavors will intensify as it chills. Make the Fish Sticks: 2. Preheat the air fryer to 175ºC. Line the two air fryer baskets with baking paper and spray lightly with oil. 3. Cut the fillets into equal-size sticks and place them in a zip-top plastic bag. 4. Add the flour to the bag, seal, and shake well until evenly coated. 5. In a shallow bowl, mix together the bread crumbs, Creole seasoning, garlic, onion powder, salt, and black pepper. 6. In a small bowl, whisk the egg. 7. Dip the fish sticks in the egg, then dredge in the bread crumb mixture until completely coated. 8. Place the fish sticks in the two prepared baskets. Do not overcrowd. Spray lightly with oil. 9. Cook for 12 to 15 minutes, or until browned and cooked through. Serve with the tartar sauce.

Cod With Avocado And Garlic Prawns

Servings: 5
Cooking Time: 10 Minutes
Ingredients:

- Cod with Avocado:
- 90 g shredded cabbage
- 60 ml full-fat sour cream
- 2 tablespoons full-fat mayonnaise
- 20 g chopped pickled jalapeños
- 2 (85 g) cod fillets
- 1 teaspoon chilli powder
- 1 teaspoon cumin
- ½ teaspoon paprika
- ¼ teaspoon garlic powder
- 1 medium avocado, peeled, pitted, and sliced
- ½ medium lime
- Garlic Prawns:
- Prawns:
- Olive or vegetable oil, for spraying
- 450 g medium raw prawns, peeled and deveined
- 6 tablespoons unsalted butter, melted
- 120 g panko bread crumbs
- 2 tablespoons garlic granules
- 1 teaspoon salt
- ½ teaspoon freshly ground black pepper
- Garlic Butter Sauce:
- 115 g unsalted butter
- 2 teaspoons garlic granules
- ¾ teaspoon salt (omit if using salted butter)

Directions:
1. Make the Cod with Avocado :

Ninja Foodi 2-Basket Air Fryer Cookbook

2. In a large bowl, place cabbage, sour cream, mayonnaise, and jalapeños. Mix until fully coated. Let sit for 20 minutes in the refrigerator.
3. Sprinkle cod fillets with chilli powder, cumin, paprika, and garlic powder. Place each fillet into the zone 1 air fryer drawer.
4. Adjust the temperature to 188ºC and set the timer for 10 minutes.
5. Flip the fillets halfway through the cooking time. When fully cooked, fish should have an internal temperature of at least 64ºC.
6. To serve, divide slaw mixture into two serving bowls, break cod fillets into pieces and spread over the bowls, and top with avocado. Squeeze lime juice over each bowl. Serve immediately.
7. Make the Garlic Prawns :
8. Make the Prawns
9. Preheat the air fryer to 204ºC. Line the zone 2 air fryer drawer with baking paper and spray lightly with oil.
10. Place the prawns and melted butter in a zip-top plastic bag, seal, and shake well, until evenly coated.
11. In a medium bowl, mix together the breadcrumbs, garlic, salt, and black pepper.
12. Add the prawns to the panko mixture and toss until evenly coated. Shake off any excess coating.
13. Place the prawns in the prepared drawer and spray lightly with oil.
14. Cook for 8 to 10 minutes, flipping and spraying with oil after 4 to 5 minutes, until golden brown and crispy. Make the Garlic Butter Sauce
15. In a microwave-safe bowl, combine the butter, garlic, and salt and microwave on 50% power for 30 to 60 seconds, stirring every 15 seconds, until completely melted.
16. Serve the prawns immediately with the garlic butter sauce on the side for dipping.

Breaded Scallops

Servings: 4
Cooking Time: 12 Minutes.
Ingredients:

- ½ cup crushed buttery crackers
- ½ teaspoon garlic powder
- ½ teaspoon seafood seasoning
- 2 tablespoons butter, melted
- 1 pound sea scallops patted dry
- cooking spray

Directions:
1. Mix cracker crumbs, garlic powder, and seafood seasoning in a shallow bowl. Spread melted butter in another shallow bowl.
2. Dip each scallop in the melted butter and then roll in the breading to coat well.
3. Grease each Air fryer basket with cooking spray and place half of the scallops in each.
4. Return the crisper plate to the Ninja Foodi Dual Zone Air Fryer.
5. Select the Air Fry mode for Zone 1 and set the temperature to 390 degrees F and the time to 12 minutes.
6. Press the "MATCH" button to copy the settings for Zone 2.
7. Initiate cooking by pressing the START/STOP button.
8. Flip the scallops with a spatula after 4 minutes and resume cooking.
9. Serve warm.
Nutrition:

- (Per serving) Calories 275 | Fat 1.4g |Sodium 582mg | Carbs 31.5g | Fiber 1.1g | Sugar 0.1g | Protein 29.8g

Stuffed Mushrooms With Crab

Servings: 4
Cooking Time: 18 Minutes
Ingredients:

- 907g baby bella mushrooms
- cooking spray
- 2 teaspoons tony chachere's salt blend
- ¼ red onion, diced
- 2 celery ribs, diced
- 227g lump crab
- ½ cup seasoned bread crumbs
- 1 large egg
- ½ cup parmesan cheese, shredded
- 1 teaspoon oregano
- 1 teaspoon hot sauce

Directions:
1. Mix all the ingredients except the mushrooms in a bowl.
2. Divide the crab filling into the mushroom caps.
3. Place the caps in the air fryer baskets.

4. Return the air fryer basket 1 to Zone 1, and basket 2 to Zone 2 of the Ninja Foodi 2-Basket Air Fryer.
5. Choose the "Air Fry" mode for Zone 1 at 400 degrees F and 18 minutes of cooking time.
6. Select the "MATCH COOK" option to copy the settings for Zone 2.
7. Initiate cooking by pressing the START/PAUSE BUTTON.
8. Serve warm.

Nutrition:
- (Per serving) Calories 399 | Fat 16g |Sodium 537mg | Carbs 28g | Fiber 3g | Sugar 10g | Protein 35g

Blackened Red Snapper

Servings: 4
Cooking Time: 8 To 10 Minutes

Ingredients:
- 1½ teaspoons black pepper
- ¼ teaspoon thyme
- ¼ teaspoon garlic powder
- ⅛ teaspoon cayenne pepper
- 1 teaspoon olive oil
- 4 red snapper fillet portions, skin on, 110 g each
- 4 thin slices lemon
- Cooking spray

Directions:
1. Mix the spices and oil together to make a paste. Rub into both sides of the fish.
2. Spray the two air fryer drawers with nonstick cooking spray and lay snapper steaks in drawers, skin-side down.
3. Place a lemon slice on each piece of fish.
4. Roast at 200ºC for 8 to 10 minutes. The fish will not flake when done, but it should be white through the center.

Rainbow Salmon Kebabs And Tuna Melt

Servings: 3
Cooking Time: 10 Minutes

Ingredients:
- Rainbow Salmon Kebabs:
- 170 g boneless, skinless salmon, cut into 1-inch cubes
- ¼ medium red onion, peeled and cut into 1-inch pieces
- ½ medium yellow bell pepper, seeded and cut into 1-inch pieces
- ½ medium courgette, trimmed and cut into ½-inch slices
- 1 tablespoon olive oil
- ½ teaspoon salt
- ¼ teaspoon ground black pepper
- Tuna Melt:
- Olive or vegetable oil, for spraying
- 140 g can tuna, drained
- 1 tablespoon mayonnaise
- ¼ teaspoon garlic granules, plus more for garnish
- 2 teaspoons unsalted butte
- 2 slices sandwich bread of choice
- 2 slices Cheddar cheese

Directions:
1. Make the Rainbow Salmon Kebabs : Using one skewer, skewer 1 piece salmon, then 1 piece onion, 1 piece bell pepper, and finally 1 piece courgette. Repeat this pattern with additional skewers to make four kebabs total. Drizzle with olive oil and sprinkle with salt and black pepper. 2. Place kebabs into the ungreased zone 1 air fryer drawer. Adjust the temperature to 204ºC and air fry for 8 minutes, turning kebabs halfway through cooking. Salmon will easily flake and have an internal temperature of at least 64ºC when done; vegetables will be tender. Serve warm.
2. Make the Tuna Melt : 1. Line the zone 2 air fryer drawer with baking paper and spray lightly with oil. In a medium bowl, mix together the tuna, mayonnaise, and garlic. 3. Spread 1 teaspoon of butter on each slice of bread and place one slice butter-side down in the prepared drawer. 4. Top with a slice of cheese, the tuna mixture, another slice of cheese, and the other slice of bread, butter-side up. 5. Air fry at 204ºC for 5 minutes, flip, and cook for another 5 minutes, until browned and crispy. 6. Sprinkle with additional garlic, before cutting in half and serving.

Sesame Honey Salmon

Servings: 4
Cooking Time: 10minutes

Ingredients:
- 4 salmon fillets
- 85g honey
- 15ml sesame oil
- 1 tbsp garlic, minced
- 2 tbsp soy sauce
- 1 tbsp sriracha
- Pepper
- Salt

Directions:

Ninja Foodi 2-Basket Air Fryer Cookbook

1. In a bowl, coat fish fillets with oil, garlic, honey, sriracha, soy sauce, pepper, and salt. Cover and place in refrigerator for 30 minutes.
2. Insert a crisper plate in the Ninja Foodi air fryer baskets.
3. Place the marinated fish fillets in both baskets.
4. Select zone 1, then select "air fry" mode and set the temperature to 375 degrees F for 10 minutes. Press "match" to match zone 2 settings to zone 1. Press "start/stop" to begin.

Nutrition:
- (Per serving) Calories 341 | Fat 14.4g |Sodium 596mg | Carbs 19.5g | Fiber 0.2g | Sugar 17.6g | Protein 35.2g

Cajun Catfish Cakes With Cheese

Servings: 4
Cooking Time: 35 Minutes
Ingredients:

- 2 catfish fillets
- 85 g butter
- 150 g shredded Parmesan cheese
- 150 g shredded Swiss cheese
- 120 ml buttermilk
- 1 teaspoon baking powder
- 1 teaspoon baking soda
- 1 teaspoon Cajun seasoning

Directions:
1. Bring a pot of salted water to a boil. Add the catfish fillets to the boiling water and let them boil for 5 minutes until they become opaque.
2. Remove the fillets from the pot to a mixing bowl and flake them into small pieces with a fork.
3. Add the remaining ingredients to the bowl of fish and stir until well incorporated.
4. Divide the fish mixture into 12 equal portions and shape each portion into a patty.
5. Preheat the air fryer to 190ºC.
6. Arrange the patties in the two air fryer baskets and air fry for 15 minutes until golden brown and cooked through. Flip the patties halfway through the cooking time.
7. Let the patties sit for 5 minutes and serve.

South Indian Fried Fish

Servings: 4
Cooking Time: 8 Minutes
Ingredients:

- 2 tablespoons olive oil
- 2 tablespoons fresh lime or lemon juice
- 1 teaspoon minced fresh ginger
- 1 clove garlic, minced
- 1 teaspoon ground turmeric
- ½ teaspoon kosher or coarse sea salt
- ¼ to ½ teaspoon cayenne pepper
- 455 g tilapia fillets (2 to 3 fillets)
- Olive oil spray
- Lime or lemon wedges (optional)

Directions:
1. In a large bowl, combine the oil, lime juice, ginger, garlic, turmeric, salt, and cayenne. Stir until well combined; set aside.
2. Cut each tilapia fillet into three or four equal-size pieces. Add the fish to the bowl and gently mix until all of the fish is coated in the marinade. Marinate for 10 to 15 minutes at room temperature.
3. Spray the air fryer basket with olive oil spray. Place the fish in the basket and spray the fish. Set the air fryer to 165ºC for 3 minutes to partially cook the fish. Set the air fryer to 205ºC for 5 minutes to finish cooking and crisp up the fish.
4. Carefully remove the fish from the basket. Serve hot, with lemon wedges if desired.

Salmon With Coconut

Servings:2
Cooking Time:15
Ingredients:

- Oil spray, for greasing
- 2 salmon fillets, 6ounces each
- Salt and ground black pepper, to taste
- 1 tablespoon butter, for frying
- 1 tablespoon red curry paste
- 1 cup of coconut cream
- 2 tablespoons fresh cilantro, chopped
- 1 cup of cauliflower florets
- ½ cup Parmesan cheese, hard

Directions:
1. Take a bowl and mix salt, black pepper, butter, red curry paste, coconut cream in a bowl and marinate the salmon in it.

2. Oil sprays the cauliflower florets and then seasons it with salt and freshly ground black pepper.
3. Put the florets in the zone 1 basket.
4. Layer the parchment paper over the zone 2 baskets, and then place the salmon fillet on it.
5. Set the zone 2 basket to AIR FRY mod at 15 minutes for4 00 degrees F
6. Hit the smart finish button to finish it at the same time.
7. Once the time for cooking is over, serve the salmon with cauliflower floret with Parmesan cheese drizzle on top.
Nutrition:
- (Per serving) Calories 774 | Fat 59g| Sodium 1223mg | Carbs 12.2g | Fiber 3.9g | Sugar5.9 g | Protein53.5 g

Tuna Patty Sliders

Servings: 4
Cooking Time: 10 To 15 Minutes
Ingredients:
- 3 cans tuna, 140 g each, packed in water
- 40 g whole-wheat panko bread crumbs
- 50 g shredded Parmesan cheese
- 1 tablespoon Sriracha
- ¾ teaspoon black pepper
- 10 whole-wheat buns
- Cooking spray

Directions:
1. Preheat the air fryer to 175ºC.
2. Spray the two air fryer baskets lightly with cooking spray.
3. In a medium bowl combine the tuna, bread crumbs, Parmesan cheese, Sriracha, and black pepper and stir to combine.
4. Form the mixture into 10 patties.
5. Place the patties in the two air fryer baskets in a single layer. Spray the patties lightly with cooking spray.
6. Air fry for 6 to 8 minutes. Turn the patties over and lightly spray with cooking spray. Air fry until golden brown and crisp, another 4 to 7 more minutes. Serve warm.

Dukkah-crusted Halibut

Servings: 2
Cooking Time: 17 Minutes
Ingredients:
- Dukkah:
- 1 tablespoon coriander seeds
- 1 tablespoon sesame seeds
- 1½ teaspoons cumin seeds
- 50 g roasted mixed nuts
- ¼ teaspoon kosher or coarse sea salt
- ¼ teaspoon black pepper
- Fish:
- 2 halibut fillets, 140 g each
- 2 tablespoons mayonnaise
- Vegetable oil spray
- Lemon wedges, for serving

Directions:
1. For the Dukkah: Combine the coriander, sesame seeds, and cumin in a small baking pan. Place the pan in the zone 1 air fryer basket. Set the air fryer to 205ºC for 5 minutes. Toward the end of the cooking time, you will hear the seeds popping. Transfer to a plate and let cool for 5 minutes. 2. Transfer the toasted seeds to a food processor or spice grinder and add the mixed nuts. Pulse until coarsely chopped. Add the salt and pepper and stir well.
2. 3. For the fish: Spread each fillet with 1 tablespoon of the mayonnaise. Press a heaping tablespoon of the Dukkah into the mayonnaise on each fillet, pressing lightly to adhere. 4. Spray the zone 2 air fryer basket with vegetable oil spray. Place the fish in the zone 2 basket. Cook for 12 minutes, or until the fish flakes easily with a fork. 5. Serve the fish with lemon wedges.

Brown Sugar Garlic Salmon

Servings: 4
Cooking Time: 10 Minutes
Ingredients:
- 455g salmon
- Salt and black pepper, to taste
- 2 tablespoons brown sugar
- 1 teaspoon chili powder
- ½ teaspoon paprika
- 1 teaspoon Italian seasoning
- 1 teaspoon garlic powder

Directions:
1. Mix brown sugar with garlic powder, Italian seasoning, paprika, and chili powder in a bowl.
2. Rub this mixture over the salmon along with black pepper and salt.

3. Place the salmon in the air fryer baskets.
4. Return the air fryer basket 1 to Zone 1, and basket 2 to Zone 2 of the Ninja Foodi 2-Basket Air Fryer.
5. Choose the "Air Fry" mode for Zone 1 and set the temperature to 400 degrees F and 10 minutes of cooking time.
6. Select the "MATCH COOK" option to copy the settings for Zone 2.
7. Initiate cooking by pressing the START/PAUSE BUTTON.
8. Flip the salmon once cooked halfway through.
9. Serve warm.

Nutrition:
- (Per serving) Calories 275 | Fat 1.4g |Sodium 582mg | Carbs 31.5g | Fiber 1.1g | Sugar 0.1g | Protein 29.8g

Seafood Shrimp Omelet

Servings:2
Cooking Time:15
Ingredients:
- 6 large shrimp, shells removed and chopped
- 6 eggs, beaten
- ½ tablespoon of butter, melted
- 2 tablespoons green onions, sliced
- 1/3 cup of mushrooms, chopped
- 1 pinch paprika
- Salt and black pepper, to taste
- Oil spray, for greasing

Directions:
1. In a large bowl whisk the eggs and add chopped shrimp, butter, green onions, mushrooms, paprika, salt, and black pepper.
2. Take two cake pans that fit inside the air fryer and grease them with oil spray.
3. Pour the egg mixture between the cake pans and place it in two baskets of the air fryer.
4. Turn on the BAKE function of zone 1, and let it cook for 15 minutes at 320 degrees F.
5. Select the MATCH button to match the cooking time for the zone 2 basket.
6. Once the cooking cycle completes, take out, and serve hot.

Nutrition:
- (Per serving) Calories 300 | Fat 17.5g| Sodium 368mg | Carbs 2.9g | Fiber 0.3g | Sugar1.4 g | Protein32.2 g

Pecan-crusted Catfish

Servings: 4
Cooking Time: 12 Minutes
Ingredients:
- 65 g pecans, finely crushed
- 1 teaspoon fine sea salt
- ¼ teaspoon ground black pepper
- 4 catfish fillets, 110g each
- For Garnish (Optional):
- Fresh oregano
- Pecan halves

Directions:
1. Spray the two air fryer drawers with avocado oil. Preheat the air fryer to 192ºC.
2. In a large bowl, mix the crushed pecan, salt, and pepper. One at a time, dredge the catfish fillets in the mixture, coating them well. Use your hands to press the pecan meal into the fillets. Spray the fish with avocado oil and place them in the two air fryer drawers.
3. Air fry the coated catfish for 12 minutes, or until it flakes easily and is no longer translucent in the center, flipping halfway through.
4. Garnish with oregano sprigs and pecan halves, if desired.
5. Store leftovers in an airtight container in the fridge for up to 3 days. Reheat in a preheated 176ºC air fryer for 4 minutes, or until heated through.

Frozen Breaded Fish Fillet

Servings:2
Cooking Time:12
Ingredients:
- 4 Frozen Breaded Fish Fillet
- Oil spray, for greasing
- 1 cup mayonnaise

Directions:
1. Take the frozen fish fillets out of the bag and place them in both baskets of the air fryer.
2. Lightly grease it with oil spray.

3. Set the Zone 1 basket to 380 degrees F fo12 minutes.
4. Select the MATCH button for the zone 2 basket.
5. hit the start button to start cooking.
6. Once the cooking is done, serve the fish hot with mayonnaise.

Nutrition:
- (Per serving) Calories 921| Fat 61.5g| Sodium 1575mg | Carbs 69g | Fiber 2g | Sugar 9.5g | Protein 29.1g

Roasted Salmon And Parmesan Asparagus

Servings: 4
Cooking Time: 27 Minutes

Ingredients:
- 2 tablespoons Montreal steak seasoning
- 3 tablespoons brown sugar
- 3 uncooked salmon fillets (6 ounces each)
- 2 tablespoons canola oil, divided
- 1-pound asparagus, ends trimmed
- Kosher salt, as desired
- Ground black pepper, as desired
- ¼ cup shredded parmesan cheese, divided

Directions:
1. Combine the steak spice and brown sugar in a small bowl.
2. Brush 1 tablespoon of oil over the salmon fillets, then thoroughly coat with the sugar mixture.
3. Toss the asparagus with the remaining 1 tablespoon of oil, salt, and pepper in a mixing bowl.
4. Place a crisper plate in both drawers. Put the fillets skin-side down in the zone 1 drawer, then place the drawer in the unit. Insert the zone 2 drawer into the device after placing the asparagus in it.
5. Select zone 1, then ROAST, then set the temperature to 390 degrees F/ 200 degrees C with a 17-minute timer. To match the zone 2 settings to zone 1, choose MATCH. To begin cooking, press the START/STOP button.
6. When the zone 2 timer reaches 7 minutes, press START/STOP. Remove the zone 2 drawer from the unit. Flip the asparagus with silicone-tipped tongs. Re-insert the drawer into the unit. Continue cooking by pressing START/STOP.
7. When the zone 2 timer has reached 14 minutes, press START/STOP. Remove the zone 2 drawer from the unit. Sprinkle half the parmesan cheese over the asparagus, and mix lightly. Re-insert the drawer into the unit. Continue cooking by pressing START/STOP.
8. Transfer the fillets and asparagus to a serving plate once they've finished cooking. Serve with the remaining parmesan cheese on top of the asparagus.

Nutrition:
- (Per serving) Calories 293 | Fat 15.8g | Sodium 203mg | Carbs 11.1g | Fiber 2.4g | Sugar 8.7g | Protein 29g

Perfect Parmesan Salmon

Servings: 4
Cooking Time:10 Minutes

Ingredients:
- 4 salmon fillets
- 1/4 cup parmesan cheese, shredded
- 1/4 tsp dried dill
- 1/2 tbsp Dijon mustard
- 4 tbsp mayonnaise
- 1 lemon juice
- Pepper
- Salt

Directions:
1. In a small bowl, mix cheese, dill, mustard, mayonnaise, lemon juice, pepper, and salt.
2. Place salmon fillets into the air fryer basket and brush with cheese mixture.
3. Cook salmon fillets at 400 F for 10 minutes.
4. Serve and enjoy.

Salmon With Cauliflower

Servings: 4
Cooking Time: 25 Minutes

Ingredients:
- 455 g salmon fillet, diced
- 100 g cauliflower, shredded
- 1 tablespoon dried coriander
- 1 tablespoon coconut oil, melted
- 1 teaspoon ground turmeric
- 60 ml coconut cream

Directions:
1. Mix salmon with cauliflower, dried cilantro, ground turmeric, coconut cream, and coconut oil.
2. Transfer the salmon mixture into the air fryer and cook the meal at 176ºC for 25 minutes. Stir the meal every 5 minutes to avoid the burning.

Herbed Prawns Pita

Servings: 4
Cooking Time: 8 Minutes
Ingredients:

- 455 g medium prawns, peeled and deveined
- 2 tablespoons olive oil
- 1 teaspoon dried oregano
- ½ teaspoon dried thyme
- ½ teaspoon garlic powder
- ¼ teaspoon onion powder
- ½ teaspoon salt
- ¼ teaspoon black pepper
- 4 whole wheat pitas
- 110 g feta cheese, crumbled
- 75 g shredded lettuce
- 1 tomato, diced
- 45 g black olives, sliced
- 1 lemon

Directions:
1. Preheat the oven to 192ºC.
2. In a medium bowl, combine the prawns with the olive oil, oregano, thyme, garlic powder, onion powder, salt, and black pepper.
3. Pour prawns in a single layer in the two air fryer drawers and roast for 6 to 8 minutes, or until cooked through.
4. Remove from the air fryer and divide into warmed pitas with feta, lettuce, tomato, olives, and a squeeze of lemon.

Prawn Dejonghe Skewers

Servings: 4
Cooking Time: 15 Minutes
Ingredients:

- 2 teaspoons sherry, or apple cider vinegar
- 3 tablespoons unsalted butter, melted
- 120 g panko bread crumbs
- 3 cloves garlic, minced
- 8 g minced flat-leaf parsley, plus more for garnish
- 1 teaspoon kosher salt
- Pinch of cayenne pepper
- 680 g prawns, peeled and deveined
- Vegetable oil, for spraying
- Lemon wedges, for serving

Directions:
1. Stir the sherry and melted butter together in a shallow bowl or pie plate and whisk until combined. Set aside. Whisk together the panko, garlic, parsley, salt, and cayenne pepper on a large plate or shallow bowl.
2. Thread the prawns onto metal skewers designed for the air fryer or bamboo skewers, 3 to 4 per skewer. Dip 1 prawns skewer in the butter mixture, then dredge in the panko mixture until each prawns is lightly coated. Place the skewer on a plate or rimmed baking sheet and repeat the process with the remaining skewers.
3. Preheat the air fryer to 175ºC. Arrange 4 skewers in the zone 1 air fryer basket. Spray the skewers with oil and air fry for 8 minutes, until the bread crumbs are golden brown and the prawns are cooked through. Transfer the cooked skewers to a serving plate and keep warm while cooking the remaining 4 skewers in the air fryer.
4. Sprinkle the cooked skewers with additional fresh parsley and serve with lemon wedges if desired.

Chapter 5 : **Poultry Recipes**

Teriyaki Chicken Skewers

Servings: 4
Cooking Time: 16 Minutes
Ingredients:
- 455g boneless chicken thighs, cubed
- 237ml teriyaki marinade
- 16 small wooden skewers
- Sesame seeds for rolling
- Teriyaki Marinade
- ⅓ cup soy sauce
- 59ml chicken broth
- ½ orange, juiced
- 2 tablespoons brown sugar
- 1 teaspoon ginger, grated
- 1 clove garlic, grated

Directions:
1. Blend teriyaki marinade ingredients in a blender.
2. Add chicken and its marinade to a Ziplock bag.
3. Seal this bag, shake it well and refrigerate for 30 minutes.
4. Thread the chicken on the wooden skewers.
5. Place these skewers in the air fryer baskets.
6. Return the air fryer basket 1 to Zone 1, and basket 2 to Zone 2 of the Ninja Foodi 2-Basket Air Fryer.
7. Choose the "Air Fry" mode for Zone 1 at 350 degrees F and 16 minutes of cooking time.
8. Select the "MATCH COOK" option to copy the settings for Zone 2.
9. Initiate cooking by pressing the START/PAUSE BUTTON.
10. Flip the skewers once cooked halfway through.
11. Garnish with sesame seeds.
12. Serve warm.

Nutrition:
- (Per serving) Calories 456 | Fat 16.4g |Sodium 1321mg | Carbs 19.2g | Fiber 2.2g | Sugar 4.2g | Protein 55.2g

Greek Chicken Meatballs

Servings: 4
Cooking Time: 9 Minutes
Ingredients:
- 455g ground chicken
- 1 large egg
- 1½ tablespoons garlic paste
- 1 tablespoon dried oregano
- 1 teaspoon lemon zest
- 1 teaspoon dried onion powder
- ¾ teaspoon salt
- ¼ teaspoon black pepper
- Oil spray

Directions:
1. Mix ground chicken with rest of the ingredients in a bowl.
2. Make 1-inch sized meatballs out of this mixture.
3. Place the meatballs in the air fryer baskets.
4. Return the air fryer basket 1 to Zone 1, and basket 2 to Zone 2 of the Ninja Foodi 2-Basket Air Fryer.
5. Choose the "Air Fry" mode for Zone 1 and set the temperature to 390 degrees F and 9 minutes of cooking time.
6. Select the "MATCH COOK" option to copy the settings for Zone 2.
7. Initiate cooking by pressing the START/PAUSE BUTTON.
8. Serve warm.

Nutrition:
- (Per serving) Calories 346 | Fat 16.1g |Sodium 882mg | Carbs 1.3g | Fiber 0.5g | Sugar 0.5g | Protein 48.2g

Apricot-glazed Turkey Tenderloin

Servings: 4
Cooking Time: 30 Minutes
Ingredients:
- Olive oil
- 80 g sugar-free apricot preserves
- ½ tablespoon spicy brown mustard
- 680 g turkey breast tenderloin
- Salt and freshly ground black pepper, to taste

Directions:
1. Spray the two air fryer drawers lightly with olive oil.
2. In a small bowl, combine the apricot preserves and mustard to make a paste.

3. Season the turkey with salt and pepper. Spread the apricot paste all over the turkey.
4. Place the turkey in the two air fryer drawers and lightly spray with olive oil.
5. Air fry at 190ºC for 15 minutes. Flip the turkey over and lightly spray with olive oil. Air fry until the internal temperature reaches at least 80ºC, an additional 10 to 15 minutes.
6. Let the turkey rest for 10 minutes before slicing and serving.

Honey Butter Chicken

Servings: 4
Cooking Time: 15 Minutes
Ingredients:

- 4 chicken breasts, boneless
- 85g honey
- 28g butter, melted
- 2 tsp lemon juice
- 15ml olive oil
- 62g Dijon mustard
- Pepper
- Salt

Directions:
1. In a small bowl, mix butter, oil, lemon juice, honey, mustard, pepper, and salt.
2. Insert a crisper plate in the Ninja Foodi air fryer baskets.
3. Brush chicken breasts with butter mixture and place them in both baskets.
4. Select zone 1 then select "bake" mode and set the temperature to 380 degrees F for 15 minutes. Press "match" to match zone 2 settings to zone 1. Press "start/stop" to begin.

Nutrition:

- (Per serving) Calories 434 | Fat 20.7g |Sodium 384mg | Carbs 18.4g | Fiber 0.6g | Sugar 17.6g | Protein 43.1g

Chicken Leg Piece

Servings:1
Cooking Time:25
Ingredients:

- 1 teaspoon of onion powder
- 1 teaspoon of paprika powder
- 1 teaspoon of garlic powder
- Salt and black pepper, to taste
- 1 tablespoon of Italian seasoning
- 1 teaspoon of celery seeds
- 2 eggs, whisked
- 1/3 cup buttermilk
- 1 cup of corn flour
- 1 pound of chicken leg

Directions:
1. Take a bowl and whisk egg along with pepper, salt, and buttermilk.
2. Set it aside for further use.
3. Mix all the spices in a small separate bowl.
4. Dredge the chicken in egg wash then dredge it in seasoning.
5. Coat the chicken legs with oil spray.
6. At the end dust it with the corn flour.
7. Divide the leg pieces into two zones.
8. Set zone 1 basket to 400 degrees F, for 25 minutes.
9. Select MATCH for zone 2 basket.
10. Let the air fryer do the magic.
11. Once it's done, serve and enjoy.

Nutrition:

- (Per serving) Calories 1511| Fat 52.3g| Sodium615 mg | Carbs 100g | Fiber 9.2g | Sugar 8.1g | Protein 154.2g

Crispy Sesame Chicken

Servings: 2
Cooking Time: 10 Minutes
Ingredients:

- 680g boneless chicken thighs, diced
- 2 tablespoons rice vinegar
- 1 tablespoon soy sauce
- 2 teaspoons minced fresh ginger
- 1 garlic clove, minced
- ¾ teaspoon salt
- ½ teaspoon black pepper
- 2 large eggs, beaten
- 1 cup cornstarch
- Sauce
- 59ml soy sauce
- 2 tablespoons rice vinegar

- ⅓ cup brown sugar
- 59ml water
- 1 tablespoon cornstarch
- 2 teaspoons sesame oil
- 2 tablespoons vegetable oil
- 2 garlic cloves, minced
- 2 teaspoons chile paste
- Garnish
- 1 tablespoon toasted sesame seeds

Directions:
1. Blend all the sauce ingredients in a saucepan and cook until it thickens then allow it to cool.
2. Mix chicken with black pepper, salt, garlic, ginger, vinegar, and soy sauce in a bowl.
3. Cover and marinate the chicken for 20 minutes.
4. Divide the chicken in the air fryer baskets.
5. Return the air fryer basket 1 to Zone 1, and basket 2 to Zone 2 of the Ninja Foodi 2-Basket Air Fryer.
6. Choose the "Air Fry" mode for Zone 1 and set the temperature to 400 degrees F and 10 minutes of cooking time.
7. Select the "MATCH COOK" option to copy the settings for Zone 2.
8. Initiate cooking by pressing the START/PAUSE BUTTON.
9. Pour the prepared sauce over the air fried chicken and drizzle sesame seeds on top.
10. Serve warm.

Nutrition:
- (Per serving) Calories 351 | Fat 16g |Sodium 777mg | Carbs 26g | Fiber 4g | Sugar 5g | Protein 28g

Maple-mustard Glazed Turkey Tenderloin With Apple And Sage Stuffing

Servings:4
Cooking Time: 35 Minutes
Ingredients:
- FOR THE TURKEY TENDERLOIN
- 2 tablespoons maple syrup
- 1 tablespoon unsalted butter, at room temperature
- 1 tablespoon Dijon mustard
- ½ teaspoon kosher salt
- ½ teaspoon freshly ground black pepper
- 1½ pounds turkey tenderloin
- FOR THE STUFFING
- 6 ounces seasoned stuffing mix
- 1½ cups chicken broth
- 1 apple, peeled, cored, and diced
- 1 tablespoon chopped fresh sage
- 2 teaspoons unsalted butter, cut into several pieces

Directions:
1. To prep the turkey tenderloin: In a small bowl, mix the maple syrup, butter, mustard, salt, and black pepper until smooth. Spread the maple mixture over the entire turkey tenderloin.
2. To prep the stuffing: In the Zone 2 basket, combine the stuffing mix and chicken broth. Stir well to ensure the bread is fully moistened. Stir in the apple and sage. Scatter the butter on top.
3. To cook the turkey and stuffing: Install a crisper plate in the Zone 1 basket. Place the turkey tenderloin in the basket and insert the basket in the unit. Insert the Zone 2 basket in the unit.
4. Select Zone 1, select AIR FRY, set the temperature to 390°F, and set the time to 35 minutes.
5. Select Zone 2, select BAKE, set the temperature to 340°F, and set the time to 20 minutes. Select SMART FINISH.
6. Press START/PAUSE to begin cooking.
7. When the Zone 2 timer reads 10 minutes, press START/PAUSE. Remove the basket and stir the stuffing. Reinsert the basket and press START/PAUSE to resume cooking.
8. When cooking is complete, the turkey will be cooked through (an instant-read thermometer should read 165°F) and the stuffing will have absorbed all the liquid and be slightly crisp on top. Serve warm.

Nutrition:
- (Per serving) Calories: 455; Total fat: 10g; Saturated fat: 3g; Carbohydrates: 42g; Fiber: 2.5g; Protein: 46g; Sodium: 1,230mg

Sweet-and-sour Chicken With Pineapple Cauliflower Rice

Servings:4
Cooking Time: 30 Minutes
Ingredients:
- FOR THE CHICKEN
- ¼ cup cornstarch, plus 2 teaspoons
- ¼ teaspoon kosher salt
- 2 large eggs
- 1 tablespoon sesame oil
- 1½ pounds boneless, skinless chicken breasts, cut into 1-inch pieces
- Nonstick cooking spray
- 6 tablespoons ketchup
- ¾ cup apple cider vinegar

- 1½ tablespoons soy sauce
- 1 tablespoon sugar
- FOR THE CAULIFLOWER RICE
- 1 cup finely diced fresh pineapple
- 1 red bell pepper, thinly sliced
- 1 small red onion, thinly sliced
- 1 tablespoon vegetable oil
- 2 cups frozen cauliflower rice, thawed
- 2 tablespoons soy sauce
- 1 teaspoon sesame oil
- 2 scallions, sliced

Directions:

1. To prep the chicken: Set up a breading station with two small shallow bowls. Combine ¼ cup of cornstarch and the salt in the first bowl. In the second bowl, beat the eggs with the sesame oil.
2. Dip the chicken pieces in the cornstarch mixture to coat, then into the egg mixture, then back into the cornstarch mixture to coat. Mist the coated pieces with cooking spray.
3. In a small bowl, whisk together the ketchup, vinegar, soy sauce, sugar, and remaining 2 teaspoons of cornstarch.
4. To prep the cauliflower rice: Blot the pineapple dry with a paper towel. In a large bowl, combine the pineapple, bell pepper, onion, and vegetable oil.
5. To cook the chicken and cauliflower rice: Install a crisper plate in each of the two baskets. Place the chicken in the Zone 1 basket and insert the basket in the unit. Place a piece of aluminum foil over the crisper plate in the Zone 2 basket and add the pineapple mixture. Insert the basket in the unit.
6. Select Zone 1, select AIR FRY, set the temperature to 400°F, and set the time to 30 minutes.
7. Select Zone 2, select AIR BROIL, set the temperature to 450°F, and set the time to 12 minutes. Select SMART FINISH.
8. Press START/PAUSE to begin cooking.
9. When the Zone 2 timer reads 4 minutes, press START/PAUSE. Remove the basket and stir in the cauliflower rice, soy sauce, and sesame oil. Reinsert the basket and press START/PAUSE to resume cooking.
10. When cooking is complete, the chicken will be golden brown and cooked through and the rice warmed through. Stir the scallions into the rice and serve.

Nutrition:

- (Per serving) Calories: 457; Total fat: 17g; Saturated fat: 2.5g; Carbohydrates: 31g; Fiber: 2.5g; Protein: 43g; Sodium: 1,526mg

Easy Chicken Thighs

Servings: 8
Cooking Time: 12 Minutes

Ingredients:

- 900g chicken thighs, boneless & skinless
- 2 tsp chilli powder
- 2 tsp olive oil
- 1 tsp garlic powder
- 1 tsp ground cumin
- Pepper
- Salt

Directions:

1. In a bowl, mix chicken with remaining ingredients until well coated.
2. Insert a crisper plate in the Ninja Foodi air fryer baskets.
3. Place chicken thighs in both baskets.
4. Select zone 1 then select "air fry" mode and set the temperature to 390 degrees F for 12 minutes. Press "match" to match zone 2 settings to zone 1. Press "start/stop" to begin. Turn halfway through.

Nutrition:

- (Per serving) Calories 230 | Fat 9.7g | Sodium 124mg | Carbs 0.7g | Fiber 0.3g | Sugar 0.2g | Protein 33g

Cornish Hen With Asparagus

Servings: 2
Cooking Time: 45

Ingredients:

- 10 spears of asparagus
- Salt and black pepper, to taste
- 1 Cornish hen
- Salt, to taste
- Black pepper, to taste
- 1 teaspoon of Paprika
- Coconut spray, for greasing
- 2 lemons, sliced

Directions:

1. Wash and pat dry the asparagus and coat it with coconut oil spray.
2. Sprinkle salt on the asparagus and place inside the first basket of the air fryer.

3. Next, take the Cornish hen and rub it well with the salt, black pepper, and paprika.
4. Oil sprays the Cornish hen and place in the second air fryer basket.
5. Press button 1 for the first basket and set it to AIR FRY mode at 350 degrees F, for 8 minutes.
6. For the second basket hit 2 and set the time to 45 minutes at 350 degrees F, by selecting the ROAST mode.
7. To start cooking, hit the smart finish button and press hit start.
8. Once the 6 minutes pass press 1 and pause and take out the asparagus.
9. Once the chicken cooking cycle complete, press 2 and hit pause.
10. Take out the Basket of chicken and let it transfer to the serving plate
11. Serve the chicken with roasted asparagus and slices of lemon.
12. Serve hot and enjoy.

Nutrition:
- (Per serving) Calories 192| Fat 4.7g| Sodium 151mg | Carbs10.7 g | Fiber 4.6g | Sugar 3.8g | Protein 30g

Turkey Burger Patties

Servings: 4
Cooking Time: 14 Minutes

Ingredients:
- 1 egg white
- 453g ground turkey
- 30ml Worcestershire sauce
- ½ tsp dried basil
- ½ tsp dried oregano
- Pepper
- Salt

Directions:
1. In a bowl, mix ground turkey with remaining ingredients until well combined.
2. Insert a crisper plate in the Ninja Foodi air fryer baskets.
3. Make patties from the turkey mixture and place them in both baskets.
4. Select zone 1, then select "air fry" mode and set the temperature to 360 degrees F for 14 minutes. Press "match" to match zone 2 settings to zone 1. Press "start/stop" to begin.

Nutrition:
- (Per serving) Calories 234 | Fat 12.5g |Sodium 251mg | Carbs 1.7g | Fiber 0.1g | Sugar 1.6g | Protein 32g

Nice Goulash

Servings: 2
Cooking Time: 17 Minutes

Ingredients:
- 2 red bell peppers, chopped
- 450 g chicken mince
- 2 medium tomatoes, diced
- 120 ml chicken broth
- Salt and ground black pepper, to taste
- Cooking spray

Directions:
1. Preheat the zone 1 air fryer drawer to 186°C. Spritz a baking pan with cooking spray.
2. Set the bell pepper in the baking pan and put in the zone 1 air fry drawer to broil for 5 minutes or until the bell pepper is tender. Shake the drawer halfway through.
3. Add the chicken mince and diced tomatoes in the baking pan and stir to mix well. Broil for 6 more minutes or until the chicken is lightly browned.
4. Pour the chicken broth over and sprinkle with salt and ground black pepper. Stir to mix well. Broil for an additional 6 minutes.
5. Serve immediately.

Pickled Chicken Fillets

Servings: 4
Cooking Time: 28 Minutes.

Ingredients:
- 2 boneless chicken breasts
- ½ cup dill pickle juice
- 2 eggs
- ½ cup milk
- 1 cup flour, all-purpose
- 2 tablespoons powdered sugar
- 2 tablespoons potato starch
- 1 teaspoon paprika
- 1 teaspoon of sea salt
- ½ teaspoon black pepper
- ½ teaspoon garlic powder
- ¼ teaspoon ground celery seed ground

- 1 tablespoon olive oil
- Cooking spray
- 4 hamburger buns, toasted
- 8 dill pickle chips

Directions:
1. Set the chicken in a suitable ziplock bag and pound it into ½ thickness with a mallet.
2. Slice the chicken into 2 halves.
3. Add pickle juice and seal the bag.
4. Refrigerate for 30 minutes approximately for marination. Whisk both eggs with milk in a shallow bowl.
5. Thoroughly mix flour with spices and flour in a separate bowl.
6. Dip each chicken slice in egg, then in the flour mixture.
7. Shake off the excess and set the chicken pieces in the crisper plate.
8. Spray the pieces with cooking oil.
9. Place the chicken pieces in the two crisper plate in a single layer and spray the cooking oil.
10. Return the crisper plate to the Ninja Foodi Dual Zone Air Fryer.
11. Choose the Air Fry mode for Zone 1 and set the temperature to 390 degrees F and the time to 28 minutes.
12. Select the "MATCH" button to copy the settings for Zone 2.
13. Initiate cooking by pressing the START/STOP button.
14. Flip the chicken pieces once cooked halfway through, and resume cooking.
15. Enjoy with pickle chips and a dollop of mayonnaise.

Nutrition:
- (Per serving) Calories 353 | Fat 5g |Sodium 818mg | Carbs 53.2g | Fiber 4.4g | Sugar 8g | Protein 17.3g

Balsamic Duck Breast

Servings: 2
Cooking Time: 20 Minutes.
Ingredients:
- 2 duck breasts
- 1 teaspoon parsley
- Salt and black pepper, to taste
- Marinade:
- 1 tablespoon olive oil
- ½ teaspoon French mustard
- 1 teaspoon dried garlic
- 2 teaspoons honey
- ½ teaspoon balsamic vinegar

Directions:
1. Mix olive oil, mustard, garlic, honey, and balsamic vinegar in a bowl.
2. Add duck breasts to the marinade and rub well.
3. Place one duck breast in each crisper plate.
4. Return the crisper plates to the Ninja Foodi Dual Zone Air Fryer.
5. Choose the Air Fry mode for Zone 1 and set the temperature to 360 degrees F and the time to 20 minutes.
6. Select the "MATCH" button to copy the settings for Zone 2.
7. Initiate cooking by pressing the START/STOP button.
8. Flip the duck breasts once cooked halfway through, then resume cooking.
9. Serve warm.

Nutrition:
- (Per serving) Calories 546 | Fat 33.1g |Sodium 1201mg | Carbs 30g | Fiber 2.4g | Sugar 9.7g | Protein 32g

Coconut Chicken Tenders With Broiled Utica Greens

Servings:4
Cooking Time: 25 Minutes
Ingredients:
- FOR THE CHICKEN TENDERS
- 2 tablespoons all-purpose flour
- 2 large eggs
- 1 cup unsweetened shredded coconut
- ¾ cup panko bread crumbs
- ½ teaspoon kosher salt
- 1½ pounds chicken tenders
- Nonstick cooking spray
- FOR THE UTICA GREENS
- 12 ounces frozen chopped escarole or Swiss chard, thawed and drained
- ¼ cup diced prosciutto
- 2 tablespoons chopped pickled cherry peppers
- ½ teaspoon garlic powder
- ½ teaspoon onion powder
- ¼ teaspoon kosher salt
- ¼ cup Italian-style bread crumbs
- ¼ cup grated Romano cheese
- Nonstick cooking spray

Directions:

1.   To prep the chicken tenders: Set up a breading station with three small shallow bowls. Place the flour in the first bowl. In the second bowl, beat the eggs. Combine the coconut, bread crumbs, and salt in the third bowl.

2.   Bread the chicken tenders in this order: First, coat them in the flour. Then, dip into the beaten egg. Finally, coat them in the coconut breading, gently pressing the breading into the chicken to help it adhere. Mist both sides of each tender with cooking spray.

3.   To prep the Utica greens: In the Zone 2 basket, mix the greens, prosciutto, cherry peppers, garlic powder, onion powder, and salt. Scatter the bread crumbs and Romano cheese over the top. Spritz the greens with cooking spray.

4.   To cook the chicken and greens: Install a crisper plate in the Zone 1 basket. Place the chicken tenders in the basket in a single layer and insert the basket in the unit. Insert the Zone 2 basket in the unit.

5.   Select Zone 1, select AIR FRY, set the temperature to 390°F, and set the time to 25 minutes.

6.   Select Zone 2, select AIR BROIL, set the temperature to 450°F, and set the time to 10 minutes. Select SMART FINISH.

7.   Press START/PAUSE to begin cooking.

8.   When cooking is complete, the chicken will be crispy and cooked through (an instant-read thermometer should read 165°F) and the greens should be warmed through and toasted on top. Serve warm.

Nutrition:

•   (Per serving) Calories: 527; Total fat: 26g; Saturated fat: 11g; Carbohydrates: 24g; Fiber: 6.5g; Protein: 50g; Sodium: 886mg

Thai Chicken With Cucumber And Chili Salad

Servings: 6
Cooking Time: 25 Minutes
Ingredients:

•   2 (570 g) small chickens, giblets discarded
•   1 tablespoon fish sauce
•   6 tablespoons chopped fresh coriander
•   2 teaspoons lime zest
•   1 teaspoon ground coriander
•   2 garlic cloves, minced
•   2 tablespoons packed light brown sugar
•   2 teaspoons vegetable oil
•   Salt and ground black pepper, to taste
•   1 English cucumber, halved lengthwise and sliced thin
•   1 Thai chili, stemmed, deseeded, and minced
•   2 tablespoons chopped dry-roasted peanuts
•   1 small shallot, sliced thinly
•   1 tablespoon lime juice
•   Lime wedges, for serving
•   Cooking spray

Directions:

1.   Arrange a chicken on a clean work surface, remove the backbone with kitchen shears, then pound the chicken breast to flat. Cut the breast in half. Repeat with the remaining chicken.

2.   Loose the breast and thigh skin with your fingers, then pat the chickens dry and pierce about 10 holes into the fat deposits of the chickens. Tuck the wings under the chickens.

3.   Combine 2 teaspoons of fish sauce, coriander, lime zest, coriander, garlic, 4 teaspoons of sugar, 1 teaspoon of vegetable oil, ½ teaspoon of salt, and ⅛ teaspoon of ground black pepper in a small bowl. Stir to mix well.

4.   Rub the fish sauce mixture under the breast and thigh skin of the game chickens, then let sit for 10 minutes to marinate.

5.   Preheat the air fryer to 200°C. Spritz the two air fryer baskets with cooking spray.

6.   Arrange the marinated chickens in the preheated air fryer, skin side down.

7.   Air fry for 15 minutes, then gently turn the game hens over and air fry for 10 more minutes or until the skin is golden brown and the internal temperature of the chickens reads at least 75°C.

8.   Meanwhile, combine all the remaining ingredients, except for the lime wedges, in a large bowl and sprinkle with salt and black pepper. Toss to mix well.

9.   Transfer the fried chickens on a large plate, then sit the salad aside and squeeze the lime wedges over before serving.

Coriander Lime Chicken Thighs

Servings: 4
Cooking Time: 22 Minutes
Ingredients:

•   4 bone-in, skin-on chicken thighs
•   1 teaspoon baking powder
•   ½ teaspoon garlic powder
•   2 teaspoons chili powder
•   1 teaspoon cumin
•   2 medium limes
•   5 g chopped fresh coriander

Directions:

1. Pat chicken thighs dry and sprinkle with baking powder.
2. In a small bowl, mix garlic powder, chili powder, and cumin and sprinkle evenly over thighs, gently rubbing on and under chicken skin.
3. Cut one lime in half and squeeze juice over thighs. Place chicken into the zone 1 air fryer drawer.
4. Adjust the temperature to 190ºC and roast for 22 minutes.
5. Cut other lime into four wedges for serving and garnish cooked chicken with wedges and coriander.

Chicken Potatoes

Servings: 4
Cooking Time: 22 Minutes.
Ingredients:
- 15 ounces canned potatoes drained
- 1 teaspoon olive oil
- 1 teaspoon Lawry's seasoned salt
- ⅛ teaspoons black pepper optional
- 8 ounces boneless chicken breast cubed
- ¼ teaspoon paprika
- ⅜ cup cheddar, shredded
- 4 bacon slices, cooked, cut into strips

Directions:
1. Dice the chicken into small pieces and toss them with olive oil and spices.
2. Drain and dice the potato pieces into smaller cubes.
3. Add potato to the chicken and mix well to coat.
4. Spread the mixture in the two crisper plates in a single layer.
5. Return the crisper plates to the Ninja Foodi Dual Zone Air Fryer.
6. Choose the Air Fry mode for Zone 1 and set the temperature to 390 degrees F and the time to 22 minutes.
7. Select the "MATCH" button to copy the settings for Zone 2.
8. Initiate cooking by pressing the START/STOP button.
9. Top the chicken and potatoes with cheese and bacon.
10. Return the crisper plates to the Ninja Foodi Dual Zone Air Fryer.
11. Select the Max Crisp mode for Zone 1 and set the temperature to 300 degrees F and the time to 5 minutes.
12. Initiate cooking by pressing the START/STOP button.
13. Repeat the same step for Zone 2 to broil the potatoes and chicken in the right drawer.
14. Enjoy with dried herbs on top.

Nutrition:
- (Per serving) Calories 346 | Fat 16.1g |Sodium 882mg | Carbs 1.3g | Fiber 0.5g | Sugar 0.5g | Protein 48.2g

Sesame Ginger Chicken

Servings: 4
Cooking Time: 30 Minutes
Ingredients:
- 4 ounces green beans
- 1 tablespoon canola oil
- 1½ pounds boneless, skinless chicken breasts
- 1/3 cup prepared sesame-ginger sauce
- Kosher salt, to taste
- Black pepper, to taste

Directions:
1. Toss the green beans with a teaspoon of salt and pepper in a medium mixing bowl.
2. Place a crisper plate in each drawer. Place the green beans in the zone 1 drawer and insert it into the unit. Place the chicken breasts in the zone 2 drawer and place it inside the unit.
3. Select zone 1, then AIR FRY, and set the temperature to 390 degrees F/ 200 degrees C with a 10-minute timer. Select zone 2, then AIR FRY, and set the temperature to 390 degrees F/ 200 degrees C with an 18-minute timer. Select SYNC. To begin cooking, press the START/STOP button.
4. Press START/STOP to pause the unit when the zone 2 timer reaches 9 minutes. Remove the chicken from the drawer and toss it in the sesame ginger sauce. To resume cooking, re-insert the drawer into the unit and press START/STOP.
5. When cooking is complete, serve the chicken breasts and green beans straight away.

Nutrition:
- (Per serving) Calories 143 | Fat 7g | Sodium 638mg | Carbs 11.6g | Fiber 1.4g | Sugar 8.5g | Protein 11.1g

Chicken & Veggies

Servings: 4
Cooking Time: 10 Minutes
Ingredients:

- 450g chicken breast, boneless & cut into pieces
- 2 garlic cloves, minced
- 15ml olive oil
- 239g frozen mix vegetables
- 1 tbsp Italian seasoning
- ½ tsp chilli powder
- ½ tsp garlic powder
- Pepper
- Salt

Directions:

1. In a bowl, toss chicken with remaining ingredients until well coated.
2. Insert a crisper plate in the Ninja Foodi air fryer baskets.
3. Add chicken and vegetables in both baskets.
4. Select zone 1 then select "air fry" mode and set the temperature to 390 degrees F for 10 minutes. Press "match" to match zone 2 settings to zone 1. Press "start/stop" to begin.

Nutrition:

- (Per serving) Calories 221 | Fat 7.6g |Sodium 126mg | Carbs 10.6g | Fiber 3.3g | Sugar 2.7g | Protein 26.3g

Chicken And Vegetable Fajitas

Servings: 6
Cooking Time: 23 Minutes
Ingredients:

- Chicken:
- 450 g boneless, skinless chicken thighs, cut crosswise into thirds
- 1 tablespoon vegetable oil
- 4½ teaspoons taco seasoning
- Vegetables:
- 50 g sliced onion
- 150 g sliced bell pepper
- 1 or 2 jalapeños, quartered lengthwise
- 1 tablespoon vegetable oil
- ½ teaspoon kosher salt
- ½ teaspoon ground cumin
- For Serving:
- Tortillas
- Sour cream
- Shredded cheese
- Guacamole
- Salsa

Directions:

1. For the chicken: In a medium bowl, toss together the chicken, vegetable oil, and taco seasoning to coat. 2. For the vegetables: In a separate bowl, toss together the onion, bell pepper, jalapeño, vegetable oil, salt, and cumin to coat. 3. Place the chicken in the air fryer basket. Set the air fryer to (190ºC for 10 minutes. Add the vegetables to the basket, toss everything together to blend the seasonings, and set the air fryer for 13 minutes more. Use a meat thermometer to ensure the chicken has reached an internal temperature of 75ºC. 4. Transfer the chicken and vegetables to a serving platter. Serve with tortillas and the desired fajita fixings.

Chicken Strips With Satay Sauce

Servings: 4
Cooking Time: 10 Minutes
Ingredients:

- 4 (170 g) boneless, skinless chicken breasts, sliced into 16 (1-inch) strips
- 1 teaspoon fine sea salt
- 1 teaspoon paprika
- Sauce:
- 60 g creamy almond butter (or sunflower seed butter for nut-free)
- 2 tablespoons chicken broth
- 1½ tablespoons coconut vinegar or unseasoned rice vinegar
- 1 clove garlic, minced
- 1 teaspoon peeled and minced fresh ginger
- ½ teaspoon hot sauce
- ⅛ teaspoon stevia glycerite, or 2 to 3 drops liquid stevia
- For Garnish/Serving (Optional):
- 15 g chopped coriander leaves
- Red pepper flakes
- Sea salt flakes
- Thinly sliced red, orange, and yellow bell peppers
- Special Equipment:
- 16 wooden or bamboo skewers, soaked in water for 15 minutes

Directions:

1. Spray the zone 1 air fryer drawer with avocado oil. Preheat the air fryer to 200ºC. 2. Thread the chicken strips onto the skewers. Season on all sides with the salt and paprika. Place the chicken skewers in the air fryer drawer and air fry for 5 minutes, flip, and cook for another 5 minutes, until the chicken is cooked through and the internal temperature reaches 76ºC. 3. While the chicken skewers cook, make the sauce: In a medium-sized bowl, stir together all the sauce ingredients until well combined. Taste and adjust the sweetness and heat to your liking. 4. Garnish the chicken with coriander, red pepper flakes, and salt flakes, if desired, and serve with sliced bell peppers, if desired. Serve the sauce on the side. 5. Store leftovers in an airtight container in the fridge for up to 4 days or in the freezer for up to a month. Reheat in a preheated 180ºC air fryer for 3 minutes per side, or until heated through.

Juicy Duck Breast

Servings: 1
Cooking Time: 20 Minutes
Ingredients:
- ½ duck breast
- Salt and black pepper, to taste
- 2 tablespoons plum sauce

Directions:
1. Rub the duck breast with black pepper and salt.
2. Place the duck breast in air fryer basket 1 and add plum sauce on top.
3. Return the basket to the Ninja Foodi 2 Baskets Air Fryer.
4. Choose the "Air Fry" mode for Zone 1 and set the temperature to 400 degrees F and 20 minutes of cooking time.
5. Initiate cooking by pressing the START/PAUSE BUTTON.
6. Flip the duck breast once cooked halfway through.
7. Serve warm.

Nutrition:
- (Per serving) Calories 379 | Fat 19g |Sodium 184mg | Carbs 12.3g | Fiber 0.6g | Sugar 2g | Protein 37.7g

Almond Chicken

Servings: 4
Cooking Time: 25 Minutes
Ingredients:
- 2 large eggs
- ½ cup buttermilk
- 2 teaspoons garlic salt
- 1 teaspoon pepper
- 2 cups slivered almonds, finely chopped
- 4 boneless, skinless chicken breast halves (6 ounces each)

Directions:
1. Whisk together the egg, buttermilk, garlic salt, and pepper in a small bowl.
2. In another small bowl, place the almonds.
3. Dip the chicken in the egg mixture, then roll it in the almonds, patting it down to help the coating stick.
4. Install a crisper plate in both drawers. Place half the chicken breasts in the zone 1 drawer and half in zone 2's, then insert the drawers into the unit.
5. Select zone 1, select AIR FRY, set temperature to 390 degrees F/ 200 degrees C, and set time to 22 minutes. Select MATCH to match zone 2 settings to zone 1. Press the START/STOP button to begin cooking.
6. When the time reaches 11 minutes, press START/STOP to pause the unit. Remove the drawers and flip the chicken. Re-insert the drawers into the unit and press START/STOP to resume cooking.
7. When cooking is complete, remove the chicken.

Nutrition:
- (Per serving) Calories 353 | Fat 18g | Sodium 230mg | Carbs 6g | Fiber 2g | Sugar 3g | Protein 41g

Whole Chicken

Servings: 8
Cooking Time: 20 Minutes
Ingredients:
- 1 whole chicken (about 2.8 pounds), cut in half
- 4 tablespoons olive oil
- 2 teaspoons paprika
- 1 teaspoon garlic powder
- 1 teaspoon onion powder
- Salt and pepper, to taste

Directions:
1. Mix the olive oil, paprika, garlic powder, and onion powder together in a bowl.

2. Place the chicken halves, breast side up, on a plate. Spread a teaspoon or two of the oil mix all over the halves using either your hands or a brush. Season with salt and pepper.

3. Flip the chicken halves over and repeat on the other side. You'll want to reserve a little of the oil mix for later, but other than that, use it liberally.

4. Install a crisper plate in both drawers. Place one half of the chicken in the zone 1 drawer and the other half in the zone 2 drawer, then insert the drawers into the unit.

5. Select zone 1, select AIR FRY, set temperature to 390 degrees F/ 200 degrees C, and set time to 20 minutes. Select MATCH to match zone 2 settings to zone 1. Press the START/STOP button to begin cooking.

6. When cooking is done, check the internal temperature of the chicken. It should read 165°F. If the chicken isn't done, add more cooking time.

Nutrition:

- (Per serving) Calories 131 | Fat 8g | Sodium 51mg | Carbs 0g | Fiber 0g | Sugar 0g | Protein 14g

Juicy Paprika Chicken Breast

Servings: 4
Cooking Time: 30 Minutes
Ingredients:

- Oil, for spraying
- 4 (170 g) boneless, skinless chicken breasts
- 1 tablespoon olive oil
- 1 tablespoon paprika
- 1 tablespoon packed light brown sugar
- ½ teaspoon cayenne pepper
- ½ teaspoon onion powder
- ½ teaspoon granulated garlic

Directions:

1. Line the two air fryer drawers with parchment and spray lightly with oil.
2. Brush the chicken with the olive oil.
3. In a small bowl, mix together the paprika, brown sugar, cayenne pepper, onion powder, and garlic and sprinkle it over the chicken.
4. Place the chicken in the two prepared drawers.
5. Air fry at 180°C for 15 minutes, flip, and cook for another 15 minutes, or until the internal temperature reaches 76°C. Serve immediately.

Chicken With Pineapple And Peach

Servings: 4
Cooking Time: 14 To 15 Minutes
Ingredients:

- 1 (450 g) low-sodium boneless, skinless chicken breasts, cut into 1-inch pieces
- 1 medium red onion, chopped
- 1 (230 g) can pineapple chunks, drained, 60 ml juice reserved
- 1 tablespoon peanut oil or safflower oil
- 1 peach, peeled, pitted, and cubed
- 1 tablespoon cornflour
- ½ teaspoon ground ginger
- ¼ teaspoon ground allspice
- Brown rice, cooked (optional)

Directions:

1. Preheat the air fryer to 195°C.
2. In a medium metal bowl, mix the chicken, red onion, pineapple, and peanut oil. Bake in the air fryer for 9 minutes. Remove and stir.
3. Add the peach and return the bowl to the air fryer. Bake for 3 minutes more. Remove and stir again.
4. In a small bowl, whisk the reserved pineapple juice, the cornflour, ginger, and allspice well. Add to the chicken mixture and stir to combine.
5. Bake for 2 to 3 minutes more, or until the chicken reaches an internal temperature of 75°C on a meat thermometer and the sauce is slightly thickened.
6. Serve immediately over hot cooked brown rice, if desired.

Air Fried Chicken Legs

Servings: 4
Cooking Time: 10 Minutes
Ingredients:

- 8 chicken legs
- 2 tablespoons olive oil
- 1 teaspoon salt
- 1 teaspoon black pepper

- 1 teaspoon smoked paprika
- 1 teaspoon garlic powder
- 1 teaspoon dried parsley

Directions:
1. Mix chicken with oil, herbs and spices in a bowl.
2. Divide the chicken legs in the air fryer baskets.
3. Return the air fryer basket 1 to Zone 1, and basket 2 to Zone 2 of the Ninja Foodi 2-Basket Air Fryer.
4. Choose the "Air Fry" mode for Zone 1 at 400 degrees F and 10 minutes of cooking time.
5. Select the "MATCH COOK" option to copy the settings for Zone 2.
6. Initiate cooking by pressing the START/PAUSE BUTTON.
7. Flip the chicken once cooked halfway through.
8. Serve warm.

Nutrition:
- (Per serving) Calories 220 | Fat 13g |Sodium 542mg | Carbs 0.9g | Fiber 0.3g | Sugar 0.2g | Protein 25.6g

Spicy Chicken Wings

Servings: 8
Cooking Time: 30 Minutes
Ingredients:
- 900g chicken wings
- 1 tsp black pepper
- 12g brown sugar
- 1 tbsp chilli powder
- 57g butter, melted
- 1 tsp smoked paprika
- 1 tsp garlic powder
- 1 tsp salt

Directions:
1. In a bowl, toss chicken wings with remaining ingredients until well coated.
2. Insert a crisper plate in the Ninja Foodi air fryer baskets.
3. Add the chicken wings to both baskets.
4. Select zone 1, then select "air fry" mode and set the temperature to 355 degrees F for 30 minutes. Press "match" to match zone 2 settings to zone 1. Press "start/stop" to begin. Turn halfway through.

Nutrition:
- (Per serving) Calories 276 | Fat 14.4g |Sodium 439mg | Carbs 2.2g | Fiber 0.5g | Sugar 1.3g | Protein 33.1g

Chicken Tenders And Curly Fries

Servings: 4
Cooking Time: 35 Minutes
Ingredients:
- 1-pound frozen chicken tenders
- 1-pound frozen curly French fries
- Dipping sauces of your choice

Directions:
1. Place a crisper plate in each drawer. In the zone 1 drawer, place the chicken tenders, then place the drawer into the unit.
2. Fill the zone 2 drawer with the curly French fries, then place the drawer in the unit.
3. Select zone 1, then AIR FRY, and set the temperature to 390 degrees F/ 200 degrees C with a 22-minute timer. Select zone 2, then AIR FRY, and set the temperature to 400 degrees F/ 200 degrees C with a 30-minute timer. Select SYNC. To begin cooking, press the START/STOP button.
4. Press START/STOP to pause the device when the zone 1 and 2 times reach 8 minutes. Shake the drawers for 10 seconds after removing them from the unit. To resume cooking, re-insert the drawers into the unit and press START/STOP.
5. Enjoy!

Nutrition:
- (Per serving) Calories 500 | Fat 19.8g | Sodium 680mg | Carbs 50.1g | Fiber 4.1g | Sugar 0g | Protein 27.9g

Glazed Thighs With French Fries

Servings:3
Cooking Time:35
Ingredients:

- 2 tablespoons of Soy Sauce
- Salt, to taste
- 1 teaspoon of Worcestershire Sauce
- 2 teaspoons Brown Sugar
- 1 teaspoon of Ginger, paste
- 1 teaspoon of Garlic, paste
- 6 Boneless Chicken Thighs
- 1 pound of hand-cut potato fries
- 2 tablespoons of canola oil

Directions:

1. Coat the French fries well with canola oil.
2. Season it with salt.
3. In a small bowl, combine the soy sauce, Worcestershire sauce, brown sugar, ginger, and garlic.
4. Place the chicken in this marinade and let it sit for 40 minutes.
5. Put the chicken thighs into the zone 1 basket and fries into the zone 2 basket.
6. Press button 1 for the first basket, and set it to ROAST mode at 350 degrees F for 35 minutes.
7. For the second basket hit 2 and set time to 30 minutes at 360 degrees F, by selecting AIR FRY mode.
8. Once the cooking cycle completely take out the fries and chicken and serve it hot.

Nutrition:

- (Per serving) Calories 858| Fat39g | Sodium 1509mg | Carbs 45.6g | Fiber 4.4g | Sugar3 g | Protein 90g

Bruschetta Chicken

Servings: 4
Cooking Time: 20 Minutes
Ingredients:

- Bruschetta Stuffing:
- 1 tomato, diced
- 3 tablespoons balsamic vinegar
- 1 teaspoon Italian seasoning
- 2 tablespoons chopped fresh basil
- 3 garlic cloves, minced
- 2 tablespoons extra-virgin olive oil
- Chicken:
- 4 (115 g) boneless, skinless chicken breasts, cut 4 slits each
- 1 teaspoon Italian seasoning
- Chicken seasoning or rub, to taste
- Cooking spray

Directions:

1. Preheat the air fryer to 190º. Spritz the two air fryer baskets with cooking spray.
2. Combine the ingredients for the bruschetta stuffing in a bowl. Stir to mix well. Set aside.
3. Rub the chicken breasts with Italian seasoning and chicken seasoning on a clean work surface.
4. Arrange the chicken breasts, slits side up, in a single layer in the two air fryer baskets and spritz with cooking spray.
5. Air fry for 7 minutes, then open the air fryer and fill the slits in the chicken with the bruschetta stuffing. Cook for another 3 minutes or until the chicken is well browned.
6. Serve immediately.

Asian Chicken

Servings: 4
Cooking Time: 12 Minutes
Ingredients:

- 8 chicken thighs, boneless
- 4 garlic cloves, minced
- 85g honey
- 120ml soy sauce
- 1 tsp dried oregano
- 2 tbsp parsley, chopped
- 1 tbsp ketchup

Directions:

1. Add chicken and remaining ingredients in a bowl and mix until well coated. Cover and place in the refrigerator for 6 hours.
2. Insert a crisper plate in the Ninja Foodi air fryer baskets.
3. Remove the chicken from the marinade and place them in both baskets.
4. Select zone 1 then select "air fry" mode and set the temperature to 390 degrees F for 12 minutes. Press "match" to match zone 2 settings to zone 1. Press "start/stop" to begin.

Nutrition:

- (Per serving) Calories 646 | Fat 21.7g |Sodium 2092mg | Carbs 22.2g | Fiber 0.6g | Sugar 18.9g | Protein 86.9g

Buttermilk Fried Chicken

Servings: 6
Cooking Time: 30 Minutes
Ingredients:

- 1½ pounds boneless, skinless chicken thighs
- 2 cups buttermilk
- 1 cup all-purpose flour
- 1 tablespoon seasoned salt
- ½ tablespoon ground black pepper
- 1 cup panko breadcrumbs
- Cooking spray

Directions:

1. Place the chicken thighs in a shallow baking dish. Cover with the buttermilk. Refrigerate for 4 hours or overnight.
2. In a large gallon-sized resealable bag, combine the flour, seasoned salt, and pepper.
3. Remove the chicken from the buttermilk but don't discard the mixture.
4. Add the chicken to the bag and shake well to coat.
5. Dip the thighs in the buttermilk again, then coat in the panko breadcrumbs.
6. Install a crisper plate in each drawer. Place half the chicken thighs in the zone 1 drawer and half in zone 2's, then insert the drawers into the unit.
7. Select zone 1, select AIR FRY, set temperature to 390 degrees F/ 200 degrees C, and set time to 30 minutes. Select MATCH to match zone 2 settings to zone 1. Press the START/STOP button to begin cooking.
8. When the time reaches 15 minutes, press START/STOP to pause the unit. Remove the drawers and flip the chicken. Re-insert the drawers into the unit and press START/STOP to resume cooking.
9. When cooking is complete, remove the chicken.

Nutrition:

- (Per serving) Calories 335 | Fat 12.8g | Sodium 687mg | Carbs 33.1g | Fiber 0.4g | Sugar 4g | Protein 24.5g

Tex-mex Chicken Roll-ups

Servings: 8
Cooking Time: 14 To 17 Minutes
Ingredients:

- 900 g boneless, skinless chicken breasts or thighs
- 1 teaspoon chili powder
- ½ teaspoon smoked paprika
- ½ teaspoon ground cumin
- Sea salt and freshly ground black pepper, to taste
- 170 g Monterey Jack cheese, shredded
- 115 g canned diced green chilies
- Avocado oil spray

Directions:

1. Place the chicken in a large zip-top bag or between two pieces of plastic wrap. Using a meat mallet or heavy skillet, pound the chicken until it is about ¼ inch thick.
2. In a small bowl, combine the chili powder, smoked paprika, cumin, and salt and pepper to taste. Sprinkle both sides of the chicken with the seasonings.
3. Sprinkle the chicken with the Monterey Jack cheese, then the diced green chilies.
4. Roll up each piece of chicken from the long side, tucking in the ends as you go. Secure the roll-up with a toothpick.
5. Set the air fryer to 180ºC. . Spray the outside of the chicken with avocado oil. Place the chicken in a single layer in the two baskets, and roast for 7 minutes. Flip and cook for another 7 to 10 minutes, until an instant-read thermometer reads 70ºC.
6. Remove the chicken from the air fryer and allow it to rest for about 5 minutes before serving.

Chapter 6 : Beef, Pork, And Lamb Recipes

Taco Seasoned Steak

Servings: 6
Cooking Time: 30 Minutes
Ingredients:
- 1 (1-pound) flank steaks
- 1½ tablespoons taco seasoning rub

Directions:
1. Grease each basket of "Zone 1" and "Zone 2" of Ninja Foodi 2-Basket Air Fryer.
2. Press "Zone 1" and "Zone 2" and then rotate the knob for each zone to select "Bake".
3. Set the temperature to 420 degrees F/ 215 degrees C for both zones and then set the time for 5 minutes to preheat.
4. Rub the steaks with taco seasoning evenly.
5. After preheating, arrange the steak into the basket of each zone.
6. Slide each basket into Air Fryer and set the time for 30 minutes.
7. After cooking time is completed, remove the steaks from Air Fryer and place onto a cutting board for about 10-15 minutes before slicing.
8. With a sharp knife, cut each steak into desired size slices and serve.

Cinnamon-beef Kofta

Servings: 12 Koftas
Cooking Time: 13 Minutes
Ingredients:
- 680 g lean beef mince
- 1 teaspoon onion granules
- ¾ teaspoon ground cinnamon
- ¾ teaspoon ground dried turmeric
- 1 teaspoon ground cumin
- ¾ teaspoon salt
- ¼ teaspoon cayenne
- 12 (3½- to 4-inch-long) cinnamon sticks
- Cooking spray

Directions:
1. Preheat the air fryer to 192°C. Spritz the two air fryer drawers with cooking spray.
2. Combine all the ingredients, except for the cinnamon sticks, in a large bowl. Toss to mix well.
3. Divide and shape the mixture into 12 balls, then wrap each ball around each cinnamon stick and leave a quarter of the length uncovered.
4. Arrange the beef-cinnamon sticks in the preheated air fryer and spritz with cooking spray.
5. Air fry for 13 minutes or until the beef is browned. Flip the sticks halfway through.
6. Serve immediately.

Sausage And Cauliflower Arancini

Servings: 6
Cooking Time: 28 To 32 Minutes
Ingredients:
- Avocado oil spray
- 170 g Italian-seasoned sausage, casings removed
- 60 ml diced onion
- 1 teaspoon minced garlic
- 1 teaspoon dried thyme
- Sea salt and freshly ground black pepper, to taste
- 120 ml cauliflower rice
- 85 g cream cheese
- 110 g Cheddar cheese, shredded
- 1 large egg
- 120 ml finely ground blanched almond flour
- 60 ml finely grated Parmesan cheese
- Keto-friendly marinara sauce, for serving

Directions:
1. Spray a large skillet with oil and place it over medium-high heat. Once the skillet is hot, put the sausage in the skillet and cook for 7 minutes, breaking up the meat with the back of a spoon.
2. Reduce the heat to medium and add the onion. Cook for 5 minutes, then add the garlic, thyme, and salt and pepper to taste. Cook for 1 minute more.
3. Add the cauliflower rice and cream cheese to the skillet. Cook for 7 minutes, stirring frequently, until the cream cheese melts and the cauliflower is tender.
4. Remove the skillet from the heat and stir in the Cheddar cheese. Using a cookie scoop, form the mixture into 1½-inch balls. Place the balls on a parchment paper-lined baking sheet. Freeze for 30 minutes.
5. Place the egg in a shallow bowl and beat it with a fork. In a separate bowl, stir together the almond flour and Parmesan cheese.

6. Dip the cauliflower balls into the egg, then coat them with the almond flour mixture, gently pressing the mixture to the balls to adhere.

7. Set the air fryer to 204ºC. Spray the cauliflower rice balls with oil, and arrange them in a single layer in the two air fryer drawers. Air fry for 5 minutes. Flip the rice balls and spray them with more oil. Air fry for 3 to 7 minutes longer, until the balls are golden brown.

8. Serve warm with marinara sauce.

Rosemary And Garlic Lamb Chops

Servings: 4
Cooking Time: 15 Minutes
Ingredients:

- 8 lamb chops
- 3 tablespoons olive oil
- 2 tablespoons chopped fresh rosemary
- 1 teaspoon garlic powder or 3 cloves garlic, minced
- 1 teaspoon salt, or to taste
- ½ teaspoon black pepper, or to taste

Directions:

1. Dry the lamb chops with a paper towel.
2. Combine the olive oil, rosemary, garlic, salt, and pepper in a large mixing bowl. Toss the lamb in the marinade gently to coat it. Cover and set aside to marinate for 1 hour or up to overnight.
3. Install a crisper plate in both drawers. Place half the lamb chops in the zone 1 drawer and half in zone 2's, then insert the drawers into the unit.
4. Select zone 1, select AIR FRY, set temperature to 390 degrees F/ 200 degrees C, and set time to 15 minutes. Select MATCH to match zone 2 settings to zone 1. Press the START/STOP button to begin cooking.
5. When the time reaches 10 minutes, press START/STOP to pause the unit. Remove the drawers and flip the chops. Re-insert the drawers into the unit and press START/STOP to resume cooking.
6. Serve and enjoy!

Nutrition:

- (Per serving) Calories 427 | Fat 34g | Sodium 668mg | Carbs 1g | Fiber 1g | Sugar 1g | Protein 31g

Beef & Broccoli

Servings:4
Cooking Time:12
Ingredients:

- 12 ounces of teriyaki sauce, divided
- ½ tablespoon garlic powder
- ¼ cup of soy sauce
- 1 pound raw sirloin steak, thinly sliced
- 2 cups broccoli, cut into florets
- 2 teaspoons of olive oil
- Salt and black pepper, to taste

Directions:

1. Take a zip-lock plastic bag and mix teriyaki sauce, salt, garlic powder, black pepper, soy sauce, and olive oil.
2. Marinate the beef in it for 2 hours.
3. Then drain the beef from the marinade.
4. Now toss the broccoli with oil, teriyaki sauce, and salt and black pepper.
5. Put it in a zone 1 basket
6. Now for the zone, 1 basket set it to AIRFRY mode at 400 degrees F for 15 minutes.
7. Place the steak in a zone 2 basket and set it to AIR FRY mode at 375 degrees F for 10-12 minutes.
8. Hit start and let the cooking cycle completes.
9. Once it's done take out the beef and broccoli and
10. serve immediately with leftover teriyaki sauce and cooked rice.

Nutrition:

- (Per serving) Calories 344| Fat 10g| Sodium 4285mg | Carbs18.2 g | Fiber 1.5g| Sugar 13.3g | Protein42 g

Bbq Pork Spare Ribs

Servings: 8
Cooking Time: 30 Minutes
Ingredients:

- ½ cup honey, divided
- 1½ cups BBQ sauce
- 4 tablespoons tomato ketchup
- 2 tablespoons Worcestershire sauce
- 2 tablespoons low-sodium soy sauce
- 1 teaspoon garlic powder

- Freshly ground white pepper, as required
- 3½ pounds pork ribs

Directions:
1. In a bowl, mix together 6 tablespoons of honey and the remaining ingredients except pork ribs.
2. Add the pork ribs and coat with the mixture generously.
3. Refrigerate to marinate for about 20 minutes.
4. Grease each basket of "Zone 1" and "Zone 2" of Ninja Foodi 2-Basket Air Fryer.
5. Press "Zone 1" and "Zone 2" and then rotate the knob for each zone to select "Air Fry".
6. Set the temperature to 355 degrees F/ 180 degrees C for both zones and then set the time for 5 minutes to preheat.
7. After preheating, arrange the ribs into the basket of each zone.
8. Slide each basket into Air Fryer and set the time for 26 minutes.
9. While cooking, flip the ribs once halfway through.
10. After cooking time is completed, remove the ribs from Air Fryer and place onto serving plates.
11. Drizzle with the remaining honey and serve immediately.

Mojito Lamb Chops

Servings: 2
Cooking Time: 5 Minutes
Ingredients:
- Marinade:
- 2 teaspoons grated lime zest
- 120 ml lime juice
- 60 ml avocado oil
- 60 ml chopped fresh mint leaves
- 4 cloves garlic, roughly chopped
- 2 teaspoons fine sea salt
- ½ teaspoon ground black pepper
- 4 (1-inch-thick) lamb chops
- Sprigs of fresh mint, for garnish (optional)
- Lime slices, for serving (optional)

Directions:
1. Make the marinade: Place all the ingredients for the marinade in a food processor or blender and purée until mostly smooth with a few small chunks. Transfer half of the marinade to a shallow dish and set the other half aside for serving. Add the lamb to the shallow dish, cover, and place in the refrigerator to marinate for at least 2 hours or overnight. 2. Spray the two air fryer drawers with avocado oil. Preheat the air fryer to 200ºC. 3. Remove the chops from the marinade and place them in the two air fryer drawers. Air fry for 5 minutes, or until the internal temperature reaches 64ºC for medium doneness. 4. Allow the chops to rest for 10 minutes before serving with the rest of the marinade as a sauce. Garnish with fresh mint leaves and serve with lime slices, if desired. Best served fresh.

Pork Chops With Apples

Servings: 2
Cooking Time: 15 Minutes
Ingredients:
- ½ small red cabbage, sliced
- 1 apple, sliced
- 1 sweet onion, sliced
- 2 tablespoons oil
- ½ teaspoon cumin
- ½ teaspoon paprika
- Salt and black pepper, to taste
- 2 boneless pork chops (1″ thick)

Directions:
1. Toss pork chops with apple and the rest of the ingredients in a bowl.
2. Divide the mixture in the air fryer baskets.
3. Return the air fryer basket 1 to Zone 1, and basket 2 to Zone 2 of the Ninja Foodi 2-Basket Air Fryer.
4. Choose the "Air Fry" mode for Zone 1 and set the temperature to 400 degrees F and 15 minutes of cooking time.
5. Select the "MATCH COOK" option to copy the settings for Zone 2.
6. Initiate cooking by pressing the START/PAUSE BUTTON.
7. Serve warm.

Nutrition:
- (Per serving) Calories 374 | Fat 25g |Sodium 275mg | Carbs 7.3g | Fiber 0g | Sugar 6g | Protein 12.3g

Minute Steak Roll-ups

Servings: 4
Cooking Time: 8 To 10 Minutes
Ingredients:

- 4 minute steaks (170 g each)
- 1 (450 g) bottle Italian dressing
- 1 teaspoon salt
- ½ teaspoon freshly ground black pepper
- 120 ml finely chopped brown onion
- 120 ml finely chopped green pepper
- 120 ml finely chopped mushrooms
- 1 to 2 tablespoons oil

Directions:

1. In a large resealable bag or airtight storage container, combine the steaks and Italian dressing. Seal the bag and refrigerate to marinate for 2 hours.
2. Remove the steaks from the marinade and place them on a cutting board. Discard the marinade. Evenly season the steaks with salt and pepper.
3. In a small bowl, stir together the onion, pepper, and mushrooms. Sprinkle the onion mixture evenly over the steaks. Roll up the steaks, jelly roll-style, and secure with toothpicks.
4. Preheat the air fryer to 204ºC.
5. Place the steaks in the two air fryer drawers.
6. Cook for 4 minutes. Flip the steaks and spritz them with oil. Cook for 4 to 6 minutes more until the internal temperature reaches 64ºC. Let rest for 5 minutes before serving.

Mustard Rubbed Lamb Chops

Servings: 4
Cooking Time: 31 Minutes.
Ingredients:

- 1 teaspoon Dijon mustard
- 1 teaspoon olive oil
- ½ teaspoon soy sauce
- ½ teaspoon garlic, minced
- ½ teaspoon cumin powder
- ½ teaspoon cayenne pepper
- ½ teaspoon Italian spice blend
- ⅛ teaspoon salt
- 4 pieces of lamb chops

Directions:

1. Mix Dijon mustard, soy sauce, olive oil, garlic, cumin powder, cayenne pepper, Italian spice blend, and salt in a medium bowl and mix well.
2. Place lamb chops into a Ziploc bag and pour in the marinade.
3. Press the air out of the bag and seal tightly.
4. Press the marinade around the lamb chops to coat.
5. Keep then in the fridge and marinate for at least 30 minutes, up to overnight.
6. Place 2 chops in each of the crisper plate and spray them with cooking oil.
7. Return the crisper plate to the Ninja Foodi Dual Zone Air Fryer.
8. Select the Roast mode for Zone 1 and set the temperature to 350 degrees F and the time to 27 minutes.
9. Select the "MATCH" button to copy the settings for Zone 2.
10. Initiate cooking by pressing the START/STOP button.
11. Flip the chops once cooked halfway through, and resume cooking.
12. Switch the Roast mode to Max Crisp mode and cook for 5 minutes.
13. Serve warm.

Nutrition:

- (Per serving) Calories 264 | Fat 17g |Sodium 129mg | Carbs 0.9g | Fiber 0.3g | Sugar 0g | Protein 27g

Italian Sausage And Cheese Meatballs

Servings: 4
Cooking Time: 20 Minutes
Ingredients:

- 230 g sausage meat with Italian seasoning added to taste
- 230 g 85% lean beef mince
- 120 ml shredded sharp Cheddar cheese
- ½ teaspoon onion granules
- ½ teaspoon garlic powder
- ½ teaspoon black pepper

Directions:

1. In a large bowl, gently mix the sausage meat, beef mince, cheese, onion granules, garlic powder, and pepper until well combined.
2. Form the mixture into 16 meatballs. Place the meatballs in a single layer in the two air fryer drawers. Set the air fryer to 176°C for 20 minutes, turning the meatballs halfway through the cooking time. Use a meat thermometer to ensure the meatballs have reached an internal temperature of 72°C .

Roast Beef With Yorkshire Pudding

Servings:6
Cooking Time: 40 Minutes
Ingredients:

- FOR THE ROAST BEEF
- 3-pound beef roast, trimmed
- 1 tablespoon vegetable oil
- ½ teaspoon kosher salt
- ½ teaspoon freshly ground black pepper
- ½ teaspoon garlic powder
- ½ teaspoon onion powder
- ½ teaspoon dried thyme

- FOR THE YORKSHIRE PUDDING
- 3 large eggs
- ¾ cup whole milk
- 2 tablespoons beef broth
- ¾ cup all-purpose flour
- ½ teaspoon kosher salt
- 2 teaspoons unsalted butter

Directions:
1. To prep the roast beef: If necessary, trim the beef roast to fit in the Zone 1 basket. Rub the beef with the oil.
2. In a small bowl, combine the salt, black pepper, garlic powder, onion powder, and thyme. Rub the spice mixture all over the beef roast.
3. To prep the Yorkshire pudding: In a large bowl, whisk the eggs, milk, and beef broth until well combined. Whisk in the flour and salt to form a thin batter.
4. To cook the beef and Yorkshire pudding: Install a crisper plate in the Zone 1 basket. Place the beef roast in the basket and insert the basket in the unit. Place the butter in the Zone 2 basket and insert the basket in the unit.
5. Select Zone 1, select AIR FRY, set the temperature to 375°F, and set the time to 40 minutes for a medium-rare roast (set to 50 minutes for medium or 60 minutes for well done).
6. Select Zone 2, select BAKE, set the temperature to 400°F, and set the time to 20 minutes. Select SMART FINISH.
7. Press START/PAUSE to begin cooking.
8. When the Zone 2 timer reads 18 minutes, press START/PAUSE. Remove the basket and pour the batter into it. Reinsert the basket and press START/PAUSE to resume cooking.
9. When cooking is complete, the beef should be cooked to your liking and the Yorkshire pudding should be fluffy on the edges and set in the center.
10. Remove the beef from the basket and let rest for at least 15 minutes before slicing.
11. Cut the Yorkshire pudding into 6 servings and serve the sliced beef on top.
Nutrition:
- (Per serving) Calories: 517; Total fat: 26g; Saturated fat: 9.5g; Carbohydrates: 13g; Fiber: 0.5g; Protein: 52g; Sodium: 354mg

Sausage And Pork Meatballs

Servings: 8
Cooking Time: 8 To 12 Minutes
Ingredients:

- 1 large egg
- 1 teaspoon gelatin
- 450 g pork mince
- 230 g Italian-seasoned sausage, casings removed, crumbled
- 80 ml Parmesan cheese
- 60 ml finely diced onion

- 1 tablespoon tomato paste
- 1 teaspoon minced garlic
- 1 teaspoon dried oregano
- ¼ teaspoon red pepper flakes
- Sea salt and freshly ground black pepper, to taste
- Keto-friendly marinara sauce, for serving

Directions:
1. Beat the egg in a small bowl and sprinkle with the gelatin. Allow to sit for 5 minutes.
2. In a large bowl, combine the pork mince, sausage, Parmesan, onion, tomato paste, garlic, oregano, and red pepper flakes. Season with salt and black pepper.
3. Stir the gelatin mixture, then add it to the other ingredients and, using clean hands, mix to ensure that everything is well combined. Form into 1½-inch round meatballs.
4. Set the air fryer to 204°C. Place the meatballs in the two air fryer drawers in a single layer. Air fry for 5 minutes. Flip and cook for 3 to 7 minutes more, or until an instant-read thermometer reads 72°C.

Roasted Beef

Servings: 8
Cooking Time: 50 Minutes
Ingredients:

- 1 (1-pound) beef roast
- Salt and ground black pepper, as required

Directions:
1. Grease each basket of "Zone 1" and "Zone 2" of Ninja Foodi 2-Basket Air Fryer.
2. Press "Zone 1" and "Zone 2" and then rotate the knob for each zone to select "Roast".
3. Set the temperature to 350 degrees F/ 175 degrees C for both zones and then set the time for 5 minutes to preheat.
4. Rub ach roast with salt and black pepper generously.
5. After preheating, arrange the roast into the basket of each zone.
6. Slide each basket into Air Fryer and set the time for 50 minutes.
7. After cooking time is completed, remove each roast from Air Fryer and place onto a platter for about 10 minutes before slicing.
8. With a sharp knife, cut each roast into desired-sized slices and serve.

Easy Breaded Pork Chops

Servings: 8
Cooking Time: 12 Minutes
Ingredients:

- 1 egg
- 118ml milk
- 8 pork chops
- 1 packet ranch seasoning
- 238g breadcrumbs
- Pepper
- Salt

Directions:
1. In a small bowl, whisk the egg and milk.
2. In a separate shallow dish, mix breadcrumbs, ranch seasoning, pepper, and salt.
3. Dip each pork chop in the egg mixture, then coat with breadcrumbs.
4. Insert a crisper plate in the Ninja Foodi air fryer baskets.
5. Place the coated pork chops in both baskets.
6. Select zone 1, then select air fry mode and set the temperature to 360 degrees F for 12 minutes. Press "match" to match zone 2 settings to zone 1. Press "start/stop" to begin. Turn halfway through.

Nutrition:

- (Per serving) Calories 378 | Fat 22.2g | Sodium 298mg | Carbs 20.2g | Fiber 1.2g | Sugar 2.4g | Protein 22.8g

Parmesan Pork Chops

Servings: 4
Cooking Time: 15 Minutes.
Ingredients:

- 4 boneless pork chops
- 2 tablespoons olive oil
- ½ cup freshly grated Parmesan
- 1 teaspoon salt
- 1 teaspoon paprika
- 1 teaspoon garlic powder
- 1 teaspoon onion powder
- ½ teaspoon black pepper

Directions:
1. Pat dry the pork chops with a paper towel and rub them with olive oil.
2. Mix parmesan with spices in a medium bowl.
3. Rub the pork chops with Parmesan mixture.
4. Place 2 seasoned pork chops in each of the two crisper plate
5. Return the crisper plate to the Ninja Foodi Dual Zone Air Fryer.
6. Choose the Air Fry mode for Zone 1 and set the temperature to 390 degrees F and the time to 15 minutes.
7. Select the "MATCH" button to copy the settings for Zone 2.
8. Initiate cooking by pressing the START/STOP button.
9. Flip the pork chops when cooked halfway through, then resume cooking.
10. Serve warm.

Nutrition:

- (Per serving) Calories 396 | Fat 23.2g | Sodium 622mg | Carbs 0.7g | Fiber 0g | Sugar 0g | Protein 45.6g

Beef Ribs Ii

Servings:2
Cooking Time:1
Ingredients:

- ¼ cup olive oil
- 4 garlic cloves, minced
- ½ cup white wine vinegar
- ¼ cup soy sauce, reduced-sodium
- ¼ cup Worcestershire sauce
- 1 lemon juice
- Salt and black pepper, to taste
- 2 tablespoons of Italian seasoning
- 1 teaspoon of smoked paprika
- 2 tablespoons of mustard
- ½ cup maple syrup
- Meat Ingredients:
- Oil spray, for greasing
- 8 beef ribs lean

Directions:

1. Take a large bowl and add all the ingredients under marinade ingredients.
2. Put the marinade in a zip lock bag and add ribs to it.
3. Let it sit for 4 hours.
4. Now take out the basket of air fryer and grease the baskets with oil spray.
5. Now dived the ribs among two baskets.
6. Set it to AIR fry mode at 220 degrees F for 30 minutes.
7. Select Pause and take out the baskets.
8. Afterward, flip the ribs and cook for 30 minutes at 250 degrees F.
9. Once done, serve the juicy and tender ribs.
10. Enjoy.

Nutrition:

- (Per serving) Calories 1927| Fat116g| Sodium 1394mg | Carbs 35.2g | Fiber 1.3g| Sugar29 g | Protein 172.3g

Kheema Burgers

Servings: 4
Cooking Time: 12 Minutes
Ingredients:

- Burgers:
- 450 g 85% lean beef mince or lamb mince
- 2 large eggs, lightly beaten
- 1 medium brown onion, diced
- 60 ml chopped fresh coriander
- 1 tablespoon minced fresh ginger
- 3 cloves garlic, minced
- 2 teaspoons garam masala
- 1 teaspoon ground turmeric
- ½ teaspoon ground cinnamon
- ⅛ teaspoon ground cardamom
- 1 teaspoon coarse or flaky salt
- 1 teaspoon cayenne pepper
- Raita Sauce:
- 235 ml grated cucumber
- 120 ml sour cream
- ¼ teaspoon coarse or flaky salt
- ¼ teaspoon black pepper
- For Serving:
- 4 lettuce leaves, hamburger buns, or naan breads

Directions:

1. For the burgers: In a large bowl, combine the beef mince, eggs, onion, coriander, ginger, garlic, garam masala, turmeric, cinnamon, cardamom, salt, and cayenne. Gently mix until ingredients are thoroughly combined. 2. Divide the meat into four portions and form into round patties. Make a slight depression in the middle of each patty with your thumb to prevent them from puffing up into a dome shape while cooking. 3. Place the patties in the zone 1 air fryer drawer. Set the temperature to 176°C for 12 minutes. Use a meat thermometer to ensure the burgers have reached an internal temperature of 72°C . 4. Meanwhile, for the sauce: In a small bowl, combine the cucumber, sour cream, salt, and pepper. 5. To serve: Place the burgers on the lettuce, buns, or naan and top with the sauce.

Air Fryer Meatloaves

Servings: 4
Cooking Time: 22 Minutes.
Ingredients:

- ⅓ cup milk
- 2 tablespoons basil pesto
- 1 egg, beaten
- 1 garlic clove, minced
- ¼ teaspoons black pepper
- 1 lb. ground beef
- ⅓ cup panko bread crumbs
- 8 pepperoni slices

- ½ cup marinara sauce, warmed
- 1 tablespoon fresh basil, chopped

Directions:
1. Mix pesto, milk, egg, garlic, and black pepper in a medium-sized bowl.
2. Stir in ground beef and bread crumbs, then mix.
3. Make the 4 small-sized loaves with this mixture and top them with 2 pepperoni slices.
4. Press the slices into the meatloaves.
5. Place the meatloaves in the two crisper plates.
6. Return the crisper plate to the Ninja Foodi Dual Zone Air Fryer.
7. Choose the Air Fry mode for Zone 1 and set the temperature to 390 degrees F and the time to 22 minutes.
8. Select the "MATCH" button to copy the settings for Zone 2.
9. Initiate cooking by pressing the START/STOP button.
10. Top them with marinara sauce and basil to serve.
11. Serve warm.

Nutrition:
- (Per serving) Calories 316 | Fat 12.2g |Sodium 587mg | Carbs 12.2g | Fiber 1g | Sugar 1.8g | Protein 25.8g

Seasoned Flank Steak

Servings: 12
Cooking Time: 30 Minutes
Ingredients:
- 2 (2-pound) flank steaks
- 3 tablespoons taco seasoning rub

Directions:
1. Grease each basket of "Zone 1" and "Zone 2" of Ninja Foodi 2-Basket Air Fryer.
2. Press "Zone 1" and "Zone 2" and then rotate the knob for each zone to select "Bake".
3. Set the temperature to 420 degrees F/ 215 degrees C for both zones and then set the time for 5 minutes to preheat.
4. Rub the steaks with taco seasoning evenly.
5. After preheating, arrange 1 steak into the basket of each zone.
6. Slide each basket into Air Fryer and set the time for 30 minutes.
7. After cooking time is completed, remove the steaks from Air Fryer and place onto a cutting board for about 10-15 minutes before slicing.
8. With a sharp knife, cut each steak into desired size slices and serve.

Cinnamon-apple Pork Chops

Servings: 4
Cooking Time: 10 Minutes
Ingredients:
- 2 tablespoons butter
- 4 boneless pork loin chops
- 3 tablespoons brown sugar
- 1 teaspoon ground cinnamon
- ½ teaspoon ground nutmeg
- ¼ teaspoon salt
- 4 medium tart apples, sliced
- 2 tablespoons chopped pecans

Directions:
1. Mix butter, brown sugar, cinnamon, nutmeg, and salt in a bowl.
2. Rub this mixture over the pork chops and place them in the air fryer baskets.
3. Top them with apples and pecans.
4. Return the air fryer basket 1 to Zone 1, and basket 2 to Zone 2 of the Ninja Foodi 2-Basket Air Fryer.
5. Choose the "Air Fry" mode for Zone 1 at 375 degrees F and 10 minutes of cooking time.
6. Select the "MATCH COOK" option to copy the settings for Zone 2.
7. Initiate cooking by pressing the START/PAUSE BUTTON.
8. Serve warm.

Nutrition:
- (Per serving) Calories 316 | Fat 17g |Sodium 271mg | Carbs 4.3g | Fiber 0.9g | Sugar 2.1g | Protein 35g

Tomahawk Steak

Servings: 4
Cooking Time: 12 Minutes
Ingredients:

- 4 tablespoons butter, softened
- 2 cloves garlic, minced
- 2 teaspoons chopped fresh parsley
- 1 teaspoon chopped chives
- 1 teaspoon chopped fresh thyme
- 1 teaspoon chopped fresh rosemary
- 2 (2 pounds each) bone-in ribeye steaks
- Kosher salt, to taste
- Freshly ground black pepper, to taste

Directions:

1. In a small bowl, combine the butter and herbs. Place the mixture in the center of a piece of plastic wrap and roll it into a log. Twist the ends together to keep it tight and refrigerate until hardened, about 20 minutes.
2. Season the steaks on both sides with salt and pepper.
3. Install a crisper plate in both drawers. Place one steak in the zone 1 drawer and one in zone 2's, then insert the drawers into the unit.
4. Select zone 1, select AIR FRY, set temperature to 390 degrees F/ 200 degrees C, and set time to 12 minutes. Select MATCH to match zone 2 settings to zone 1. Press the START/STOP button to begin cooking.
5. When the time reaches 10 minutes, press START/STOP to pause the unit. Remove the drawers and flip the steaks. Add the herb-butter to the tops of the steaks. Re-insert the drawers into the unit and press START/STOP to resume cooking.
6. Serve and enjoy!

Nutrition:

- (Per serving) Calories 338 | Fat 21.2g | Sodium 1503mg | Carbs 5.1g | Fiber 0.3g | Sugar 4.6g | Protein 29.3g

Yogurt Lamb Chops

Servings:2
Cooking Time:20
Ingredients:

- 1½ cups plain Greek yogurt
- 1 lemon, juice only
- 1 teaspoon ground cumin
- 1 teaspoon ground coriander
- ¾ teaspoon ground turmeric
- ¼ teaspoon ground allspice
- 10 rib lamb chops (1–1¼ inches thick cut)
- 2 tablespoons olive oil, divided

Directions:

1. Take a bowl and add lamb chop along with listed ingredients.
2. Rub the lamb chops well.
3. and let it marinate in the refrigerator for 1 hour.
4. Afterward takeout the lamb chops from the refrigerator.
5. Layer parchment paper on top of the baskets of the air fryer.
6. Divide it between ninja air fryer baskets.
7. Set the time for zone 1 to 20 minutes at 400 degrees F.
8. Select the MATCH button for the zone 2 basket.
9. Hit start and then wait for the chop to be cooked.
10. Once the cooking is done, the cool sign will appear on display.
11. Take out the lamb chops and let the chops serve on plates.

Nutrition:

- (Per serving) Calories1973 | Fat90 g | Sodium228 mg | Carbs 109.2g | Fiber 1g | Sugar 77.5g | Protein 184g

Strip Steaks With Hasselback Potatoes

Servings:4
Cooking Time: 30 Minutes
Ingredients:

- FOR THE STRIP STEAK
- 2 boneless strip steaks (8 ounces each)
- 2 teaspoons vegetable oil
- 1 tablespoon steak seasoning
- FOR THE HASSELBACK POTATOES
- 4 russet potatoes
- 1 tablespoon vegetable oil
- 1 teaspoon kosher salt
- 1 tablespoon salted butter, at room temperature
- 2 teaspoons minced garlic
- 2 teaspoons minced fresh parsley

Directions:

1. To prep the strip steak: Brush both sides of the steaks with the oil and season with the steak seasoning.
2. To prep the Hasselback potatoes: Set a potato on a work surface and lay the handles of two wooden spoons lengthwise on either side of the potato. Make crosswise slits along the potato, spacing them ⅛ inch apart, being careful to not cut the potato completely through (the spoon handles will prevent you from cutting all the way through). Repeat with the remaining potatoes.
3. Rub the potatoes with the oil and season with salt.
4. In a small bowl, mix the butter, garlic, and parsley until smooth.
5. To cook the steak and potatoes: Install a crisper plate in each of the two baskets. Place the steaks in the Zone 1 basket and insert the basket in the unit. Place the potatoes in the Zone 2 basket and insert the basket in the unit.
6. Select Zone 1, select AIR FRY, set the temperature to 375°F, and set the time to 20 minutes.
7. Select Zone 2, select BAKE, set the temperature to 375°F, and set the time to 30 minutes. Select SMART FINISH.
8. Press START/PAUSE to begin cooking.
9. When both timers read 6 minutes, press START/PAUSE. Remove the Zone 1 basket and use silicone-tipped tongs to flip the steaks. Reinsert the basket in the unit. Remove the Zone 2 basket and spread the herb butter into the potatoes, being sure to work the butter in between the slices. Reinsert the basket and press START/PAUSE to resume cooking.
10. When cooking is complete, the steak should be cooked to your liking and the potato soft when pierced with a fork.
11. Remove the steaks from the basket and let rest for 5 minutes before slicing.

Nutrition:

- (Per serving) Calories: 361; Total fat: 15g; Saturated fat: 5g; Carbohydrates: 31g; Fiber: 2g; Protein: 25g; Sodium: 694mg

Garlic Butter Steak Bites

Servings: 3
Cooking Time: 16 Minutes
Ingredients:

- Oil, for spraying
- 450 g boneless steak, cut into 1-inch pieces
- 2 tablespoons olive oil
- 1 teaspoon Worcestershire sauce
- ½ teaspoon granulated garlic
- ½ teaspoon salt
- ¼ teaspoon freshly ground black pepper

Directions:

1. Preheat the air fryer to 204ºC. Line the two air fryer drawers with parchment and spray lightly with oil.
2. In a medium bowl, combine the steak, olive oil, Worcestershire sauce, garlic, salt, and black pepper and toss until evenly coated.
3. Place the steak in a single layer in the two prepared drawers.
4. Cook for 10 to 16 minutes, flipping every 3 to 4 minutes. The total cooking time will depend on the thickness of the meat and your preferred doneness. If you want it well done, it may take up to 5 additional minutes.

Garlic Sirloin Steak

Servings: 4
Cooking Time: 10 Minutes
Ingredients:

- 4 sirloin steak
- 30ml olive oil
- 28g steak sauce
- ½ tsp ground coriander
- 1 tsp garlic, minced
- 1 tbsp thyme, chopped
- Pepper
- Salt

Directions:

1. In a bowl, mix steak with thyme, oil, steak sauce, coriander, garlic, pepper, and salt. Cover and set aside for 2 hours.
2. Insert a crisper plate in Ninja Foodi air fryer baskets.
3. Place the marinated steaks in both baskets.
4. Select zone 1 then select air fry mode and set the temperature to 360 degrees F for 10 minutes. Press "match" and then "start/stop" to begin.

Nutrition:

- (Per serving) Calories 348 | Fat 18.1g |Sodium 39mg | Carbs 0.7g | Fiber 0.3g | Sugar 0g | Protein 0.1g

Smothered Chops

Servings: 4
Cooking Time: 30 Minutes
Ingredients:

- 4 bone-in pork chops (230 g each)
- 2 teaspoons salt, divided
- 1½ teaspoons freshly ground black pepper, divided
- 1 teaspoon garlic powder
- 235 ml tomato purée
- 1½ teaspoons Italian seasoning
- 1 tablespoon sugar
- 1 tablespoon cornflour
- 120 ml chopped onion
- 120 ml chopped green pepper
- 1 to 2 tablespoons oil

Directions:
1. Evenly season the pork chops with 1 teaspoon salt, 1 teaspoon pepper, and the garlic powder.
2. In a medium bowl, stir together the tomato purée, Italian seasoning, sugar, remaining 1 teaspoon of salt, and remaining ½ teaspoon of pepper.
3. In a small bowl, whisk 180 ml water and the cornflour until blended. Stir this slurry into the tomato purée, with the onion and green pepper. Transfer to a baking pan.
4. Preheat the air fryer to 176°C.
5. Place the sauce in the fryer and cook for 10 minutes. Stir and cook for 10 minutes more. Remove the pan and keep warm.
6. Increase the air fryer temperature to 204°C. Line the two air fryer drawers with parchment paper.
7. Place the pork chops on the parchment and spritz with oil.
8. Cook for 5 minutes. Flip and spritz the chops with oil and cook for 5 minutes more, until the internal temperature reaches 64°C. Serve with the tomato mixture spooned on top.

Goat Cheese-stuffed Bavette Steak

Servings: 6
Cooking Time: 14 Minutes
Ingredients:

- 450 g bavette or skirt steak
- 1 tablespoon avocado oil
- ½ teaspoon sea salt
- ½ teaspoon garlic powder
- ¼ teaspoon freshly ground black pepper
- 60 g goat cheese, crumbled
- 235 ml baby spinach, chopped

Directions:
1. Place the steak in a large zip-top bag or between two pieces of plastic wrap. Using a meat mallet or heavy-bottomed skillet, pound the steak to an even ¼-inch thickness.
2. Brush both sides of the steak with the avocado oil.
3. Mix the salt, garlic powder, and pepper in a small dish. Sprinkle this mixture over both sides of the steak.
4. Sprinkle the goat cheese over top, and top that with the spinach.
5. Starting at one of the long sides, roll the steak up tightly. Tie the rolled steak with kitchen string at 3-inch intervals.
6. Set the zone 1 air fryer drawer to 204°C. Place the steak roll-up in the zone 1 air fryer drawer. Air fry for 7 minutes. Flip the steak and cook for an additional 7 minutes, until an instant-read thermometer reads 49°C for medium-rare .

Honey-baked Pork Loin

Servings: 6
Cooking Time: 22 To 25 Minutes
Ingredients:

- 60 ml honey
- 60 ml freshly squeezed lemon juice
- 2 tablespoons soy sauce
- 1 teaspoon garlic powder
- 1 (900 g) pork loin
- 2 tablespoons vegetable oil

Directions:
1. In a medium bowl, whisk together the honey, lemon juice, soy sauce, and garlic powder. Reserve half of the mixture for basting during cooking.
2. Cut 5 slits in the pork loin and transfer it to a resealable bag. Add the remaining honey mixture. Seal the bag and refrigerate to marinate for at least 2 hours.
3. Preheat the air fryer to 204°C. Line the two air fryer drawers with parchment paper.
4. Remove the pork from the marinade, and place it on the parchment. Spritz with oil, then baste with the reserved marinade.
5. Cook for 15 minutes. Flip the pork, baste with more marinade and spritz with oil again. Cook for 7 to 10 minutes more until the internal temperature reaches 64°C. Let rest for 5 minutes before serving.

Filet Mignon Wrapped In Bacon

Servings: 2
Cooking Time: 20 Minutes
Ingredients:

- 2 (2-ounce) filet mignon
- 2 bacon slices
- Olive oil cooking spray
- Salt and ground black pepper, as required

Directions:
1. Wrap 1 bacon slice around each filet mignon and secure with toothpicks.
2. Season the filets with salt and black pepper lightly.
3. Grease each basket of "Zone 1" and "Zone 2" of Ninja Foodi 2-Basket Air Fryer.
4. Press "Zone 1" and "Zone 2" and then rotate the knob for each zone to select "Air Fry".
5. Set the temperature to 400 degrees F/ 200 degrees C for both zones and then set the time for 5 minutes to preheat.
6. After preheating, arrange the filets into the basket of each zone.
7. Slide each basket into Air Fryer and set the time for 15 minutes.
8. While cooking, flip the filets once halfway through.
9. After cooking time is completed, remove the filets from Air Fryer and serve hot.

Rosemary Ribeye Steaks And Mongolian-style Beef

Servings: 6
Cooking Time: 15 Minutes
Ingredients:

- Rosemary Ribeye Steaks:
- 60 ml butter
- 1 clove garlic, minced
- Salt and ground black pepper, to taste
- 1½ tablespoons balsamic vinegar
- 60 ml rosemary, chopped
- 2 ribeye steaks
- Mongolian-Style Beef:
- Oil, for spraying
- 60 ml cornflour
- 450 g bavette or skirt steak, thinly sliced
- 180 ml packed light brown sugar
- 120 ml soy sauce
- 2 teaspoons toasted sesame oil
- 1 tablespoon minced garlic
- ½ teaspoon ground ginger
- 120 ml water
- Cooked white rice or ramen noodles, for serving

Directions:
1. Make the Rosemary Ribeye Steaks :
2. Melt the butter in a skillet over medium heat. Add the garlic and fry until fragrant.
3. Remove the skillet from the heat and add the salt, pepper, and vinegar. Allow it to cool.
4. Add the rosemary, then pour the mixture into a Ziploc bag.
5. Put the ribeye steaks in the bag and shake well, coating the meat well. Refrigerate for an hour, then allow to sit for a further twenty minutes.
6. Preheat the zone 1 air fryer drawer to 204ºC.
7. Air fry the ribeye steaks for 15 minutes.
8. Take care when removing the steaks from the air fryer and plate up.
9. Serve immediately.
10. Make the Mongolian-Style Beef :
11. Line the zone 2 air fryer drawer with parchment and spray lightly with oil.
12. Place the cornflour in a bowl and dredge the steak until evenly coated. Shake off any excess cornflour.
13. Place the steak in the prepared drawer and spray lightly with oil.
14. Roast at 200ºC for 5 minutes, flip, and cook for another 5 minutes.
15. In a small saucepan, combine the brown sugar, soy sauce, sesame oil, garlic, ginger, and water and bring to a boil over medium-high heat, stirring frequently. Remove from the heat.
16. Transfer the meat to the sauce and toss until evenly coated. Let sit for about 5 minutes so the steak absorbs the flavors. Serve with white rice or ramen noodles.

Bell Peppers With Sausages

Servings:4
Cooking Time:20
Ingredients:

- 6 beef or pork Italian sausages
- 4 bell peppers, whole
- Oil spray, for greasing
- 2 cups of cooked rice
- 1 cup of sour cream

Directions:
1. Put the bell pepper in the zone 1 basket and sausages in the zone 2 basket of the air fryer.
2. Set zone 1 to AIR FRY MODE for 10 minutes at 400 degrees F.
3. For zone 2 set it to 20 minutes at 375 degrees F.
4. Hit the smart finish button, so both finish at the same time.
5. After 5 minutes take out the sausage basket and break or mince it with a plastic spatula.
6. Then, let the cooking cycle finish.
7. Once done serve the minced meat with bell peppers and serve over cooked rice with a dollop of sour cream.

Nutrition:
- (Per serving) Calories1356 | Fat 81.2g| Sodium 3044 mg | Carbs 96g | Fiber 3.1g | Sugar 8.3g | Protein 57.2 g

New York Strip Steak

Servings: 2
Cooking Time: 10 Minutes
Ingredients:

- 1 (4½-ounce) New York strip steaks
- 1½ teaspoons olive oil
- Salt and ground black pepper, as required

Directions:
1. Grease each basket of "Zone 1" and "Zone 2" of Ninja Foodi 2-Basket Air Fryer.
2. Press "Zone 1" and "Zone 2" and then rotate the knob for each zone to select "Air Fry".
3. Set the temperature to 400 degrees F/ 200 degrees C for both zones and then set the time for 5 minutes to preheat.
4. Coat the steaks with oil and then sprinkle with salt and black pepper evenly.
5. After preheating, arrange the steak into the basket of each zone.
6. Slide each basket into Air Fryer and set the time for 10 minutes.
7. While cooking, flip the steak once halfway through.
8. After cooking time is completed, remove the steaks from Air Fryer and place onto a platter for about 10 minutes.
9. Cut each steak into desired size slices and serve immediately.

Panko Crusted Calf's Liver Strips

Servings: 4
Cooking Time: 23 To 25 Minutes
Ingredients:

- 450 g sliced calf's liver, cut into ½-inch wide strips
- 2 eggs
- 2 tablespoons milk
- 120 ml whole wheat flour
- 475 ml panko breadcrumbs
- Salt and ground black pepper, to taste
- Cooking spray

Directions:
1. Preheat the air fryer to 200ºC and spritz with cooking spray.
2. Rub the calf's liver strips with salt and ground black pepper on a clean work surface.
3. Whisk the eggs with milk in a large bowl. Pour the flour in a shallow dish. Pour the panko on a separate shallow dish.
4. Dunk the liver strips in the flour, then in the egg mixture. Shake the excess off and roll the strips over the panko to coat well.
5. Arrange the liver strips in a single layer in the two preheated air fryer drawers and spritz with cooking spray.
6. Air fry for 5 minutes or until browned. Flip the strips halfway through.
7. Serve immediately.

Simple Strip Steak

Servings: 4
Cooking Time: 10 Minutes
Ingredients:

- 2 (9½-ounce) New York strip steaks
- Salt and ground black pepper, as required
- 3 teaspoons olive oil

Directions:

1. Grease each basket of "Zone 1" and "Zone 2" of Ninja Foodi 2-Basket Air Fryer.
2. Press "Zone 1" and "Zone 2" and then rotate the knob for each zone to select "Air Fry".
3. Set the temperature to 400 degrees F/ 200 degrees C for both zones and then set the time for 5 minutes to preheat.
4. Coat the steaks with oil and then sprinkle with salt and black pepper evenly.
5. After preheating, arrange 1 steak into the basket of each zone.
6. Slide each basket into Air Fryer and set the time for 10 minutes.
7. While cooking, flip the steak once halfway through.
8. After cooking time is completed, remove the steaks from Air Fryer and place onto a platter for about 10 minutes.
9. Cut each steak into desired size slices and serve immediately.

Chapter 7 : Vegetables And Sides Recipes

Healthy Air Fried Veggies

Servings: 4
Cooking Time: 15 Minutes
Ingredients:

- 52g onion, sliced
- 71g broccoli florets
- 116g radishes, sliced
- 15ml olive oil
- 100g Brussels sprouts, cut in half
- 325g cauliflower florets
- 1 tsp balsamic vinegar
- ½ tsp garlic powder
- Pepper
- Salt

Directions:

1. In a bowl, toss veggies with oil, vinegar, garlic powder, pepper, and salt.
2. Insert a crisper plate in the Ninja Foodi air fryer baskets.
3. Add veggies in both baskets.
4. Select zone 1 then select "air fry" mode and set the temperature to 380 degrees F for 15 minutes. Press "match" to match zone 2 settings to zone 1. Press "start/stop" to begin. Stir halfway through.

Nutrition:

- (Per serving) Calories 71 | Fat 3.8g |Sodium 72mg | Carbs 8.8g | Fiber 3.2g | Sugar 3.3g | Protein 2.5g

Broccoli, Squash, & Pepper

Servings: 4
Cooking Time: 12 Minutes
Ingredients:

- 175g broccoli florets
- 1 red bell pepper, diced
- 1 tbsp olive oil
- ½ tsp garlic powder
- ¼ onion, sliced
- 1 zucchini, sliced
- 2 yellow squash, sliced
- Pepper
- Salt

Directions:

1. In a bowl, toss veggies with oil, garlic powder, pepper, and salt.
2. Insert a crisper plate in the Ninja Foodi air fryer baskets.
3. Add the vegetable mixture in both baskets.
4. Select zone 1 then select "air fry" mode and set the temperature to 390 degrees F for 12 minutes. Press "match" to match zone 2 settings to zone 1. Press "start/stop" to begin. Stir halfway through.

Nutrition:

- (Per serving) Calories 75 | Fat 3.9g |Sodium 62mg | Carbs 9.6g | Fiber 2.8g | Sugar 4.8g | Protein 2.9g

Air-fried Radishes

Servings: 6
Cooking Time: 15 Minutes
Ingredients:

- 1020g radishes, quartered
- 3 tablespoons olive oil
- 1 tablespoon fresh oregano, minced
- ¼ teaspoon salt
- ⅛ teaspoon black pepper

Directions:

1. Toss radishes with oil, black pepper, salt and oregano in a bowl.
2. Divide the radishes into the Ninja Foodi 2 Baskets Air Fryer baskets.
3. Return the air fryer basket 1 to Zone 1, and basket 2 to Zone 2 of the Ninja Foodi 2-Basket Air Fryer.
4. Choose the "Air Fry" mode for Zone 1 at 375 degrees F and 15 minutes of cooking time.
5. Select the "MATCH COOK" option to copy the settings for Zone 2.
6. Initiate cooking by pressing the START/PAUSE BUTTON.
7. Toss the radishes once cooked halfway through.
8. Serve.

Nutrition:

- (Per serving) Calories 270 | Fat 14.6g |Sodium 394mg | Carbs 31.3g | Fiber 7.5g | Sugar 9.7g | Protein 6.4g

Quinoa Patties

Servings: 4
Cooking Time: 32 Minutes.
Ingredients:

- 1 cup quinoa red
- 1½ cups water
- 1 teaspoon salt
- black pepper, ground
- 1½ cups rolled oats
- 3 eggs beaten
- ¼ cup minced white onion
- ½ cup crumbled feta cheese
- ¼ cup chopped fresh chives
- Salt and black pepper, to taste
- Vegetable or canola oil
- 4 hamburger buns
- 4 arugulas
- 4 slices tomato sliced
- Cucumber yogurt dill sauce
- 1 cup cucumber, diced
- 1 cup Greek yogurt
- 2 teaspoons lemon juice
- ¼ teaspoon salt
- Black pepper, ground
- 1 tablespoon chopped fresh dill
- 1 tablespoon olive oil

Directions:
1. Add quinoa to a saucepan filled with cold water, salt, and black pepper, and place it over medium-high heat.
2. Cook the quinoa to a boil, then reduce the heat, cover, and cook for 20 minutes on a simmer.
3. Fluff and mix the cooked quinoa with a fork and remove it from the heat.
4. Spread the quinoa in a baking stay.
5. Mix eggs, oats, onion, herbs, cheese, salt, and black pepper.
6. Stir in quinoa, then mix well. Make 4 patties out of this quinoa cheese mixture.
7. Divide the patties in the two crisper plates and spray them with cooking oil.
8. Return the crisper plates to the Ninja Foodi Dual Zone Air Fryer.
9. Choose the Air Fry mode for Zone 1 and set the temperature to 390 degrees F and the time to 13 minutes.
10. Select the "MATCH" button to copy the settings for Zone 2.
11. Initiate cooking by pressing the START/STOP button.
12. Flip the patties once cooked halfway through, and resume cooking.
13. Meanwhile, prepare the cucumber yogurt dill sauce by mixing all of its ingredients in a mixing bowl.
14. Place each quinoa patty in a burger bun along with arugula leaves.
15. Serve with yogurt dill sauce.

Nutrition:
- (Per serving) Calories 231 | Fat 9g |Sodium 271mg | Carbs 32.8g | Fiber 6.4g | Sugar 7g | Protein 6.3g

Curly Fries

Servings: 6
Cooking Time: 20 Minutes.
Ingredients:

- 2 spiralized zucchinis
- 1 cup flour
- 2 tablespoons paprika
- 1 teaspoon cayenne pepper
- 1 teaspoon garlic powder
- 1 teaspoon black pepper
- 1 teaspoon salt
- 2 eggs
- Olive oil or cooking spray

Directions:
1. Mix flour with paprika, cayenne pepper, garlic powder, black pepper, and salt in a bowl.
2. Beat eggs in another bowl and dip the zucchini in the eggs.
3. Coat the zucchini with the flour mixture and divide it into two crisper plates.
4. Spray the zucchini with cooking oil.
5. Return the crisper plate to the Ninja Foodi Dual Zone Air Fryer.
6. Choose the Air Fry mode for Zone 1 and set the temperature to 400 degrees F and the time to 20 minutes.
7. Select the "MATCH" button to copy the settings for Zone 2.
8. Initiate cooking by pressing the START/STOP button.
9. Toss the zucchini once cooked halfway through, then resume cooking.
10. Serve warm.

Nutrition:
- (Per serving) Calories 212 | Fat 11.8g |Sodium 321mg | Carbs 24.6g | Fiber 4.4g | Sugar 8g | Protein 7.3g

Green Beans With Baked Potatoes

Servings:2
Cooking Time:45
Ingredients:

- 2 cups of green beans
- 2 large potatoes, cubed
- 3 tablespoons of olive oil
- 1 teaspoon of seasoned salt
- ½ teaspoon chili powder
- 1/6 teaspoon garlic powder
- 1/4 teaspoon onion powder

Directions:

1. Take a large bowl and pour olive oil into it.
2. Now add all the seasoning in the olive oil and whisk it well.
3. Toss the green bean in it, then transfer it to zone 1 basket of the air fryer.
4. Now season the potatoes with the seasoning and add them to the zone 2 basket.
5. Now set the zone one basket to AIRFRY mode at 350 degrees F for 18 minutes.
6. Now hit 2 for the second basket and set it to AIR FRY mode at 350 degrees F, for 45 minutes.
7. Once the cooking cycle is complete, take out and serve it by transferring it to the serving plates.

Nutrition:

- (Per serving) Calories473 | Fat21.6g | Sodium796 mg | Carbs 66.6g | Fiber12.9 g | Sugar6 g | Protein8.4 g

Jerk Tofu With Roasted Cabbage

Servings:4
Cooking Time: 20 Minutes
Ingredients:

- FOR THE JERK TOFU
- 1 (14-ounce) package extra-firm tofu, drained
- 1 tablespoon apple cider vinegar
- 1 tablespoon reduced-sodium soy sauce
- 2 tablespoons jerk seasoning
- Juice of 1 lime
- ½ teaspoon kosher salt
- 2 tablespoons olive oil
- FOR THE CABBAGE
- 1 (14-ounce) bag coleslaw mix
- 1 red bell pepper, thinly sliced
- 2 scallions, thinly sliced
- 2 tablespoons water
- 3 garlic cloves, minced
- ¼ teaspoon fresh thyme leaves
- ¼ teaspoon onion powder
- ¼ teaspoon kosher salt
- ¼ teaspoon freshly ground black pepper

Directions:

1. To prep the jerk tofu: Cut the tofu horizontally into 4 slabs.
2. In a shallow dish (big enough to hold the tofu slabs), whisk together the vinegar, soy sauce, jerk seasoning, lime juice, and salt.
3. Place the tofu in the marinade and turn to coat both sides. Cover and marinate for at least 15 minutes (or up to overnight in the refrigerator).
4. To prep the cabbage: In the Zone 2 basket, combine the coleslaw, bell pepper, scallions, water, garlic, thyme, onion powder, salt, and black pepper.
5. To cook the tofu and cabbage: Install a crisper plate in the Zone 1 basket and add the tofu in a single layer. Brush the tofu with the oil and insert the basket in the unit. Insert the Zone 2 basket in the unit.
6. Select Zone 1, select AIR FRY, set the temperature to 390°F, and set the timer to 15 minutes.
7. Select Zone 2, select ROAST, set the temperature to 330°F, and set the timer to 20 minutes. Select SMART FINISH.
8. Press START/PAUSE to begin cooking.
9. When both timers read 5 minutes, press START/PAUSE. Remove the Zone 1 basket and use silicone-tipped tongs to flip the tofu. Reinsert the basket in the unit. Remove the Zone 2 basket and stir the cabbage. Reinsert the basket and press START/PAUSE to resume cooking.
10. When cooking is complete, the tofu will be crispy and browned around the edges and the cabbage soft.
11. Transfer the tofu to four plates and serve with the cabbage on the side.

Nutrition:

- (Per serving) Calories: 220; Total fat: 12g; Saturated fat: 1.5g; Carbohydrates: 21g; Fiber: 5g; Protein: 12g; Sodium: 817mg

Potatoes & Beans

Servings: 4
Cooking Time: 25 Minutes
Ingredients:

- 453g potatoes, cut into pieces
- 15ml olive oil
- 1 tsp garlic powder
- 160g green beans, trimmed
- Pepper
- Salt

Directions:
1. In a bowl, toss green beans, garlic powder, potatoes, oil, pepper, and salt.
2. Insert a crisper plate in the Ninja Foodi air fryer baskets.
3. Add green beans and potato mixture to both baskets.
4. Select zone 1 then select "air fry" mode and set the temperature to 380 degrees F for 25 minutes. Press "match" to match zone 2 settings to zone 1. Press "start/stop" to begin. Stir halfway through.

Nutrition:
- (Per serving) Calories 128 | Fat 3.7g |Sodium 49mg | Carbs 22.4g | Fiber 4.7g | Sugar 2.3g | Protein 3.1g

Delicious Potatoes & Carrots

Servings: 8
Cooking Time: 25 Minutes
Ingredients:

- 453g carrots, sliced
- 2 tsp smoked paprika
- 21g sugar
- 30ml olive oil
- 453g potatoes, diced
- ¼ tsp thyme
- ½ tsp dried oregano
- 1 tsp garlic powder
- Pepper
- Salt

Directions:
1. In a bowl, toss carrots and potatoes with 1 tablespoon of oil.
2. Insert a crisper plate in the Ninja Foodi air fryer baskets.
3. Add carrots and potatoes to both baskets.
4. Select zone 1 then select "air fry" mode and set the temperature to 390 degrees F for 15 minutes. Press "match" to match zone 2 settings to zone 1. Press "start/stop" to begin.
5. In a mixing bowl, add cooked potatoes, carrots, smoked paprika, sugar, oil, thyme, oregano, garlic powder, pepper, and salt and toss well.
6. Return carrot and potato mixture into the air fryer basket and cook for 10 minutes more.

Nutrition:
- (Per serving) Calories 101 | Fat 3.6g |Sodium 62mg | Carbs 16.6g | Fiber 3g | Sugar 5.1g | Protein 1.6g

Lime Glazed Tofu

Servings: 6
Cooking Time: 14 Minutes.
Ingredients:

- ⅔ cup coconut aminos
- 2 (14-oz) packages extra-firm, water-packed tofu, drained
- 6 tablespoons toasted sesame oil
- ⅔ cup lime juice

Directions:
1. Pat dry the tofu bars and slice into half-inch cubes.
2. Toss all the remaining ingredients in a small bowl.
3. Marinate for 4 hours in the refrigerator. Drain off the excess water.
4. Divide the tofu cubes in the two crisper plates.
5. Return the crisper plates to the Ninja Foodi Dual Zone Air Fryer.
6. Choose the Air Fry mode for Zone 1 and set the temperature to 400 degrees F and the time to 14 minutes.
7. Select the "MATCH" button to copy the settings for Zone 2.
8. Initiate cooking by pressing the START/STOP button.
9. Toss the tofu once cooked halfway through, then resume cooking.
10. Serve warm.

Nutrition:
- (Per serving) Calories 284 | Fat 7.9g |Sodium 704mg | Carbs 38.1g | Fiber 1.9g | Sugar 1.9g | Protein 14.8g

Chickpea Fritters

Servings: 6
Cooking Time: 6 Minutes
Ingredients:

- 237ml plain yogurt
- 2 tablespoons sugar
- 1 tablespoon honey
- ½ teaspoon salt
- ½ teaspoon black pepper
- ½ teaspoon crushed red pepper flakes
- 1 can (28g) chickpeas, drained
- 1 teaspoon ground cumin
- ½ teaspoon salt
- ½ teaspoon garlic powder
- ½ teaspoon ground ginger
- 1 large egg
- ½ teaspoon baking soda
- ½ cup fresh coriander, chopped
- 2 green onions, sliced

Directions:

1. Mash chickpeas with rest of the ingredients in a food processor.
2. Layer the two air fryer baskets with a parchment paper.
3. Drop the batter in the baskets spoon by spoon.
4. Return the air fryer basket 1 to Zone 1, and basket 2 to Zone 2 of the Ninja Foodi 2-Basket Air Fryer.
5. Choose the "Air Fry" mode for Zone 1 at 400 degrees F and 6 minutes of cooking time.
6. Select the "MATCH COOK" option to copy the settings for Zone 2.
7. Initiate cooking by pressing the START/PAUSE BUTTON.
8. Flip the fritters once cooked halfway through.
9. Serve warm.

Nutrition:

- (Per serving) Calories 284 | Fat 7.9g |Sodium 704mg | Carbs 38.1g | Fiber 1.9g | Sugar 1.9g | Protein 14.8g

Fried Olives

Servings: 6
Cooking Time: 9 Minutes.
Ingredients:

- 2 cups blue cheese stuffed olives, drained
- ½ cup all-purpose flour
- 1 cup panko breadcrumbs
- ½ teaspoon garlic powder
- 1 pinch oregano
- 2 eggs

Directions:

1. Mix flour with oregano and garlic powder in a bowl and beat two eggs in another bowl.
2. Spread panko breadcrumbs in a bowl.
3. Coat all the olives with the flour mixture, dip in the eggs and then coat with the panko breadcrumbs.
4. As you coat the olives, place them in the two crisper plates in a single layer, then spray them with cooking oil.
5. Return the crisper plates to the Ninja Foodi Dual Zone Air Fryer.
6. Choose the Air Fry mode for Zone 1 and set the temperature to 375 degrees F and the time to 9 minutes.
7. Select the "MATCH" button to copy the settings for Zone 2.
8. Initiate cooking by pressing the START/STOP button.
9. Flip the olives once cooked halfway through, then resume cooking.
10. Serve.

Nutrition:

- (Per serving) Calories 166 | Fat 3.2g |Sodium 437mg | Carbs 28.8g | Fiber 1.8g | Sugar 2.7g | Protein 5.8g

Air Fried Okra

Servings: 2
Cooking Time: 13 Minutes.
Ingredients:

- ½ lb. okra pods sliced
- 1 teaspoon olive oil
- ¼ teaspoon salt
- ⅛ teaspoon black pepper

Directions:

1. Preheat the Ninja Foodi Dual Zone Air Fryer to 350 degrees F.
2. Toss okra with olive oil, salt, and black pepper in a bowl.
3. Spread the okra in a single layer in the two crisper plates.
4. Return the crisper plate to the Ninja Foodi Dual Zone Air Fryer.

5. Choose the Air Fry mode for Zone 1 and set the temperature to 375 degrees F and the time to 13 minutes.
6. Select the "MATCH" button to copy the settings for Zone 2.
7. Initiate cooking by pressing the START/STOP button.
8. Toss the okra once cooked halfway through, and resume cooking.
9. Serve warm.
Nutrition:
- (Per serving) Calories 208 | Fat 5g |Sodium 1205mg | Carbs 34.1g | Fiber 7.8g | Sugar 2.5g | Protein 5.9g

Rosemary Asparagus & Potatoes

Servings: 6
Cooking Time: 30 Minutes
Ingredients:
- 125g asparagus, trimmed & cut into pieces
- 2 tsp garlic powder
- 2 tbsp rosemary, chopped
- 30ml olive oil
- 679g baby potatoes, quartered
- ½ tsp red pepper flakes
- Pepper
- Salt

Directions:
1. Insert a crisper plate in the Ninja Foodi air fryer baskets.
2. Toss potatoes with 1 tablespoon of oil, pepper, and salt in a bowl until well coated.
3. Add potatoes into in zone 1 basket.
4. Toss asparagus with remaining oil, red pepper flakes, pepper, garlic powder, and rosemary in a mixing bowl.
5. Add asparagus into the zone 2 basket.
6. Select zone 1, then select "air fry" mode and set the temperature to 390 degrees F for 20 minutes. Select zone 2, then select "air fry" mode and set the temperature to 390 degrees F for 10 minutes. Press "match" mode, then press "start/stop" to begin.
Nutrition:
- (Per serving) Calories 121 | Fat 5g |Sodium 40mg | Carbs 17.1g | Fiber 4.2g | Sugar 1g | Protein 4g

Bacon Wrapped Corn Cob

Servings: 4
Cooking Time: 10 Minutes
Ingredients:
- 4 trimmed corns on the cob
- 8 bacon slices

Directions:
1. Wrap the corn cobs with two bacon slices.
2. Place the wrapped cobs into the Ninja Foodi 2 Baskets Air Fryer baskets.
3. Return the air fryer basket 1 to Zone 1, and basket 2 to Zone 2 of the Ninja Foodi 2-Basket Air Fryer.
4. Choose the "Air Fry" mode for Zone 1 and set the temperature to 355 degrees F and 10 minutes of cooking time.
5. Select the "MATCH COOK" option to copy the settings for Zone 2.
6. Initiate cooking by pressing the START/PAUSE BUTTON.
7. Flip the corn cob once cooked halfway through.
8. Serve warm.
Nutrition:
- (Per serving) Calories 350 | Fat 2.6g |Sodium 358mg | Carbs 64.6g | Fiber 14.4g | Sugar 3.3g | Protein 19.9g

Chapter 8 : **Snacks And Appetizers Recipes**

Crab Rangoon Dip With Crispy Wonton Strips

Servings:6
Cooking Time: 15 Minutes
Ingredients:

- FOR THE DIP
- 1 (6-ounce) can pink crab, drained
- 8 ounces (16 tablespoons) cream cheese, at room temperature
- ½ cup sour cream
- 1 tablespoon chopped scallions
- ½ teaspoon garlic powder
- 1 teaspoon Worcestershire sauce
- ¼ teaspoon kosher salt
- 1 cup shredded part-skim mozzarella cheese
- FOR THE WONTON STRIPS
- 12 wonton wrappers
- 1 tablespoon olive oil
- ¼ teaspoon kosher salt

Directions:

1. To prep the dip: In a medium bowl, mix the crab, cream cheese, sour cream, scallions, garlic powder, Worcestershire sauce, and salt until smooth.
2. To prep the wonton strips: Brush both sides of the wonton wrappers with the oil and sprinkle with salt. Cut the wonton wrappers into ¾-inch-wide strips.
3. To cook the dip and strips: Pour the dip into the Zone 1 basket, top with the mozzarella cheese, and insert the basket in the unit. Install a crisper plate in the Zone 2 basket, add the wonton strips, and insert the basket in the unit.
4. Select Zone 1, select BAKE, set the temperature to 330°F, and set the time to 15 minutes.
5. Select Zone 2, select AIR FRY, set the temperature to 350°F, and set the time to 6 minutes. Select SMART FINISH.
6. Press START/PAUSE to begin cooking.
7. When the Zone 2 timer reads 4 minutes, press START/PAUSE. Remove the basket and shake well to redistribute the wonton strips. Reinsert the basket and press START/PAUSE to resume cooking.
8. When the Zone 2 timer reads 2 minutes, press START/PAUSE. Remove the basket and shake well to redistribute the wonton strips. Reinsert the basket and press START/PAUSE to resume cooking.
9. When cooking is complete, the dip will be bubbling and golden brown on top and the wonton strips will be crunchy. Serve warm.

Nutrition:

- (Per serving) Calories: 315; Total fat: 23g; Saturated fat: 12g; Carbohydrates: 14g; Fiber: 0.5g; Protein: 14g; Sodium: 580mg

Fried Pickles

Servings: 4
Cooking Time: 15 Minutes
Ingredients:

- 2 cups sliced dill pickles
- 1 cup flour
- 1 tablespoon garlic powder
- 1 tablespoon Cajun spice
- ½ tablespoon cayenne pepper
- Olive Oil or cooking spray

Directions:

1. Mix together the flour and spices in a bowl.
2. Coat the sliced pickles with the flour mixture.
3. Place a crisper plate in each drawer. Put the pickles in a single layer in each drawer. Insert the drawers into the unit.
4. Select zone 1, then AIR FRY, then set the temperature to 400 degrees F/ 200 degrees C with a 15-minute timer. To match zone 2 settings to zone 1, choose MATCH. To begin, select START/STOP.

Nutrition:

- (Per serving) Calories 161 | Fat 4.1g | Sodium 975mg | Carbs 27.5g | Fiber 2.2g | Sugar 1.5g | Protein 4g

Jalapeño Poppers And Greek Potato Skins With Olives And Feta

Servings: 8
Cooking Time: 45 Minutes
Ingredients:

- Jalapeño Poppers:
- Oil, for spraying
- 227 g soft white cheese
- 177 ml gluten-free breadcrumbs, divided
- 2 tablespoons chopped fresh parsley
- ½ teaspoon granulated garlic
- ½ teaspoon salt
- 10 jalapeño peppers, halved and seeded
- Greek Potato Skins with Olives and Feta:
- 2 russet or Maris Piper potatoes

- 3 tablespoons olive oil, divided, plus more for drizzling (optional)
- 1 teaspoon rock salt, divided
- ¼ teaspoon black pepper
- 2 tablespoons fresh coriander, chopped, plus more for serving
- 60 ml Kalamata olives, diced
- 60 ml crumbled feta
- Chopped fresh parsley, for garnish (optional)

Directions:
1. Make the Jalapeño Popper s: Line the zone 1 air fryer basket with parchment and spray lightly with oil. 2. In a medium bowl, mix together the soft white cheese, half of the breadcrumbs, the parsley, garlic, and salt. 3. Spoon the mixture into the jalapeño halves. Gently press the stuffed jalapeños in the remaining breadcrumbs. 4. Place the stuffed jalapeños in the prepared basket. 5. Air fry at 190ºC for 20 minutes, or until the cheese is melted and the breadcrumbs are crisp and golden brown.
2. Make the Greek Potato Skins with Olives and Feta :
3. Preheat the air fryer to 190ºC.
4. Using a fork, poke 2 to 3 holes in the potatoes, then coat each with about ½ tablespoon olive oil and ½ teaspoon salt.
5. Place the potatoes into the zone 2 air fryer basket and bake for 30 minutes.
6. Remove the potatoes from the air fryer, and slice in half. Using a spoon, scoop out the flesh of the potatoes, leaving a ½-inch layer of potato inside the skins, and set the skins aside.
7. In a medium bowl, combine the scooped potato middles with the remaining 2 tablespoons of olive oil, ½ teaspoon of salt, black pepper, and coriander. Mix until well combined.
8. Divide the potato filling into the now-empty potato skins, spreading it evenly over them. Top each potato with a tablespoon each of the olives and feta.
9. Place the loaded potato skins back into the air fryer and bake for 15 minutes.
10. Serve with additional chopped coriander or parsley and a drizzle of olive oil, if desired.

Fried Okra

Servings: 4
Cooking Time: 10 Minutes
Ingredients:
- 455g fresh okra
- 240ml buttermilk
- 125g plain flour
- 160g polenta
- 1 teaspoon salt
- 1 teaspoon fresh ground pepper

Directions:
1. Wash and trim the ends of the okra before slicing it into 30cm chunks.
2. In a small dish, pour the buttermilk.
3. Combine flour, polenta, salt, and pepper in a separate dish.
4. Coat all sides of okra slices in buttermilk and then in flour mixture.
5. Place a baking sheet on the baskets.
6. Press either "Zone 1" or "Zone 2" and then rotate the knob to select "Air Fryer".
7. Set the temperature to 175 degrees C, and then set the time for 5 minutes to preheat.
8. After preheating, arrange them into the basket.
9. Slide the basket into the Air Fryer and set the time for 8 minutes.
10. After cooking time is completed, place on a wire rack for a few minutes, then transfer onto serving plates and serve.

Fried Halloumi Cheese

Servings: 6
Cooking Time: 12 Minutes.
Ingredients:
- 1 block of halloumi cheese, sliced
- 2 teaspoons olive oil

Directions:
1. Divide the halloumi cheese slices in the crisper plate.
2. Drizzle olive oil over the cheese slices.
3. Return the crisper plate to the Ninja Foodi Dual Zone Air Fryer.
4. Choose the Air Fry mode for Zone 1 and set the temperature to 360 degrees F and the time to 12 minutes.
5. Flip the cheese slices once cooked halfway through.
6. Serve.
Nutrition:
- (Per serving) Calories 186 | Fat 3g |Sodium 223mg | Carbs 31g | Fiber 8.7g | Sugar 5.5g | Protein 9.7g

Miso-glazed Shishito Peppers Charred Lemon Shishito Peppers

Servings:4
Cooking Time: 10 Minutes
Ingredients:

- FOR THE MISO-GLAZED PEPPERS
- 2 tablespoons vegetable oil
- 2 tablespoons water
- 1 tablespoon white miso
- 1 teaspoon grated fresh ginger
- ½ pound shishito peppers

- FOR THE CHARRED LEMON PEPPERS
- ½ pound shishito peppers
- 1 lemon, cut into ⅛-inch-thick rounds
- 2 garlic cloves, minced
- 2 tablespoons vegetable oil
- ½ teaspoon kosher salt

Directions:
1. To prep the miso-glazed peppers: In a large bowl, mix the vegetable oil, water, miso, and ginger until well combined. Add the shishitos and toss to coat.
2. To prep the charred lemon peppers: In a large bowl, combine the shishitos, lemon slices, garlic, vegetable oil, and salt. Toss to coat.
3. To cook the peppers: Install a crisper plate in each of the two baskets. Place the miso-glazed peppers in the Zone 1 basket and insert the basket in the unit. Place the peppers with lemons in the Zone 2 basket and insert the basket in the unit.
4. Select Zone 1, select AIR FRY, set the temperature to 390°F, and set the time to 10 minutes. Select MATCH COOK to match Zone 2 settings to Zone 1.
5. Press START/PAUSE to begin cooking.
6. When both timers read 4 minutes, press START/PAUSE. Remove both baskets and shake well. Reinsert the baskets and press START/PAUSE to resume cooking.
7. When cooking is complete, serve immediately.

Nutrition:
- (Per serving) Calories: 165; Total fat: 14g; Saturated fat: 2g; Carbohydrates: 9g; Fiber: 2g; Protein: 2g; Sodium: 334mg

Parmesan Crush Chicken

Servings:4
Cooking Time:18
Ingredients:

- 4 chicken breasts
- 1 cup parmesan cheese
- 1 cup bread crumb

- 2 eggs, whisked
- Salt, to taste
- Oil spray, for greasing

Directions:
1. Whisk egg in a large bowl and set aside.
2. Season the chicken breast with salt and then put it in egg wash.
3. Next, dredge it in breadcrumb then parmesan cheese.
4. Line both the basket of the air fryer with parchment paper.
5. Divided the breast pieces between the backsets, and oil spray the breast pieces.
6. Set zone 1 basket to air fry mode at 350 degrees F for 18 minutes.
7. Select the MATCH button for the zone 2 basket.
8. Once it's done, serve.

Nutrition:
- (Per serving) Calories574 | Fat25g | Sodium848 mg | Carbs 21.4g | Fiber 1.2g| Sugar 1.8g | Protein 64.4g

Crispy Chickpeas

Servings: 4
Cooking Time: 15 Minutes
Ingredients:

- 1 (15-ounce) can unsalted chickpeas, rinsed and drained
- 1½ tablespoons toasted sesame oil
- ¼ teaspoon smoked paprika

- ¼ teaspoon crushed red pepper
- ⅛ teaspoon salt
- Cooking spray
- 2 lime wedges

Directions:
1. The chickpeas should be spread out over multiple layers of paper towels. Roll the chickpeas under the paper towels to dry both sides, then top with more paper towels and pat until completely dry.

2. In a medium mixing bowl, combine the chickpeas and oil. Add the paprika, crushed red pepper, and salt to taste.
3. Place a crisper plate in each drawer. Put the chickpeas in a single layer in each drawer. Insert the drawers into the unit.
4. Select zone 1, then ROAST, then set the temperature to 400 degrees F/ 200 degrees C with a 15-minute timer. To match zone 2 settings to zone 1, choose MATCH. To begin, select START/STOP.

Nutrition:
- (Per serving) Calories 169 | Fat 5g | Sodium 357mg | Carbs 27.3g | Fiber 5.7g | Sugar 0.6g | Protein 5.9g

Dried Apple Chips Dried Banana Chips

Servings:6
Cooking Time: 6 To 10 Hours
Ingredients:
- FOR THE APPLE CHIPS
- ½ teaspoon ground cinnamon
- ¼ teaspoon ground nutmeg
- ⅛ teaspoon ground allspice
- ⅛ teaspoon ground ginger
- 2 Gala apples, cored and cut into ⅛-inch-thick rings
- FOR THE BANANA CHIPS
- 2 firm-ripe bananas, cut into ¼-inch slices

Directions:
1. To prep the apple chips: In a small bowl, mix the cinnamon, nutmeg, allspice, and ginger until combined. Sprinkle the spice mixture over the apple slices.
2. To dehydrate the fruit: Arrange half of the apple slices in a single layer in the Zone 1 basket. It is okay if the edges overlap a bit as they will shrink as they cook. Place a crisper plate on top of the apples. Arrange the remaining apple slices on top of the crisper plate and insert the basket in the unit.
3. Repeat this process with the bananas in the Zone 2 basket and insert the basket in the unit.
4. Select Zone 1, select DEHYDRATE, set the temperature to 135°F, and set the time to 8 hours.
5. Select Zone 2, select DEHYDRATE, set the temperature to 135°F, and set the time to 10 hours. Select SMART FINISH.
6. Press START/PAUSE to begin cooking.
7. When both timers read 2 hours, press START/PAUSE. Remove both baskets and check the fruit for doneness; note that juicier fruit will take longer to dry than fruit that starts out drier. Reinsert the basket and press START/PAUSE to continue cooking if necessary.

Nutrition:
- (Per serving) Calories: 67; Total fat: 0g; Saturated fat: 0g; Carbohydrates: 16g; Fiber: 3g; Protein: 0g; Sodium: 1mg

Healthy Spinach Balls

Servings: 4
Cooking Time: 10 Minutes
Ingredients:
- 1 egg
- 29g breadcrumbs
- ½ medium onion, chopped
- 225g spinach, blanched & chopped
- 1 carrot, peel & grated
- 1 tbsp cornflour
- 1 tbsp nutritional yeast
- 1 tsp garlic, minced
- ½ tsp garlic powder
- Pepper
- Salt

Directions:
1. Add spinach and remaining ingredients into the mixing bowl and mix until well combined.
2. Insert a crisper plate in the Ninja Foodi air fryer baskets.
3. Make small balls from the spinach mixture and place them in both baskets.
4. Select zone 1, then select "air fry" mode and set the temperature to 390 degrees F for 10 minutes. Press "match" to match zone 2 settings to zone 1. Press "start/stop" to begin.

Nutrition:
- (Per serving) Calories 74 | Fat 1.7g |Sodium 122mg | Carbs 11.1g | Fiber 1.9g | Sugar 2g | Protein 4.2g

Avocado Fries With Sriracha Dip

Servings: 4
Cooking Time: 6 Minutes
Ingredients:

- Avocado Fries
- 4 avocados, peeled and cut into sticks
- ¾ cup panko breadcrumbs
- ¼ cup flour
- 2 eggs, beaten
- ½ teaspoon garlic powder
- ½ teaspoon salt
- SRIRACHA-RANCH SAUCE
- ¼ cup ranch dressing
- 1 teaspoon sriracha sauce

Directions:

1. Mix flour with garlic powder and salt in a bowl.
2. Dredge the avocado sticks through the flour mixture.
3. Dip them in the eggs and coat them with breadcrumbs.
4. Place the coated fries in the air fryer baskets.
5. Return the air fryer basket 1 to Zone 1, and basket 2 to Zone 2 of the Ninja Foodi 2-Basket Air Fryer.
6. Choose the "Air Fry" mode for Zone 1 at 400 degrees F and 6 minutes of cooking time.
7. Select the "MATCH COOK" option to copy the settings for Zone 2.
8. Initiate cooking by pressing the START/PAUSE BUTTON.
9. Flip the fries once cooked halfway through.
10. Mix all the dipping sauce ingredients in a bowl.
11. Serve the fries with dipping sauce.

Nutrition:

- (Per serving) Calories 229 | Fat 1.9 |Sodium 567mg | Carbs 1.9g | Fiber 0.4g | Sugar 0.6g | Protein 11.8g

Crab Cakes

Servings: 4
Cooking Time: 10 Minutes
Ingredients:

- 227g lump crab meat
- 1 red capsicum, chopped
- 3 green onions, chopped
- 3 tablespoons mayonnaise
- 3 tablespoons breadcrumbs
- 2 teaspoons old bay seasoning
- 1 teaspoon lemon juice

Directions:

1. Mix crab meat with capsicum, onions and the rest of the ingredients in a food processor.
2. Make 4 inch crab cakes out of this mixture.
3. Divide the crab cakes into the Ninja Foodi 2 Baskets Air Fryer baskets.
4. Return the air fryer basket 1 to Zone 1, and basket 2 to Zone 2 of the Ninja Foodi 2-Basket Air Fryer.
5. Choose the "Air Fry" mode for Zone 1 at 370 degrees F and 10 minutes of cooking time.
6. Select the "MATCH COOK" option to copy the settings for Zone 2.
7. Initiate cooking by pressing the START/PAUSE BUTTON.
8. Flip the crab cakes once cooked halfway through.
9. Serve warm.

Nutrition:

- (Per serving) Calories 163 | Fat 11.5g |Sodium 918mg | Carbs 8.3g | Fiber 4.2g | Sugar 0.2g | Protein 7.4g

Caramelized Onion Dip With White Cheese

Servings: 8 To 10
Cooking Time: 30 Minutes
Ingredients:

- 1 tablespoon butter
- 1 medium onion, halved and thinly sliced
- ¼ teaspoon rock salt, plus additional for seasoning
- 113 g soft white cheese
- 120 ml sour cream
- ¼ teaspoon onion powder
- 1 tablespoon chopped fresh chives
- Black pepper, to taste
- Thick-cut potato crisps or vegetable crisps

Directions:

1. Place the butter in a baking pan. Place the pan in the zone 1 air fryer basket. Set the air fryer to 90ºC for 1 minute, or until the butter is melted. Add the onions and salt to the pan.

2.   Set the air fryer to 90ºC for 15 minutes, or until onions are softened. Set the air fryer to 190ºC for 15 minutes, until onions are a deep golden brown, stirring two or three times during the cooking time. Let cool completely.
3.   In a medium bowl, stir together the cooked onions, soft white cheese, sour cream, onion powder, and chives. Season with salt and pepper. Cover and refrigerate for 2 hours to allow the flavours to blend.
4.   Serve the dip with potato crisps or vegetable crisps.

Bacon-wrapped Dates Bacon-wrapped Scallops

Servings:6
Cooking Time: 12 Minutes
Ingredients:
- FOR THE SCALLOPS
- 6 slices bacon, halved crosswise
- 12 large sea scallops, patted dry

- FOR THE DATES
- 4 slices bacon, cut into thirds
- 12 pitted dates

Directions:
1.   To prep the dates: Wrap each piece of bacon around a date and secure with a toothpick.
2.   To cook the dates and the bacon for the scallops: Install a crisper plate in each of the two baskets. Place the bacon for the scallops in the Zone 1 basket in a single layer and insert the basket in the unit. Place the bacon-wrapped dates in the Zone 2 basket in a single layer and insert the basket in the unit.
3.   Select Zone 1, select AIR FRY, set the temperature to 400ºF, and set the time to 12 minutes.
4.   Select Zone 2, select AIR FRY, set the temperature to 360ºF, and set the time to 10 minutes. Select SMART FINISH.
5.   Press START/PAUSE to begin cooking.
6.   When the Zone 1 timer reads 9 minutes, press START/PAUSE. Remove the basket from the unit. Wrap each piece of bacon around a scallop and secure with a toothpick. Place the bacon-wrapped scallops in the basket. Reinsert the basket and press START/PAUSE to resume cooking.
7.   When the Zone 1 timer reads 4 minutes, press START/PAUSE. Remove the basket and use silicone-tipped tongs to flip the scallops. Reinsert the basket and press START/PAUSE to resume cooking.
8.   When cooking is complete, the scallops will be opaque and the bacon around both the scallops and dates will be crisp. Arrange the bacon-wrapped scallops and dates on a serving platter. Serve warm.
Nutrition:
- (Per serving) Calories: 191; Total fat: 2.5g; Saturated fat: 1g; Carbohydrates: 39g; Fiber: 4g; Protein: 3g; Sodium: 115mg

Taco-spiced Chickpeas And Black Bean Corn Dip

Servings: 7
Cooking Time: 17 Minutes
Ingredients:
- Taco-Spiced Chickpeas:
- Oil, for spraying
- 1 (439 g) can chickpeas, drained
- 1 teaspoon chilli powder
- ½ teaspoon ground cumin
- ½ teaspoon salt
- ½ teaspoon granulated garlic
- 2 teaspoons lime juice
- Black Bean Corn Dip:

- ½ (425 g) can black beans, drained and rinsed
- ½ (425 g) can corn, drained and rinsed
- 60 ml chunky salsa
- 57 g low-fat soft white cheese
- 60 ml shredded low-fat Cheddar cheese
- ½ teaspoon ground cumin
- ½ teaspoon paprika
- Salt and freshly ground black pepper, to taste

Directions:
1.   Make the Taco-Spiced Chickpeas :
2.   Line the zone 1 air fryer basket with parchment and spray lightly with oil. Place the chickpeas in the prepared basket.
3.   Air fry at 200ºC for 17 minutes, shaking or stirring the chickpeas and spraying lightly with oil every 5 to 7 minutes.
4.   In a small bowl, mix together the chilli powder, cumin, salt, and garlic.
5.   When 2 to 3 minutes of cooking time remain, sprinkle half of the seasoning mix over the chickpeas. Finish cooking.
6.   Transfer the chickpeas to a medium bowl and toss with the remaining seasoning mix and the lime juice. Serve immediately.
7.   Make the Black Bean Corn Dip :
8.   Preheat the air fryer to 165ºC.
9.   In a medium bowl, mix together the black beans, corn, salsa, soft white cheese, Cheddar cheese, cumin, and paprika. Season with salt and pepper and stir until well combined.
10. Spoon the mixture into a baking dish.
11. Place baking dish in the zone 2 air fryer basket and bake until heated through, about 10 minutes.
12. Serve hot.

Buffalo Wings Honey-garlic Wings

Servings:6
Cooking Time: 40 Minutes
Ingredients:

- FOR THE BUFFALO WINGS
- 2 pounds chicken wings
- ¼ teaspoon kosher salt
- ¼ teaspoon freshly ground black pepper
- ¼ teaspoon paprika
- 1 tablespoon vegetable oil
- ⅓ cup Buffalo wing sauce
- FOR THE HONEY-GARLIC WINGS

- 2 pounds chicken wings
- 2 tablespoons all-purpose flour
- ½ teaspoon garlic powder
- 1 tablespoon vegetable oil
- ¼ cup honey
- 2 tablespoons reduced-sodium soy sauce
- ½ teaspoon ground ginger (optional)

Directions:
1. To prep the Buffalo wings: In a large bowl, combine the wings, salt, black pepper, and paprika and toss to coat the wings with the seasonings. Drizzle with the oil.
2. To prep the honey-garlic wings: In another large bowl, combine the wings, flour, and garlic powder and toss to coat the wings. Drizzle with the oil.
3. In a small bowl, whisk together the honey, soy sauce, and ginger (if using). Set the honey-soy sauce aside.
4. To cook the wings: Install a crisper plate in each of the two baskets. Place the Buffalo wings in the Zone 1 basket and insert the basket in the unit. Place the honey-garlic wings in the Zone 2 basket and insert the basket in the unit.
5. Select Zone 1, select AIR FRY, set the temperature to 390°F, and set the time to 40 minutes. Select MATCH COOK to match Zone 2 settings to Zone 1.
6. Press START/PAUSE to begin cooking.
7. When both timers read 8 minutes, press START/PAUSE. Remove the Zone 1 basket, drizzle the Buffalo sauce over the wings, and shake to coat the wings with the sauce. Reinsert the basket. Remove the Zone 2 basket, drizzle the honey-soy sauce over the wings, and shake to coat the wings with the sauce. Reinsert the basket. Press START/PAUSE to resume cooking.
8. When cooking is complete, the wings will be golden brown and cooked through. Use silicone-tipped tongs to transfer the wings to a serving plate. Serve warm.

Nutrition:
- (Per serving) Calories: 399; Total fat: 28g; Saturated fat: 7.5g; Carbohydrates: 0g; Fiber: 0g; Protein: 34g; Sodium: 1,049mg

Kale Chips

Servings: 4
Cooking Time: 3 Minutes
Ingredients:

- 1 head fresh kale, stems and ribs removed and cut into 4cm pieces
- 1 tablespoon olive oil

- 1 teaspoon soy sauce
- ⅛ teaspoon cayenne pepper
- Pinch of freshly ground black pepper

Directions:
1. In a large bowl, add all the ingredients and mix well.
2. Grease basket of Ninja Foodi 2-Basket Air Fryer.
3. Press your chosen zone - "Zone 1" or "Zone 2" and then rotate the knob to select "Air Fry".
4. Set the temperature to 200 degrees C and then set the time for 5 minutes to preheat.
5. After preheating, arrange the kale pieces into the basket of each zone.
6. Slide the basket into the Air Fryer and set the time for 3 minutes.
7. While cooking, toss the kale pieces once halfway through.
8. After cooking time is completed, remove the kale chips and baking pans from Air Fryer.
9. Place the kale chips onto a wire rack to cool for about 10 minutes before serving.

Onion Pakoras

Servings: 2
Cooking Time: 10 Minutes
Ingredients:

- 2 medium brown or white onions, sliced (475 ml)
- 120 ml chopped fresh coriander
- 2 tablespoons vegetable oil
- 1 tablespoon chickpea flour
- 1 tablespoon rice flour, or 2 tablespoons chickpea flour
- 1 teaspoon ground turmeric
- 1 teaspoon cumin seeds
- 1 teaspoon rock salt
- ½ teaspoon cayenne pepper
- Vegetable oil spray

Directions:

1. In a large bowl, combine the onions, coriander, oil, chickpea flour, rice flour, turmeric, cumin seeds, salt, and cayenne. Stir to combine. Cover and let stand for 30 minutes or up to overnight. Mix well before using.
2. Spray the air fryer baskets generously with vegetable oil spray. Drop the batter in 6 heaping tablespoons into the two baskets. Set the air fryer to 175ºC for 8 minutes. Carefully turn the pakoras over and spray with oil spray. Set the air fryer for 2 minutes, or until the batter is cooked through and crisp, checking at 6 minutes for doneness. Serve hot.

Onion Rings

Servings: 4
Cooking Time: 7 Minutes
Ingredients:

- 170g onion, sliced into rings
- ½ cup breadcrumbs
- 2 eggs, beaten
- ½ cup flour
- Salt and black pepper to taste

Directions:

1. Mix flour, black pepper and salt in a bowl.
2. Dredge the onion rings through the flour mixture.
3. Dip them in the eggs and coat with the breadcrumbs.
4. Place the coated onion rings in the air fryer baskets.
5. Return the air fryer basket 1 to Zone 1, and basket 2 to Zone 2 of the Ninja Foodi 2-Basket Air Fryer.
6. Choose the "Air Fry" mode for Zone 1 at 350 degrees F and 7 minutes of cooking time.
7. Select the "MATCH COOK" option to copy the settings for Zone 2.
8. Initiate cooking by pressing the START/PAUSE BUTTON.
9. Shake the rings once cooked halfway through.
10. Serve warm.

Nutrition:

- (Per serving) Calories 185 | Fat 11g |Sodium 355mg | Carbs 21g | Fiber 5.8g | Sugar 3g | Protein 4.7g

Crispy Popcorn Shrimp

Servings: 4
Cooking Time: 6 Minutes
Ingredients:

- 170g shrimp, peeled and diced
- ½ cup breadcrumbs
- Salt and black pepper to taste
- 2 eggs, beaten

Directions:

1. Mix breadcrumbs with black pepper and salt in a bowl.
2. Dip the shrimp pieces in the eggs and coat each with breadcrumbs.
3. Divide the shrimp popcorn into the 2 Air Fryer baskets.
4. Return the air fryer basket 1 to Zone 1, and basket 2 to Zone 2 of the Ninja Foodi 2-Basket Air Fryer.
5. Choose the "Air Fry" mode for Zone 1 at 400 degrees F and 6 minutes of cooking time.
6. Select the "MATCH COOK" option to copy the settings for Zone 2.
7. Initiate cooking by pressing the START/PAUSE BUTTON.
8. Serve warm.

Nutrition:

- (Per serving) Calories 180 | Fat 3.2g |Sodium 133mg | Carbs 32g | Fiber 1.1g | Sugar 1.8g | Protein 9g

Chapter 9 : Desserts Recipes

Air Fried Beignets

Servings: 6
Cooking Time: 17 Minutes.
Ingredients:

- Cooking spray
- ¼ cup white sugar
- ⅛ cup water
- ½ cup all-purpose flour
- 1 large egg, separated

- 1 ½ teaspoons butter, melted
- ½ teaspoon baking powder
- ½ teaspoon vanilla extract
- 1 pinch salt
- 2 tablespoons confectioners' sugar, or to taste

Directions:
1. Beat flour with water, sugar, egg yolk, baking powder, butter, vanilla extract, and salt in a large bowl until lumps-free.
2. Beat egg whites in a separate bowl and beat using an electric hand mixer until it forms soft peaks.
3. Add the egg white to the flour batter and mix gently until fully incorporated.
4. Divide the dough into small beignets and place them in the crisper plate.
5. Return the crisper plate to the Ninja Foodi Dual Zone Air Fryer.
6. Choose the Air Fry mode for Zone 1 and set the temperature to 390 degrees F and the time to 17 minutes.
7. Select the "MATCH" button to copy the settings for Zone 2.
8. Initiate cooking by pressing the START/STOP button.
9. And cook for another 4 minutes. Dust the cooked beignets with sugar.
10. Serve.

Nutrition:
- (Per serving) Calories 327 | Fat 14.2g |Sodium 672mg | Carbs 47.2g | Fiber 1.7g | Sugar 24.8g | Protein 4.4g

Peanut Butter, Honey & Banana Toast

Servings: 4
Cooking Time: 9 Minutes
Ingredients:

- 2 tablespoons unsalted butter, softened
- 4 slices white bread
- 4 tablespoons peanut butter

- 2 bananas, peeled and thinly sliced
- 4 tablespoons honey
- 1 teaspoon ground cinnamon

Directions:
1. Spread butter on one side of each slice of bread, then peanut butter on the other side. Arrange the banana slices on top of the peanut butter sides of each slice . Drizzle honey on top of the banana and sprinkle with cinnamon.
2. Cut each slice in half lengthwise so that it will better fit into the air fryer basket. Arrange the bread slices, butter sides down, in the two air fryer baskets. Set the air fryer to 190ºC cooking for 5 minutes. Then set the air fryer to 205ºC and cook for an additional 4 minutes, or until the bananas have started to brown. Serve hot.

Walnuts Fritters

Servings: 6
Cooking Time: 15 Minutes.
Ingredients:

- 1 cup all-purpose flour
- ½ cup walnuts, chopped
- ¼ cup white sugar
- ¼ cup milk
- 1 egg
- 1 ½ teaspoons baking powder
- 1 pinch salt
- Cooking spray

- 2 tablespoons white sugar
- ½ teaspoon ground cinnamon
- Glaze:
- ½ cup confectioners' sugar
- 1 tablespoon milk
- ½ teaspoon caramel extract
- ¼ teaspoons ground cinnamon

Directions:
1. Layer both crisper plate with parchment paper.
2. Grease the parchment paper with cooking spray.
3. Whisk flour with milk, ¼ cup of sugar, egg, baking powder, and salt in a small bowl.
4. Separately mix 2 tablespoons of sugar with cinnamon in another bowl, toss in walnuts and mix well to coat.
5. Stir in flour mixture and mix until combined.
6. Drop the fritters mixture using a cookie scoop into the two crisper plate.
7. Return the crisper plate to the Ninja Foodi Dual Zone Air Fryer.

8. Choose the Air Fry mode for Zone 1 and set the temperature to 375 degrees F and the time to 15 minutes.
9. Select the "MATCH" button to copy the settings for Zone 2.
10. Initiate cooking by pressing the START/STOP button.
11. Flip the fritters once cooked halfway through, then resume cooking.
12. Meanwhile, whisk milk, caramel extract, confectioners' sugar, and cinnamon in a bowl.
13. Transfer fritters to a wire rack and allow them to cool.
14. Drizzle with a glaze over the fritters.

Nutrition:
- (Per serving) Calories 391 | Fat 24g |Sodium 142mg | Carbs 38.5g | Fiber 3.5g | Sugar 21g | Protein 6.6g

Pumpkin Cookie With Cream Cheese Frosting

Servings: 6
Cooking Time: 7 Minutes
Ingredients:
- 50 g blanched finely ground almond flour
- 50 g powdered sweetener, divided
- 2 tablespoons butter, softened
- 1 large egg
- ½ teaspoon unflavored gelatin
- ½ teaspoon baking powder
- ½ teaspoon vanilla extract
- ½ teaspoon pumpkin pie spice
- 2 tablespoons pure pumpkin purée
- ½ teaspoon ground cinnamon, divided
- 40 g low-carb, sugar-free chocolate chips
- 85 g full-fat cream cheese, softened

Directions:
1. In a large bowl, mix almond flour and 25 gsweetener. Stir in butter, egg, and gelatin until combined. 2. Stir in baking powder, vanilla, pumpkin pie spice, pumpkin purée, and ¼ teaspoon cinnamon, then fold in chocolate chips. 3. Pour batter into a round baking pan. Place pan into the zone 1 air fryer basket. 4. Adjust the temperature to 150ºC and bake for 7 minutes. 5. When fully cooked, the top will be golden brown, and a toothpick inserted in center will come out clean. Let cool at least 20 minutes. 6. To make the frosting: mix cream cheese, remaining ¼ teaspoon cinnamon, and remaining 25 g sweetener in a large bowl. Using an electric mixer, beat until it becomes fluffy. Spread onto the cooled cookie. Garnish with additional cinnamon if desired.

Homemade Mini Cheesecake

Servings: 2
Cooking Time: 15 Minutes
Ingredients:
- ½ cup walnuts
- 2 tablespoons salted butter
- 2 tablespoons granular erythritol
- 4 ounces full-fat cream cheese, softened
- 1 large egg
- ½ teaspoon vanilla extract
- ⅛ cup powdered erythritol

Directions:
1. Place butter, granular erythritol, and walnuts in a food processor. Pulse until all the ingredients stick together to form a dough.
2. Place dough into 4&quot| springform pan then put the pan into the air fryer basket.
3. Set the temperature to 400°F, then set the timer for 5 minutes.
4. When timer goes off, remove the crust and allow it rest.
5. Stir cream cheese with vanilla extract, powdered erythritol and egg until smooth in a medium bowl.
6. Pour mixture on top of baked walnut crust and then put into the air fryer basket.
7. Set the temperature to 300°F, then set the timer for 10 minutes.
8. Once cooked fully, allow to cool for 2 hours before serving.

Double Chocolate Brownies

Servings: 8
Cooking Time: 15 To 20 Minutes
Ingredients:
- 110 g almond flour
- 50 g unsweetened cocoa powder
- ½ teaspoon baking powder
- 35 g powdered sweetener
- ¼ teaspoon salt
- 110 g unsalted butter, melted and cooled
- 3 eggs
- 1 teaspoon vanilla extract
- 2 tablespoons mini semisweet chocolate chips

Directions:
1. Preheat the air fryer to 175ºC. Line a cake pan with baking paper and brush with oil.
2. In a large bowl, combine the almond flour, cocoa powder, baking powder, sweetener, and salt. Add the butter, eggs, and vanilla. Stir until thoroughly combined Spread the batter into the prepared pan and scatter the chocolate chips on top.
3. Air fry in the zone 1 basket for 15 to 20 minutes until the edges are set Let cool completely before slicing. To store, cover and refrigerate the brownies for up to 3 days.

Fried Oreos

Servings: 8
Cooking Time: 8 Minutes
Ingredients:
- 1 can Pillsbury Crescent Dough (or equivalent)
- 8 Oreo cookies
- 1–2 tablespoons powdered sugar

Directions:
1. Open the crescent dough up and cut it into the right-size pieces to completely wrap each cookie.
2. Wrap each Oreo in dough. Make sure that there are no air bubbles and that the cookies are completely covered.
3. Install a crisper plate in both drawers. Place half the Oreo cookies in the zone 1 drawer and half in zone 2's. Sprinkle the tops with the powdered sugar, then insert the drawers into the unit.
4. Select zone 1, select AIR FRY, set temperature to 390 degrees F/ 200 degrees C, and set time to 8 minutes. Select MATCH to match zone 2 settings to zone 1. Press the START/STOP button to begin cooking.
5. Serve warm and enjoy!

Nutrition:
- (Per serving) Calories 338 | Fat 21.2g | Sodium 1503mg | Carbs 5.1g | Fiber 0.3g | Sugar 4.6g | Protein 29.3g

Chocolate Muffins

Servings: 12
Cooking Time: 20 Minutes
Ingredients:
- 2 cup all-purpose flour
- 4 tablespoons cocoa powder
- ½ teaspoon baking soda
- 2 teaspoons baking powder
- ½ teaspoon salt
- 1 cup coconut milk
- ½ cup granulated sugar
- 6 tablespoons coconut oil, melted
- 1 teaspoon vanilla extract
- 1 cup dark chocolate chips
- ½ cup pistachios, chopped

Directions:
1. In a bowl, add the flour, cocoa powder, baking powder, baking soda, and salt and mix well.
2. In another bowl, add the coconut milk, sugar, coconut oil and vanilla extract and beat until well combined.
3. Add the flour mixture and mix until just combined.
4. Fold in the chocolate chips and pistachios.
5. Grease 2 silicone muffin tins.
6. Place the mixture into prepared muffin cups about ¾ full.
7. Press "Zone 1" and "Zone 2" and then rotate the knob for each zone to select "Air Fry".
8. Set the temperature to 300 degrees F/ 150 degrees C for both zones and then set the time for 5 minutes to preheat.
9. After preheating, arrange 1 muffin tin into the basket of each zone.
10. Slide each basket into Air Fryer and set the time for 15 minutes.
11. After cooking time is completed, remove the muffin tin from Air Fryer.
12. Place the muffin molds onto a wire rack to cool for about 10 minutes.
13. Carefully invert the muffins onto the wire rack to completely cool before serving.

Fried Dough With Roasted Strawberries

Servings:4
Cooking Time: 20 Minutes
Ingredients:
- FOR THE FRIED DOUGH
- 6 ounces refrigerated pizza dough, at room temperature
- 2 tablespoons all-purpose flour, for dusting
- 4 tablespoons vegetable oil
- 2 tablespoons powdered sugar
- FOR THE ROASTED STRAWBERRIES
- 2 cups frozen whole strawberries

- 2 tablespoons granulated sugar

Directions:
1. To prep the fried dough: Divide the dough into four equal portions.
2. Dust a clean work surface with the flour. Place one dough portion on the surface and use a rolling pin to roll to a ⅛-inch thickness. Rub both sides of the dough with 1 tablespoon of oil. Repeat with remaining dough portions and oil.
3. To prep the strawberries: Place the strawberries in the Zone 2 basket. Sprinkle the granulated sugar on top.
4. To cook the fried dough and strawberries: Install a crisper plate in the Zone 1 basket. Place 2 dough portions in the basket and insert the basket in the unit. Insert the Zone 2 basket in the unit.
5. Select Zone 1, select AIR FRY, set the temperature to 400°F, and set the timer to 18 minutes.
6. Select Zone 2, select ROAST, set the temperature to 330°F, and set the timer to 20 minutes. Select SMART FINISH.
7. Press START/PAUSE to begin cooking.
8. When both timers read 8 minutes, press START/PAUSE. Remove the Zone 1 basket and transfer the fried dough to a cutting board. Place the 2 remaining dough portions in the basket, then reinsert the basket. Remove the Zone 2 basket and stir the strawberries. Reinsert the basket and press START/PAUSE to resume cooking.
9. When cooking is complete, the dough should be cooked through and the strawberries soft and jammy.
10. Sprinkle the fried dough with powdered sugar. Gently mash the strawberries with a fork. Spoon the strawberries onto each fried dough portion and serve.

Nutrition:
- (Per serving) Calories: 304; Total fat: 15g; Saturated fat: 2.5g; Carbohydrates: 38g; Fiber: 0.5g; Protein: 3g; Sodium: 421mg

Crispy Pineapple Rings

Servings: 6
Cooking Time: 6 To 8 Minutes
Ingredients:
- 240 ml rice milk
- 85 g plain flour
- 120 ml water
- 25 g unsweetened flaked coconut
- 4 tablespoons granulated sugar
- ½ teaspoon baking soda
- ½ teaspoon baking powder
- ½ teaspoon vanilla essence
- ½ teaspoon ground cinnamon
- ¼ teaspoon ground star anise
- Pinch of kosher, or coarse sea salt
- 1 medium pineapple, peeled and sliced

Directions:
1. Preheat the air fryer to 190ºC.
2. In a large bowl, stir together all the ingredients except the pineapple.
3. Dip each pineapple slice into the batter until evenly coated.
4. Arrange the pineapple slices in the zone 1 basket and air fry for 6 to 8 minutes until golden brown.
5. Remove from the basket to a plate and cool for 5 minutes before serving warm

Honey Lime Pineapple

Servings: 4
Cooking Time: 10 Minutes
Ingredients:
- 562g pineapple chunks
- 55g brown sugar
- 30ml lime juice
- 63g honey

Directions:
1. In a bowl, mix pineapple, honey, lime juice, and brown sugar. Cover and place in refrigerator for 1 hour.
2. Insert a crisper plate in Ninja Foodi air fryer baskets.
3. Remove pineapple chunks from the marinade and place in both baskets.
4. Select zone 1 then select "air fry" mode and set the temperature to 390 degrees F for 10 minutes. Press "match" to match zone 2 settings to zone 1. Press "start/stop" to begin. Stir halfway through.

Nutrition:
- (Per serving) Calories 153 | Fat 0.2g |Sodium 5mg | Carbs 40.5g | Fiber 2g | Sugar 35.7g | Protein 0.8g

Bread Pudding

Servings: 4
Cooking Time: 15 Minutes
Ingredients:

- 2 cups bread cubes
- 1 egg
- ⅔ cup heavy cream
- ½ teaspoon vanilla extract
- ¼ cup sugar
- ¼ cup chocolate chips

Directions:

1. Grease two 4 inches baking dish with a cooking spray.
2. Divide the bread cubes in the baking dishes and sprinkle chocolate chips on top.
3. Beat egg with cream, sugar and vanilla in a bowl.
4. Divide this mixture in the baking dishes.
5. Place one pan in each air fryer basket.
6. Return the air fryer basket 1 to Zone 1, and basket 2 to Zone 2 of the Ninja Foodi 2-Basket Air Fryer.
7. Choose the "Air Fry" mode for Zone 1 at 350 degrees F and 15 minutes of cooking time.
8. Select the "MATCH COOK" option to copy the settings for Zone 2.
9. Initiate cooking by pressing the START/PAUSE BUTTON.
10. Allow the pudding to cool and serve.

Nutrition:

- (Per serving) Calories 149 | Fat 1.2g |Sodium 3mg | Carbs 37.6g | Fiber 5.8g | Sugar 29g | Protein 1.1g

Caramelized Fruit Skewers

Servings: 4
Cooking Time: 3 To 5 Minutes
Ingredients:

- 2 peaches, peeled, pitted, and thickly sliced
- 3 plums, halved and pitted
- 3 nectarines, halved and pitted
- 1 tablespoon honey
- ½ teaspoon ground cinnamon
- ¼ teaspoon ground allspice
- Pinch cayenne pepper
- Special Equipment:
- 8 metal skewers

Directions:

1. Preheat the air fryer to 204ºC.
2. Thread, alternating peaches, plums, and nectarines, onto the metal skewers that fit into the air fryer.
3. Thoroughly combine the honey, cinnamon, allspice, and cayenne in a small bowl. Brush the glaze generously over the fruit skewers.
4. Transfer the fruit skewers to the two air fryer drawers.
5. Air fry for 3 to 5 minutes, or until the fruit is caramelized.
6. Remove from the drawers.
7. Let the fruit skewers rest for 5 minutes before serving.

Cinnamon Bread Twists

Servings: 4
Cooking Time: 15 Minutes
Ingredients:

- Bread Twists Dough
- 120g all-purpose flour
- 1 teaspoon baking powder
- ¼ teaspoon salt
- 150g fat free Greek yogurt
- Brushing
- 2 tablespoons light butter
- 2 tablespoons granulated sugar
- 1-2 teaspoons ground cinnamon, to taste

Directions:

1. Mix flour, salt and baking powder in a bowl.
2. Stir in yogurt and the rest of the dough ingredients in a bowl.
3. Mix well and make 8 inches long strips out of this dough.
4. Twist the strips and place them in the air fryer baskets.
5. Return the air fryer basket 1 to Zone 1, and basket 2 to Zone 2 of the Ninja Foodi 2-Basket Air Fryer.
6. Choose the "Air Fry" mode for Zone 1 at 375 degrees F and 15 minutes of cooking time.
7. Select the "MATCH COOK" option to copy the settings for Zone 2.

8. Initiate cooking by pressing the START/PAUSE BUTTON.
9. Flip the twists once cooked halfway through.
10. Mix butter with cinnamon and sugar in a bowl.
11. Brush this mixture over the twists.
12. Serve.

Nutrition:
- (Per serving) Calories 391 | Fat 24g |Sodium 142mg | Carbs 38.5g | Fiber 3.5g | Sugar 21g | Protein 6.6g

Dessert Empanadas

Servings: 12
Cooking Time: 10 Minutes

Ingredients:
- 12 empanada wrappers thawed
- 2 apples, chopped
- 2 tablespoons raw honey
- 1 teaspoon vanilla extract
- 1 teaspoon cinnamon
- ⅛ teaspoon nutmeg
- 2 teaspoons cornstarch
- 1 teaspoon water
- 1 egg beaten

Directions:
1. Mix apples with vanilla, honey, nutmeg, and cinnamon in a saucepan.
2. Cook for 3 minutes then mix cornstarch with water and pour into the pan.
3. Cook for 30 seconds.
4. Allow this filling to cool and keep it aside.
5. Spread the wrappers on the working surface.
6. Divide the apple filling on top of the wrappers.
7. Fold the wrappers in half and seal the edges by pressing them.
8. Brush the empanadas with the beaten egg and place them in the air fryer basket 1.
9. Return the air fryer basket 1 to Zone 1 of the Ninja Foodi 2-Basket Air Fryer.
10. Choose the "Air Fry" mode for Zone 1 at 400 degrees F and 10 minutes of cooking time.
11. Initiate cooking by pressing the START/PAUSE BUTTON.
12. Flip the empanadas once cooked halfway through.
13. Serve.

Nutrition:
- (Per serving) Calories 204 | Fat 9g |Sodium 91mg | Carbs 27g | Fiber 2.4g | Sugar 15g | Protein 1.3g

Gluten-free Spice Cookies

Servings: 4
Cooking Time: 12 Minutes

Ingredients:
- 4 tablespoons unsalted butter, at room temperature
- 2 tablespoons agave nectar
- 1 large egg
- 2 tablespoons water
- 240 g almond flour
- 100 g granulated sugar
- 2 teaspoons ground ginger
- 1 teaspoon ground cinnamon
- ½ teaspoon freshly grated nutmeg
- 1 teaspoon baking soda
- ¼ teaspoon kosher, or coarse sea salt

Directions:
1. Line the bottom of the air fryer basket with baking paper cut to fit.
2. In a large bowl, using a hand mixer, beat together the butter, agave, egg, and water on medium speed until light and fluffy.
3. Add the almond flour, sugar, ginger, cinnamon, nutmeg, baking soda, and salt. Beat on low speed until well combined.
4. Roll the dough into 2-tablespoon balls and arrange them on the baking paper in the basket. Set the air fryer to 165°C, and cook for 12 minutes, or until the tops of cookies are lightly browned.
5. Transfer to a wire rack and let cool completely. Store in an airtight container for up to a week.

Quickie Cinnamon Sugar Pork Rinds

Servings: 2
Cooking Time: 5 Minutes

Ingredients:

- 2 ounces pork rinds
- 2 tablespoons unsalted butter, melted
- ½ teaspoon ground cinnamon
- ¼ cup powdered erythritol

Directions:

1. Stir butter and pork rinds in a large bowl. Sprinkle with erythritol and cinnamon, then toss to coat well.
2. Put pork rinds into the air fryer basket.
3. Set the temperature to 400°F, then set the timer for 5 minutes.
4. Serve warm.

Strawberry Nutella Hand Pies

Servings: 8
Cooking Time: 10 Minutes

Ingredients:

- 1 tube pie crust dough
- 3–4 strawberries, finely chopped
- Nutella
- Sugar
- Coconut oil cooking spray

Directions:

1. Roll out the pie dough and place it on a baking sheet. Cut out hearts using a 3-inch heart-shaped cookie cutter as precisely as possible.
2. Gather the leftover dough into a ball and roll it out thinly to make a few more heart shapes. For 8 hand pies, I was able to get 16 hearts from one tube of pie crust.
3. Set aside a baking tray lined with parchment paper.
4. Spread a dollop of Nutella (approximately 1 teaspoon) on one of the hearts. Add a few strawberry pieces to the mix. Add a pinch of sugar to the top.
5. Place another heart on top and use a fork to tightly crimp the edges. Gently poke holes in the top of the pie with a fork. Place on a baking sheet. Repeat for all the pies.
6. All of the pies on the tray should be sprayed with coconut oil.
7. Install a crisper plate in both drawers. Place half the pies in the zone 1 drawer and half in zone 2's, then insert the drawers into the unit.
8. Select zone 1, select BAKE, set temperature to 390 degrees F/ 200 degrees C, and set time to 10 minutes. Select MATCH to match zone 2 settings to zone 1. Press the START/STOP button to begin cooking.

Nutrition:

- (Per serving) Calories 41 | Fat 2.1g | Sodium 18mg | Carbs 5.5g | Fiber 0.4g | Sugar 4.1g | Protein 0.4g

Fruity Blackberry Crisp

Servings: 4
Cooking Time: 15 Minutes

Ingredients:

- 2 cups blackberries
- ⅓ cup powdered erythritol
- 2 tablespoons lemon juice
- ¼ teaspoon xanthan gum
- 1 cup Crunchy Granola

Directions:

1. Mix erythritol, blackberries, xanthan gum, and lemon juice in a large bowl.
2. Place into 6&quot| round baking dish and cover with a sheet of foil. Put into the air fryer basket.
3. Set the temperature to 350°F, then set the timer for 12 minutes.
4. When the goes off, remove the foil and shake well.
5. Sprinkle granola on the top of mixture and place back to the air fryer basket.
6. Set the temperature to 320°F, then set the timer for 3 minutes or until the top is golden brown.
7. Serve immediately.

Soft Pecan Brownies

Servings: 6
Cooking Time: 20 Minutes
Ingredients:
- ½ cup blanched finely ground almond flour
- ½ cup powdered erythritol
- 2 tablespoons unsweetened cocoa powder
- ½ teaspoon baking powder
- ¼ cup unsalted butter, softened
- 1 large egg
- ¼ cup chopped pecans
- ¼ cup low-carb, sugar-free chocolate chips

Directions:
1. Stir erythritol, almond flour, baking powder and cocoa powder in a large bowl. Add in egg and butter, mix well.
2. Fold in chocolate chips and pecans. Pour mixture into 6&quot| round baking pan. Put pan into the air fryer basket.
3. Set the temperature to 300°F, then set the timer for 20 minutes.
4. A toothpick inserted in center will come out clean when completely cooked. Let it rest for 20 minutes to fully cool and firm up. Serve immediately.

Mini Strawberry And Cream Pies

Servings:2
Cooking Time:10
Ingredients:
- 1 box Store-Bought Pie Dough, Trader Joe's
- 1 cup strawberries, cubed
- 3 tablespoons of cream, heavy
- 2 tablespoons of almonds
- 1 egg white, for brushing

Directions:
1. Take the store brought pie dough and flatten it on a surface.
2. Use a round cutter to cut it into 3-inch circles.
3. Brush the dough with egg white all around the parameters.
4. Now add almonds, strawberries, and cream in a very little amount in the center of the dough, and top it with another circular.
5. Press the edges with the fork to seal it.
6. Make a slit in the middle of the dough and divide it into the baskets.
7. Set zone 1 to AIR FRY mode 360 degrees for 10 minutes.
8. Select MATCH for zone 2 basket.
9. Once done, serve.

Nutrition:
- (Per serving) Calories 203| Fat12.7g| Sodium 193mg | Carbs20 g | Fiber 2.2g | Sugar 5.8g | Protein 3.7g

Glazed Cherry Turnovers

Servings: 8
Cooking Time: 14 Minutes
Ingredients:
- 2 sheets frozen puff pastry, thawed
- 600 g can premium cherry pie filling
- 2 teaspoons ground cinnamon
- 1 egg, beaten
- 90 g sliced almonds
- 120 g icing sugar
- 2 tablespoons milk

Directions:
1. Roll a sheet of puff pastry out into a square that is approximately 10-inches by 10-inches. Cut this large square into quarters.
2. Mix the cherry pie filling and cinnamon together in a bowl. Spoon ¼ cup of the cherry filling into the center of each puff pastry square. Brush the perimeter of the pastry square with the egg wash. Fold one corner of the puff pastry over the cherry pie filling towards the opposite corner, forming a triangle. Seal the two edges of the pastry together with the tip of a fork, making a design with the tines. Brush the top of the turnovers with the egg wash and sprinkle sliced almonds over each one. Repeat these steps with the second sheet of puff pastry. You should have eight turnovers at the end.
3. Preheat the air fryer to 188ºC.
4. Air fry turnovers in the two drawers for 14 minutes, carefully turning them over halfway through the cooking time.
5. While the turnovers are cooking, make the glaze by whisking the icing sugar and milk together in a small bowl until smooth. Let the glaze sit for a minute so the sugar can absorb the milk. If the consistency is still too thick to drizzle, add a little more milk, a drop at a time, and stir until smooth.
6. Let the cooked cherry turnovers sit for at least 10 minutes. Then drizzle the glaze over each turnover in a zigzag motion. Serve warm or at room temperature.

Pumpkin Muffins With Cinnamon

Servings: 4
Cooking Time: 20 Minutes
Ingredients:

- 1 and ½ cups all-purpose flour
- ½ teaspoon baking soda
- ½ teaspoon baking powder
- 1 and ¼ teaspoons cinnamon, groaned
- ¼ teaspoon ground nutmeg, grated
- 2 large eggs
- Salt, pinch
- ¾ cup granulated sugar
- ½ cup dark brown sugar
- 1 and ½ cups pumpkin puree
- ¼ cup coconut milk

Directions:
1. Take 4 ramekins and layer them with muffin paper.
2. In a bowl, add the eggs, brown sugar, baking soda, baking powder, cinnamon, nutmeg, and sugar and whisk well with an electric mixer.
3. In a second bowl, mix the flour, and salt.
4. Slowly add the dry ingredients to the wet ingredients.
5. Fold in the pumpkin puree and milk and mix it in well.
6. Divide this batter into 4 ramekins.
7. Place two ramekins in each air fryer basket.
8. Set the time for zone 1 to 18 minutes at 360 degrees F/ 180 degrees C on AIR FRY mode.
9. Select the MATCH button for the zone 2 basket.
10. Check after the time is up and if not done, and let it AIR FRY for one more minute.
11. Once it is done, serve.

Nutrition:
- (Per serving) Calories 291 | Fat 6.4g | Sodium 241mg | Carbs 57.1g | Fiber 4.4g | Sugar 42g | Protein 5.9g

Funnel Cake

Servings: 4
Cooking Time: 5 Minutes
Ingredients:

- Coconut, or avocado oil, for spraying
- 110 g self-raising flour, plus more for dusting
- 240 ml fat-free vanilla Greek yogurt
- ½ teaspoon ground cinnamon
- ¼ cup icing sugar

Directions:
1. Preheat the air fryer to 192°C. Line the two air fryer drawers with baking paper, and spray lightly with oil.
2. In a large bowl, mix together the flour, yogurt and cinnamon until the mixture forms a ball.
3. Place the dough on a lightly floured work surface and knead for about 2 minutes.
4. Cut the dough into 4 equal pieces, then cut each of those into 6 pieces. You should have 24 pieces in total.
5. Roll the pieces into 8- to 10-inch-long ropes. Loosely mound the ropes into 4 piles of 6 ropes.
6. Place the dough piles in the two prepared drawers, and spray liberally with oil.
7. Cook for 5 minutes, or until lightly browned.
8. Dust with the icing sugar before serving.

Butter And Chocolate Chip Cookies

Servings: 8
Cooking Time: 11 Minutes
Ingredients:

- 110 g unsalted butter, at room temperature
- 155 g powdered sweetener
- 60 g chunky peanut butter
- 1 teaspoon vanilla paste
- 1 fine almond flour
- ¼ teaspoon ginger
- 85 g unsweetened, or dark chocolate chips
- 75 g coconut flour
- 35 g cocoa powder, unsweetened
- 1 ½ teaspoons baking powder
- ¼ teaspoon ground cinnamon

Directions:
1. In a mixing dish, beat the butter and sweetener until creamy and uniform. Stir in the peanut butter and vanilla.
2. In another mixing dish, thoroughly combine the flour, cocoa powder, baking powder, cinnamon, and ginger.
3. Add the flour mixture to the peanut butter mixture; mix to combine well. Afterwards, fold in the chocolate chips. Drop by large spoonsful onto two baking paper-lined air fryer drawers. Bake at 185°C for 11 minutes or until golden brown on the top. Bon appétit!

RECIPE INDEX

Printed in Great Britain
by Amazon

24182919R00057